Manual for Tutors and Teachers of Reading

Joseph Strayhorn, Jr.

Second Edition

Psychological Skills Press

Wexford, Pennsylvania

Published by
Psychological Skills Press
263 Seasons Drive
Wexford, PA 15090
www.psyskills.com

Author's email: joestrayhorn@gmail.com.

Original art work by Catherine Fischer (three phoneme words, primer illustrations), Elizabeth Strayhorn (alphabet page), Jillian Strayhorn (horse picture in spatial awareness exercises); Joe Strayhorn (the other original drawings in spatial awareness exercises). All other art is in the public domain; it came from Wayne Winterton (www.oldtimeclipart.com), Mark Best (www.besmark.com) and The Gilbert and Sullivan Very Light Opera Company (scynthius@aol.com, http://members.aol.com/gsvloc/).

ISBN: 978-1-931773-12-6

Contents

Preface

This is a book for classroom teachers, reading tutors, parents who want to help their children with reading, homeschooling parents, trainers of adult literacy, or anyone else who is involved in teaching another person to read.

If you're a classroom teacher, you have permission to photocopy any of the pages of this book to display by overhead transparencies or large posters. I have tried to include in this book all that is necessary to get beginning readers off the ground.

If you're interested in tutoring someone in reading, I think you will do it well if you follow the directions here. If you undertake tutoring someone by telephone, I believe you'll find that this task is much easier to accomplish than most people would have thought possible. If you're a homeschooling parent, I hope that the activities here will be as useful as they have been for my homeschooled children and me.

If you're a principal or school administrator, consider the following plan. Let older students study this book in a course. Let the older students practice the methods described here, through role-playing. Let those who do well enough in role-played practice spend time in actual tutoring with younger students. Let those who shine at tutoring be given responsibility to teach and supervise and monitor other students who are also learning to be tutors. The interpersonal skills of tutoring and teaching (which this book emphasizes heavily) are helpful in any human relationships. Thus if your educational system turns out good tutors, you will have made a great accomplishment. If all schools made this accomplishment, the world would be truly transformed.

The methods described here are useful for learners of all sorts: gifted children, dyslexic people, or adults who were never taught properly. My colleagues and I have used these techniques successfully with people with IQ scores that cover a very wide range. I am very confident that these techniques can work in a wide range of circumstances.

There are three books you may want to consider as supplements to this one. The first, entitled *The Letter Stories*, is a series of stories involving characters who are letters with arms and legs. They can not talk in the usual way to people, but communicate by joining up with other letters and saying their phonetic sounds. The second, *Illustrated Stories that Model Psychological Skills*, contains stories that are meant to model kindness, productivity, frustration tolerance, good decision-making, and so forth. In both of these volumes, black and white line drawings, like the ones in the *Primer* that you will find in this book, make the stories easier and more enjoyable. The third, *Programmed Readings for Psychological Skills*, contains about a thousand brief sections. Each is meant to model a psychological skills concept. There is a quick comprehension question for each one. The stories start at kindergarten level and work their way up in complexity.

What are the connections between reading and "psychological skills?" The process of learning to read can be a form of "work therapy." It can give the learner practice in such psychological skills as patience and self-discipline, pleasure from accomplishments, persistence, joyousness, verbal fluency, social conversation, and the building of positive relationships. This book gives special attention to how to foster both of these paths of development at once.

There's another psychological skills connection. In order to do the best possible job, the teacher or tutor needs to become a master of several psychological skills: gracious social skills; patience and frustration tolerance when the learner is resistant or uncooperative; empathy and listening when the learner wants to talk; joyousness whenever the learner makes an accomplishment; dogged persistence, and others.

Finally, reading difficulties can create lots of failure experiences that are not good for psychological well-being. Conversely, overcoming reading difficulties can sometimes be the most "therapeutic" activity for the learner that one can carry out.

The central idea of this book is that learning to read should not be a failure experience for anyone, no matter what the person's native talent. I have arranged the skills of reading into an ordered series of tasks. Almost anyone can do the easiest ones successfully; each task prepares the learner for the subsequent ones; no jump from one step to the next is very large. The teacher can prevent reading from being a failure experience by following the "eighty percent rule": locate the point on this ordered series where the learner can be successful at least eighty percent of the time, and proceed up the hierarchy of difficulty, at a rate such that the fraction of successes stays at eighty per cent or above. In addition: the teacher celebrates each of the learner's successes with genuine and heartfelt joyousness. Given this combination, it's hard to go wrong.

The Big Ideas

In just a few pages we can preview the "big ideas" behind this book. All the specific techniques of teaching reading are consequences of these principles. Many of these principles also apply to almost all other learning.

1. A positive relationship makes the best context for learning.

The information necessary to learn to read is available on videotapes and computer programs and books. But most learners, particularly those who have been demoralized by their experiences so far, need more than just information: they need a positive relationship with a person who helps them learn. This is what you can supply, which no "technology" can supply. A positive relationship results from your wishing very strongly for the best for the learner, being a stable, dependable presence in the learner's life for the duration of the teaching, rigging the challenges so that you are able to give lots more approval than disapproval, being very honest with the learner, using differential reinforcement expertly, enjoying getting to know the learner, being a good listener when the learner talks to you, remembering and caring about what's going on in the learner's life.

Having a good relationship does *not* mean that you pander to the learner and let him do whatever he wants. The best relationships result when the tutor demands the best out of the learner – effort, and more effort. Having a good relationship with a learner entails that the instructor *not* give the learner a message of "Please like me." Your purpose is to get a job done, not to get approval or validation from the learner. Paradoxically, this allows the learner to respect you more, and makes for a better relationship.

2. The tasks of learning should be arranged in a hierarchy, a series of small steps.

You are best equipped to teach a certain skill when you have a series of tasks or challenges in mind, starting from the very easiest level, and moving up to the level required for mastery, with each step between challenges being so small that the learner is adequately prepared for each challenge by all the previous challenges. You will find that for reading, it is possible to arrange tasks in such an order. The easiest tasks are simple for most young children (some two-year-olds find them amusing). The challenges gradually move up to the point where the learner is reading very demanding texts. I hope that this manual is successful at communicating to you enough steps on this hierarchy to get anyone started on a lifetime of successful reading.

3. The instructor should locate the correct point on the hierarchy for each learner at each time.

A tutor can move freely along the hierarchy of challenges, so that you are working at just the right level at any given time. A classroom teacher should also strive toward this ideal. You want to usually work at the level where the learner is succeeding in at least 80% of the challenges he attempts. If the success rate is lower than this, move down the hierarchy and prepare for the challenge with an easier task, that then allows the learner to succeed at least 80% of the time when he moves back up the hierarchy.

If you are a tutor, you should find the right level of difficulty without regard for what homework the learner is getting assigned. The classroom may be working at the wrong level for this learner. Likewise, if you are a classroom teacher, you need to disregard what the learner "should" be able to do by a certain age or grade, and focus on what the learner can and cannot do successfully now.

To repeat: What the learner's peers are doing is totally irrelevant to finding the correct level. The relevant data are how the learner performs on the tasks. If the learner does them easily, you move up. If the learner struggles and is frustrated, you move down.

Demoralized learners have come to expect failure. It is a wonderful experience to help the learner find out that he can be successful, and that he can gradually be successful at more and more difficult undertakings. The transition from having "given up" to getting an expectation that "if I work hard enough I can do it" can be a life-transforming experience.

4. We learn to do something correctly by practicing doing it correctly. Therefore, aim toward errorless practice.

When we activate neural circuits over and over, they become strengthened in our repertoires, whether they are desirable or undesirable ones. In the words of some neuroscientists, the neuronal pathways that "get fired, get wired." If we practice doing something wrong, we may be setting up a habit which will compete with the habit of doing it right. Thus if possible, it's good to start practicing it "right, from the start." This principle implies that we can improve on the 80% rule I just mentioned. Suppose we can arrange that the learner moves along a hierarchy of tasks so well-planned that the practice of the skills being learned is close to errorless. Then the learner does not need to constantly to lay down memory traces and undo them. The correct memory traces are laid down from the start, and they are gradually strengthened with further practice.

When using this principle to teach piano, a teacher might ask the beginning student to listen repeatedly to a recording of a song before even starting to play it, so that the memory traces of the correct rhythms and pitch get laid down at the beginning. Later the student practices playing very slowly, so that there will be time to make sure that the correct notes are played in the correct rhythm. Gradually the speed is increased.

Let's look at another example of this principle in the teaching of spelling. Suppose an instructor asks a student to write a word ten times. The instructor has not checked first to make sure that the student has spelled it correctly the first time. If the student recopies an incorrect spelling over and over, the effort and practice subtracts from the goal of good spelling rather than adding to it.

The procedure for working on reading lists of "words in word families" that I advocate in this book gives a series of tasks, each of which is only a small jump up in difficulty from previous tasks. They are meant to get the student to correct reading of the word lists with minimal experiences of "I don't know how to do this." It is easy for the student to repeat each word after the instructor says it. The next step is to say the word after the instructor says the separate sounds. Then the student "sounds and blends" the words, immediately after the instructor models how to do this, for each word. Next the student sounds and blends, without the immediately previous model of the instructor. Finally, the student reads the words without saying the separate sounds.

The rule of aiming for errorless practice should not be taken overly seriously. In the progression toward expert performance, a very large amount of imperfect and incorrect performance should be tolerated and even celebrated, especially if it is an improvement on the past level of performance. We learn from mistakes. Still, if the instructor has a choice of two acceptable and workable pathways for the learner to progress toward expertise, that which requires the least "unlearning" of incorrect patterns is usually preferable.

5. Contingent reinforcement is an antidepressant.

Contingent reinforcement means that your effort brings forth fruit. It means that by working, you are able to get something you want, but you don't get what you want without effort. It means that you are able to control whether you get certain things that you want – the rewards or reinforcers in your life come depending upon what you do. A tiger in a zoo who has meat dumped in his cage at a certain time each day is getting noncontingent reinforcement. A tiger in the wilds who has to hunt for his food gets contingent reinforcement. If someone goes to a trophy store, buys you a trophy, and gives it to you for no reason, that's noncontingent reinforcement. For most people, it would not lift your spirits. On the other hand, if you worked extremely hard over a long period of time practicing something, giving your peak efforts, and you get a trophy as a result, that's contingent reinforcement. Your spirits are much more likely to be lifted. Many studies, with both animals and people, reveal that contingent reinforcement is better for us – it tends to be an antidepressant. On the other hand, the absence of contingent reinforcement tends to be depressing. If all reinforcement in your life is noncontingent, you are very justified in saying, "What's the point of doing anything? It doesn't make any difference." This is the conclusion that many demoralized learners have come to, even though they may not have put it into words.

If you are working with a demoralized learner, the more reinforcers you can make contingent upon effort, the better. The more important reinforcers from junk food to new possessions to the praise and approval of the people you care about are to be won by effort, the more you can overcome the condition of "learned helplessness" that often goes with a history of failure.

6. The instructor's tone of voice is crucial.

Through tone of voice, emotion gets communicated. When the tutor says, "You did it right," in a bland monotone, the learner gets the message that there is nothing to feel good about. When the tutor says, "You did it RIGHT!" with excitement and enthusiasm, the positive emotion of the tutor is communciated to the learner. That emotion is probably the most important reinforcer. One of your foremost goals is that you can help the learner sing the tune of excitement and approval to himself.

7. Monitoring and quantification of effort are good for the learner.

Effort is what we are after, and that which measured gets attained. This is the reason why every activity in this program can be given "points" of some sort. There are phonemic awareness points, spatial awareness points, letter-sound correspondence points, word list points, and text reading points.

8. Measure progress in ways sensitive to the behavior you are trying to reinforce.

There are two ways of measuring a student's accomplishment. One is by comparing her to other people her age. We can call this a "between-person" comparison, at one point in time. A second is by comparing what the student can do now, to what the student could do previously. We can call this a "within-person" comparison, over time.

Traditional grades make use of between-person comparisons. You give a test to a classroom of same-age peers. You give the students that do the best high grades, and those that do the worst low grades. The trouble with this system is that low grades are very punishing, and such punishment is often the opposite of what is needed for the students who get low grades.

Suppose there's a child beginning third grade child who for various reasons has remained at square one regarding reading – the child can't sound out any unfamiliar words, and scores at kindergarten level on tests of word recognition. The student's rate of progress so far has been approximately zero grade levels per year. Suppose someone identifies this child as in need of help, and tutors the child. With this help, and with a lot of hard work, the child learns what sounds the letters make, learns how to sound and blend, and develops enough automaticity to read simple text. By the end of the year, his test scores are close to the end of first grade level. He has made over a year and a half of progress in a year of school. At this rate, he will eventually learn to be a proficient reader. If the process is enjoyable for him, he has a lifetime of pleasant and successful reading ahead of him.

So far so good. Now, however, it is time for him to get a final reading grade. He is compared to his fellow students, and he just doesn't measure up to them. His reading is also compared to the standards that have been set for his grade level, and again he doesn't measure up. So he is given an "F" in reading on his report card. On tests standardized for his age and grade level, his percentile scores and standard scores remain discouragingly low.

What if no one pays attention to, or even calculates the numbers to reveal the fact that the child has made over a year and a half of progress in the last year? Then it is too easy for everyone, including the child, to get demoralized. There should be much celebration of the child's greater-than-average rate of advance in reading skill. But too often this accomplishment is eclipsed by the fact that the child is still behind his age-mates.

The moral of the story is that when anyone is behind in reading, you want to measure, celebrate, and be uplifted by improvement in reading grade level, and not to be demoralized by low achievement relative to peers. If we can measure, over time, the student's skill levels, and demonstrate progress, then there is reason to celebrate the student's success, even if the student is not up to where peers are. Any student who gets better and better at decoding reading each year until she finally can sound out almost any word given to her has scored a great success. If peers have scored that success sooner, that should not dampen the celebration.

This is why we should mainly be concerned with "within-person" comparisons over time, rather than "between person" comparisons at any given time. If Johnny is gaining in reading skills at more than a grade level per year, we have reason to be happy, even if he's still behind his peers at this point in time. Or, even if Johnny for some reason is not talented at picking up reading skills, but is gaining at half a grade level per year, we still have reason to be happy if he's enjoying the process and eventually attaining a high enough level to be able to use his skills to make the world a better place. Students differ in aptitudes, and nothing will erase that. No student should be punished for having a low aptitude. Every student deserves to be in a situation where the progress he or she makes can be a source of pleasure for the student as well as for the tutor. In the real world, millions of students each day get punished or criticized or disapproved of for having lower aptitudes than their age-mates, and they learn to associate academic pursuits with bad feelings. If you give these learners positive success experiences by focussing on what they can do now that they couldn't do before, you've made a wonderful accomplishment.

9. Persistence, or the development of work capacity, is an even more important skill than reading.

Many learners get a feeling of fatigue after just a small amount of mental exertion. Getting fatigued so quickly does not serve them well. It can severely limit what they are able to accomplish. On the other hand, the person who is able to keep persisting, keep practicing, keep working at something, has a skill which enables the person to improve in almost any other skill. If we can give the gift of work capacity to our learners, we have given them something literally more precious than gold.

10. Developing mental work capacity very much resembles physical conditioning. In both, gradually reducing the discomfort of effort is important.

When someone is very out of shape, physically, the first efforts at exercise are often unpleasant. But if the person persists, the sensation of expending physical effort can gradually lose its unpleasantness, and actually take on a feeling of great pleasantness. The same thing happens as one develops mental work capacity through mental conditioning. The process happens in very much the same way. You start out gradually, and slowly increase the amount of work you demand from yourself. You don't have to ever experience great pain, but you should not be afraid of feelings of minor discomfort as you stretch your limits. You grow your capacity by making demands upon yourself. It is pushing yourself that stimulates your body to grow its capacity. Over time, if expending mental effort gets you things you want, the sensation of effort can become "secondarily reinforcing" – it can begin to really feel good.

11. It will be helpful to explain to the learner the process of increasing work capacity, and to frequently remind the learner of this.

The learner who understands the process of "getting into shape" both physically and mentally is better armed to carry it out. One of the instructor's jobs, then, is to teach the learner about this and to provide frequent reminders. One of the ways of doing this is to celebrate in a major way any pieces of evidence that the learner's work capacity is increasing – including primarily, the learner's being able to get more "points" at one time than previously.

12. We can think of reading in five stages.

This idea is connected to the "big idea" of a hierarchy of tasks for reading. The five stages are as follows.

1. Oral language development. This means being able to talk well and understand someone talking or reading to you.

2. Phonemic and spatial awareness. Phonemic awareness is being able to hear words as separate sounds; spatial awareness is being able to recognize shapes and distinguish shapes from their mirror images, such as b from d.

3. Letter-sound correspondence. This means knowing the sounds that letters and combinations of letters make.

4. Sounding and blending individual words. This means saying the sounds of the letters and blending them to say words.

5. Text-reading. This means reading sentences rather than lists of words, sentences that mean something, and comprehending what those sentences mean.

13. Phonemic and spatial awareness are important foundation skills for reading.

There are ways of practicing phonemic and spatial awareness, and this manual will go into detail on this.

The big idea is that such practice exercises help some learners have a foundation for learning to read that they otherwise wouldn't get. Other learners seem to be able to do phonemic or spatial awareness tasks without any formal training. If we find learners who find phonemic and spatial awareness tasks very difficult, we should start low on the hierarchy of difficulty for these skills and work our way up. The benefits can be tremendous.

14. The sounding and blending exercise is very useful for beginning readers.

The sounding and blending exercise means, for example, looking at the written word cat and calling out "kuh ă tuh … cat." In other words, you say each individual sound (or phoneme) in the word and then blend them together to form the word. Why is this such an all-purpose exercise? Because it lets the learner simultaneously work on phonemic awareness (hearing the sounds of a word separately and then blending them together), letter-sound correspondence (calling out the sounds that each letter or letter combination makes) and word-reading. Some statistical analyses I have done suggest that doing this exercise about 6000 times, with words chosen to be at the proper level of difficulty, tends to raise the reading grade level by about one year, at least in the range from about kindergarten up to fourth grade level.

15. Sounding and blending by syllables takes the reader to the next higher level.

After the learner is able to sound and blend one-syllable words with all sorts of phonetic variations, the learner practices reading off these words quickly, without saying the individual phonemes. This prepares the learner for the next big step: sounding and blending polysyllabic words, not phoneme by phoneme, but syllable by syllable. So, for example, the learner sees the word phonetic and instead of saying "fuh oh nnn eh tuh ih kuh, phonetic," says "pho net ic, phonetic."

I've found that when learning the skill of reading polysyllabic words, it helps if the learner sees the words broken into syllables and written as a whole. That's the reason why in the back of this book you see lots of words written first in separate syllables and then joined together.

Lots of practice in sounding and blending by syllables is very effective in raising reading abilities from about the third or fourth grade level to much higher levels.

16. Accuracy first, but then get speed.

Almost all the challenges of reading go through stages where the learner at first can do them successfully, but slowly. With more repetition and practice, the learner can pick up speed.

Explain to the learner that eventually you'll want him to learn to do various tasks quickly. For example, the faster the learner can call out the sounds of the letters of the alphabet when they are presented in random order, easier it will be to sound and blend words. For another example, if a student can read word lists fast, the student is better equipped to read and understand text. Finally, the student has not fully mastered reading a certain passage of text until the student can read the passage at least as quickly as normal speech. Educators often use the word *fluency* to refer to automaticity and speed.

17. Reading aloud is a magical way to get more fluent.

When someone reads silently, she could be misreading words, skipping words, or skipping whole lines without realizing it. She could also be running the eyes over the words without even verbalizing them to herself. If the reader is doing any of these things without realizing it, she is practicing bad habits rather than good ones.

On the other hand, when the learner reads aloud, particularly to someone else, there is instant feedback to the reader, because she hears the words coming out of her mouth. Errors tend to make the sentences not make as much sense. The need to choose proper inflections for the words requires a certain amount of comprehension and with it, attention to what is being said. And, of course, if the learner is reading with a tutor, the tutor can also give both positive and corrective feedback.

Thus a major useful activity is simply for a tutor and a learner to take a book (one at the "just right" level of difficulty), and take turns reading it to each other. One reads one page, for example, and the other reads the next page. The tutor gets to model how to choose vocal inflection well. Many hours of this alternate reading aloud can work wonders for reading fluency, especially when combined with sounding and blending exercises.

18. The skill of decoding and pronouncing written words, out of context, even before you know what they mean, is extremely useful.

A large part of reading comprehension depends of knowing vocabulary. And although formal vocabulary training is good, we learn lots more words simply by picking up their meaning from hearing or seeing them used. We run across many, many more new words in written language than we do in spoken language.

When we run across a new word in written language, we have a major head start on making that word our own if we have the decoding skills to give that word a reasonably correct pronunciation. Here's a hypothesis, which I'd bet very strongly on: poor decoders pick up vocabulary much less quickly through reading than good decoders do, because the good decoders can hear new words in their minds, giving it the same pronunciation each time it's encountered, reinforcing memory traces having to do with word meaning rather than having those memory traces get jumbled up or actually interfere with one another.

This is one of the reasons why this book unabashedly focuses so much energy on the fundamental skill of decoding, of just calling out words. This is a teachable skill that makes vastly easier the much more complex intellectual activities of reading comprehension and writing.

19. It's good to remind ourselves what reading and writing are for.

What's the major reason for reading and writing? It's that certain thoughts, images, and ideas are worth remembering. When we put them down in writing, we can preserve them, and get them back when we need them. We write things down because we don't want them forgotten. We read them because we want to get into our minds this memorial that we or someone else has created.

What is not the major reason for reading and writing? Because someone is telling us to, to pass a test, to please someone, to put on a performance for someone, to get a good grade.

Writing is worthwhile in proportion to how much the thoughts are worth remembering. Reading is worthwhile in proportion to how much the recovered thoughts are worth thinking about. If the student doesn't have any inkling as to why the thoughts are worth remembering or thinking about, the education game is lost.

What makes certain thoughts, encoded into words, worth remembering and thinking about? Perhaps they are entertaining, as in a story that has a funny or suspenseful plot. Perhaps they teach us something we are curious about, as in a science book that tells why we get sick and how we get well. Perhaps the words have some beauty, and appeal to our esthetic sense, as in a beautiful poem. Perhaps the words tell us how to do something we want to do, or how to solve a problem, as in directions for putting together an appliance. Perhaps they fulfill our wish for socializing, as in reading a letter from someone we know. Perhaps we want to encode them because they are ours and we want to keep owning them, as in a story that I make up and want to keep. Or maybe they do something else I haven't listed. But the point is that insofar as possible, we want the student to be able to see and experience, without our even having to explain it, what the point is of encoding and decoding thoughts via words.

20. Psychological skills are learnable and teachable just as any others.

Psychological skills are abilities such as productivity, joyousness, kindness, honesty, fortitude, self-discipline, and so forth. We can teach people how to do these skills well, and we should, because they are so crucial to successful living.

21. People learn by observing models.

One of the major ways people learn is by imitating what they see and hear. They can learn a lot by fictional models, from movies, television shows, and stories. Obviously they can learn bad behavior patterns as well as good ones.

22. You accomplish two things at once by reading models of psychological skill.

In reading instruction it's necessary to practice text reading, and in psychological skills instruction it's useful to read about positive models. We are using our time best if we do both of these things at once. The volume I wrote called *Programmed Readings for Psychological Skills* is meant to simultaneously teach about psychological skills and give practice in reading.

23. Psychological skill is promoted by learning the meaning of certain concepts.

"Knowing the meaning of certain concepts" means the the same thing as "having certain words in your working vocabulary." If you know the meaning of the concept *fortitude*, you have the capacity to say to yourself, "Here's a situation that will take some fortitude." Otherwise, you can't think that to yourself so easily. If you know what "blaming someone else" and "learning from the experience" mean, you can think to yourself, "I think that in this situation I want to quit doing so much blaming someone else, and do more learning from the experience." Without these concepts in your vocabulary, you can't think thoughts like this so easily. Therefore the book, *Programmed Readings for Psychological Skills*, attempts to teach the meaning of many important psychological skill concepts.

24. Practicing classifying vignettes by psychological skill concepts accomplishes two things at once.

A person wanted to go to a party, but the party was cancelled. The person handled it without getting upset, and found something else useful or fun to do. Does this example have more to do with fortitude or honesty?

If you read the above passage and answer the question, you are practicing the use of psychological skill concepts such as fortitude, and you are also making sure that you understood what you read, in other words you are doing a "comprehension check." Comprehension checks are what the SAT exam and many other standardized tests do when they ask you to read a passage and answer questions on it.

This is another reason that *Programmed Readings for Psychological Skills*, one of your main textbooks for the course you will teach the student, is written the way it is.

25. Your self-talk greatly influences your emotions and behavior.

If you say to yourself, "This is awful! I can't stand it!" your reaction to the event will be much different than if you say to yourself, "What are my priorities now? What are my options for how to handle this?" The idea that your thoughts greatly influence your emotions and behaviors is the major idea behind cognitive therapy. But this idea is too good to confine it to therapy. It should be part of education.

In the *Programmed Readings for Psychological Skills*, there is much that has to do with identifying and classifying what people say to themselves. When children learn to label and classify the types of thoughts they have, they become more able to direct their thoughts into the most beneficial channels.

26. Reading rich and entertaining books aloud with a learner accomplishes two more things at once.

In our instruction sessions, usually the more tedious work is followed by a time when the instructor either reads to the learner, or the instructor and the learner take turns reading something that is fun and enriching to read. This provides reinforcement for doing the more self-discipline requiring work, and it also provides the learner a positive emotional experience of the power of written words, a motive for learning to read better. Of course, if you are not just reading to the learner, but are taking turns reading, a third goal is being accomplished, i.e. practice in reading. But the goals of reinforcement and motivation come first, so if the learner is struggling with whatever book you end-of-session reinforcement is, just read it yourself and let the learner enjoy it.

27. Reading competence and psychological skill competence nourish each other.

This is the converse of the idea that behavioral problems make it harder to learn to read, and not knowing how to read well in most educational settings is conducive to behavioral problems. Lots of kids who are "inattentive" in school could probably pay attention lots better if they could read better. Kids who can't read nearly as well as their classmates often experience a great deal of frustration and failure that leads to negative emotions and behaviors.

Learning to read well gives a child confidence about handling the tasks of school. Learning to read well permits the child to learn more about psychological skills by reading about them. Getting greater skills of self-discipline and persistence and confidence allows a child to be more successful at reading.

These are some of the reasons why it seems natural to work on psychological skills and reading skills together.

28. The interpersonal skills of the instructor are crucial.

In this manual I try to break down and explain as much as possible the various interpersonal skills required of the instructor. These are by far more complicated than mastering the reading exercises per se. I hope that the checklists and concepts here will help even those instructors with a good intuitive sense of interpersonal relations to make the interpersonal climate conducive to productivity and joyousness.

29. Role-playing is a great way for instructors to practice.

It's a good idea to role-play the activities described here with an adult who can give you good feedback on whether you are likely to be putting a bad taste in the student's mouth about the activities. Make your mistakes doing these activities in role-playing with adults, however silly you feel doing it, rather than risk turning off the student to learning. When you have done a good number of activities with the student or several students in ways that are pleasant, you can relax this prescription with the confidence that you have what it takes to make activities fun. In the role-playing, the main thing to practice is knowing how to be positive when a student gets an answer right, how not to be negative when a student gets an answer wrong, knowing when and how to make the activity easier or abandon it if the student isn't catching on to it, and to pick up on the signals that allow you to predict a "just right" amount of productivity to shoot for in any given activity before resting or switching to another.

30. Structure lessons so that self-discipline-requiring parts come first and the more fun parts come last.

You use more entertaining activities to reinforce the learner for doing the less entertaining ones, by arranging them in order of fun. Typically in the first part of the session, you do exercises. Drill and practice are not dirty words, if they are balanced by more entertaining activities. This manual will describe drills for learning the meaning of some words, learning how to take words apart into their sounds and put sounds together to make words, learning the sounds that letters make; sounding and blending words, reading word lists, and others. In the second half of the session, you either read to the learner or the two of you take turns reading text. The first part of the text-reading usually uses the psychological skills materials that I've written; the second part often uses entertaining materials written by others. At every point you are seeking the correct level on the hierarchy of difficulty. If the learner wants to chat with you, you want to be a very active listener. Sometimes at the end of sessions if the learner wants to celebrate by playing a game with you, that's another useful activity. At the end of the session, it's good to give a very brief review of the good things that the learner did during the session.

31. Make the ending of activities contingent upon goal attainment, not upon the student's acting bored, restless, or oppositional.

Almost any learning activity, any mental exercise, can cause some fatigue. Thus stopping an exercise to rest or do a different activity should usually be considered to the a reinforcer. What does it reinforce? If you play your cards right, it will reinforce sustained effort and persistence. If you play your cards wrong, it will reinforce getting off task, getting fatigued, and whining. The difference depends upon what the finishing of an activity is contingent upon.

Suppose I start out doing a drill in sounding out words with a student, and I simply keep going until the student acts so bored, complaining, and restless that I figure the student has reached the end of his attention span. If I do this over and over, then I'm repetitively reinforcing the student for the signs of fatigue and discomfort that he shows me.

Suppose, on the other hand, that we set a goal for a hundred points in a given activity. Whether the student appears fatigued or comfortable, we push on, and we stop as soon as the hundred points are reached. Now what is being repetitively reinforced is the self-discipline to keep working until goals are attained.

If the number of points was a too easy goal for the student, then the instructor makes a mental note to increase the point goal for the next session. Conversely, if the goal was too easy, the instructor plans to set an easier goal for the next session. The instructor avoids punishing easy responding by the immediate assigning of more work or reinforcing pained responding by the immediate termination of work.

The difference between the good strategy and the bad strategy for terminating work can be quite subtle. I believe that over time, the effects can be very substantial.

32. Adjust the interval of reviewing to be right for the memory decay curve of the individual learner.

For a given person and for a given type of information, there is a "memory decay curve." This is an imaginary graph of what per cent of material the person remembers as a function of the time after learning it. A curve that slopes downward steeply represents quick forgetting; a flat curve represents perfect retention.

It's much quicker and easier to bump the curve up from 90% to 100% by reviewing it than it is to wait until the material is totally forgotten and learn it all over again. Frequent quick reviewing is thus one of the secrets of successful students.

If a certain learner forgets quickly, you will want to review very soon after learning. If the learner has a flatter curve, you can afford to wait longer before reviewing previously learned material.

If educators could customize this interval for the individual learner, much of the frustration of learning – for both teacher and learner – could be eliminated. To do this requires careful experimentation to notice how frequent review is necessary.

33. The telephone has many advantages as a medium for communication between teacher and learner.

Teaching people to read over the telephone is in many ways an unusual idea. There are some disadvantages. You can't point to a letter and say, "This is an A." You can't pat the student on the back or have him see the smile on your face. You can't sit next to each other and look at the same book and turn the pages together, and point to the pictures together. You can't show the learner how to write letters. You can't write a story the learner has dictated and show the learner the results immediately. If the learner loses track of where he is in a passage, you can't point to each word with your finger to help him.

On the other hand, there are major advantages to telephone tutoring. People can be brought together instantly without having to travel. There is no waiting for buses or fighting traffic. The convenience for both tutor and student in getting together is drastically improved, and thus the sessions are more likely to actually take place. Finding a space to work together is less of a problem. Long distance phone rates have gotten low enough that learners everywhere can be served with fairly minor expense. In my experience, it is much easier to make phone sessions happen regularly and often than it is to make face-to-face sessions happen.

More interestingly: reading is a skill that relies on communicating through words. Telephone communication forces reliance on words. Anything that gets communicated must be translated into the verbal channel. Thus telephone conversations are in many ways a perfect avenue toward reading.

For the last several years I have been trying to find out which sorts of learners are responsive to telephone tutoring. Experience so far has led me to believe that a much larger fraction of learners will find this suitable than I originally thought possible.

34. Teaching older students to be expert reading tutors is a great way to improve the world.

Envision a school, with students K-12. Every student in the lower grades gets an hour or two, or more, of individual instruction per day from older students who have been trained to be expert tutors. At about fourth grade, students begin to be trained as tutors, reading about how to do the job well, observing the sessions of expert tutors, rating taped tutoring sessions, role-playing with same-aged peers, and having closely supervised sessions with younger students. As the students get older, they gradually refine the skills of tutoring, both the teaching techniques and the interpersonal skills. They become able, over years, to take on more and more responsibility for teaching younger students and for training and supervising younger tutors. By the time a student has finished twelfth grade, if all has gone as planned, the student has become expert at tutoring, training tutors, and supervising the activity of younger tutors.

If this vision could be put into effect, it is highly likely that the current high rate of reading difficulties in older children could be eradicated. One-on-one tutoring, beginning early and conducted well, can do wonders for the reading skills of young learners.

But the benefits would go far beyond this. The interpersonal skills of tutoring overlap highly with those of being a good spouse, parent, boss, or friend. Learning tutoring can become a context where people study closely the skills of getting along with each other. The benefits for tutors might even exceed the benefits for the developing readers.

In addition, the climate of adolescent culture might be vastly improved if they were able, as a group, to take part in highly useful service to younger children. I believe that one of the biggest problems of adolescent culture is a perception of "uselessness" – a life revolving around the pursuit of passing tests at school and being entertained elsewhere, without the pleasure of having a very meaningful impact on someone else's life.

Finally, if much of the curriculum of reading materials involved models of psychological skills and instructions about these skills, students could learn a great deal about how to handle life well, at the same time that they are practicing reading or practicing tutoring in reading.

Hierarchies, Steps, and The Challenge Zone

This chapter focusses on one of the most important and powerful ideas in education. This idea has to do with the phrases "hierarchy of challenges" or "successive steps toward a goal" or the "correct instructional level" or "finding the challenge zone." The notion is that it is possible to arrange complex skills, such as reading or doing higher mathematics or showing expert psychological functioning or playing the piano into a set of steps, ranging from very simple to very complex. Learning the steps lower on the hierarchy prepares you for learning the higher ones, and makes learning them easier.

If you have arranged the hierarchy of steps in enough detail, it should be possible to find a point on that hierarchy that is not too hard, not too easy, but just right, for any given learner. We call that point of "just right" difficulty the "challenge zone" or the "correct level." If the first task you choose is too hard, you quickly move down the hierarchy. If the first task you choose is too easy, you quickly move up. It takes lots of knowledge of a subject to know the entire hierarchy, and how to make things easier and harder at a moment's notice. You can be an expert reader without knowing the steps on the hierarchy well enough to be a good reading teacher. Part of the job of the instructor is to know the steps well enough to zero in on the challenge zone.

You can depart from the correct instructional level by having tasks that are too hard or too easy. In the frustration level, the challenge is too great for the learner's skills, and in the boredom zone, in the challenge is too little.

One of the most important parts of this theory is that working at the challenge zone on something worthwhile seems to be inherently pleasurable. It is fun to try challenges that are not too hard, not to easy, but just right for you. One of the major tasks for an instructor is to come up with activities at the challenge zone for each individual student.

One of the reasons this task is complex is that no activity makes just one demand upon the student; never is a challenge met with just one skill. For example, if the student is asked to read a story out loud and retell what he remembers from it, his skills in reading decoding, reading comprehension, compliance, sustaining attention, and probably delay of gratification, enjoying successes, and handling mistakes and failures are all being challenged. Low skill development in any one of these can lead to the student's being unsuccessful at the activity.

Finding the challenge zone is complex for another reason: the challenge zone constantly changes. As the student does activities at her challenge zone, she gradually becomes more and more skilled, and the challenge zone moves up to a slightly higher level of complexity.

A good bit of the unpleasantness of life comes from finding ourselves outside the challenge zone, taking on activities that are either too difficult or not challenging enough.

As we work with learners, we want to think constantly about what stage they have reached in reading and several psychological skills. We will at various times give tests to tell us where the student is on those hierarchies. If the student is frustrated or not making progress, you usually need to move down the hierarchy, to the point where the student can be successful on at least 80% of the things you want him to do. If you play your cards right, you can teach in such a way that the student is almost always successful. As the student becomes more and more successful and skilled, you gradually move up the hierarchy, so as to keep in the challenge zone.

Our dream is that each student will spend the vast majority of educational time doing activities at the challenge zone. If this can be fulfilled, learning becomes associated with pleasure, and the student becomes "hooked" on it for a lifetime.

Obviously the task of finding the best level of challenge is easier if you are an individual tutor than if you are aiming instruction at a whole classroom at a time. If you are a classroom teacher, think about harnessing the skills of older students, parent volunteers, or even same-age classroom peers for one-on-one tutoring. Older tutors can read this book to get help in finding the correct level of challenge for the student!

What an Instructor Must Know, in the Language of Hierarchies and Zones and Steps

In order to be a good instructor, you must know, first of all, what tasks and challenges and steps there are on the road from almost no skill to very great skill at whatever you are trying to teach. In other words, you have to know the points on the hierarchy. Second, you have to know how to do all these activities with the student, and to do them in a funloving and enthusiastic way. Third, you have to have a method of finding out where a given student is on this hierarchy, so that you can quickly locate and work at the challenge zone. There are two ways of doing this. The first is formal tests. By testing you can get valid numbers rating the student's skill. You need to know the correspondence between certain levels of performance on tests and certain types of tasks for training. The second way of finding the challenge zone is noting the student's response to your initial guesses about the right level of challenge. That is, when you have the tasks and challenges arranged in order, if your first guess seems to be too hard, you drop back, and if it seems to be too easy, you move up in difficulty. To be a good instructor you have to know how to make any given activity harder or easier, so as to tune into the right degree of challenge.

Therefore let's think about the hierarchy of steps in learning to read.

Stages in Learning Reading

1. Oral language development and interest in books
2. Phonemic awareness (also known as phonological awareness) and spatial awareness
3. Letter-sound correspondence
4. Sounding and blending individual words in word families
5. Reading and comprehending "decodable text"

Oral Language Development

What's the first step in learning to read? It is not learning the alphabet. It's learning how to use words, and to take interest in what words say. Early in life we start to get information into the brain by understanding spoken language. Listening comprehension is the skill of hearing language and understanding it. To comprehend spoken language, you have to know what words mean, and you have to understand the grammatical forms in which these words are put together. Hearing someone chat with you gives practice in this skill; hearing someone read to you also gives practice. If you are way behind in listening comprehension, you have a big disadvantage in learning to read. After all, what sense does it make to learn to call out words from print on a page, if you can't make sense of those words when they're called out for you? Listening comprehension skills are a major foundation for reading. Some children start school without good listening comprehension skills, and would greatly benefit from hundreds of hours of conversation, story reading, and dramatic play to practice these skills. If the whole school day is filled with messages to "Be quiet!" and "Stop talking!" then these children miss out on the practice they need the most. In tutoring sessions you can let children practice chatting for large amounts of time if this is what's best for the student.

You can get a fairly quick impression of where a student is in listening comprehension by reading stories to the student and asking the student to tell back what she remembers. The task becomes more complex as the stories gradually become less fully illustrated, longer, and more abstract. If the child can not keep listening to a very short (under one minute long) picture book, with a very simple plot and every action pictured as well as put in words, either listening comprehension skills or attention skills or both are at a very low level. At the other end of the scale, if the child can listen to a story without pictures, where there are fairly abstract concepts used, and tell back the story in some detail, and enjoy the whole process of doing so, the student's listening comprehension is much greater.

If your main task is building up enough language fluency in the student, then the first priority is to do activities that give the student lots of practice in hearing and using language. Three major ways the student can practice are by chatting, listening to stories, and doing dramatic play.

Even if the learner starts the reading program with lots of oral language skill, listening to you read aloud can further exercise the comprehension abilities. And, it can be pleasant and fun. I recommend that no one outgrow the activity of taking turns reading aloud with someone else. It's too good to save for young children.

Phonemic Awareness and Spatial Awareness

The step after oral language development is being able to hear words as combinations of separate sounds rather than indivisible wholes. This is called phonemic awareness, or phonological awareness. Another way of defining this skill is that of taking words apart into sounds and putting sounds back together into words. One phonemic awareness activity is called the blending exercise. In this, you hear someone say sounds like "buh ă tuh" and then you blend those sounds together to guess that the word was "bat." Suppose that a student can't do the blending exercise. How can the student possibly sound out words? If you can't put buh and ă and tuh together to make bat when someone else is saying the sounds for you, how can you do it when you're saying the sounds yourself?

Thus it makes logical sense that if a student isn't good at phonemic awareness, we should teach phonemic awareness skills before expecting the student to be able to sound out words. In addition to this logical evidence that phonemic awareness is important, there's empirical evidence. Kids with reading disabilities tend to do badly on tests of phonemic awareness. Many of them seem to have been laboring for years in efforts to learn sounding and blending, without having the adequate foundation laid under those efforts in the form of phonemic awareness.

There are several other phonemic awareness challenges other than the blending exercise. In a later chapter I'll go over these.

The phrase "phonemic awareness" is a commonly used one. The phrase "spatial awareness" is one that I chose to apply to a skill that I regard at the same foundation level as phonemic awareness. Phonemic awareness has to do with hearing. Spatial awareness has to do with seeing. Reading involves such visual memory tasks as remembering which letter is which, which side of the word and the page you start at, and which direction you go in. Particularly challenging spatial awareness tasks are remembering the difference between b, d, p, and q. Learning to distinguish designs from their mirror images is one of the big tasks of spatial awareness. Just as with phonemic awareness, we can take the learner through a hierarchy of challenges for this skill.

Letter-Sound Correspondence

The next stage is learning letter-sound correspondences. This means that for example, you can look b and say buh; it also means that when asked "What letter makes the sound buh?" you can say or write b. Learning letter-sound correspondences is at the center of what people call phonics.

Letter-sound correspondence is different from letter recognition. Letter-sound correspondence is looking at an h and saying "huh." Letter recognition is looking at an h and saying "aitch." Letter recognition is useful; among other things it helps to keep straight what you're talking about when you learn about the sounds made by combinations of letters. But it has much less to do with beginning reading than letter-sound correspondence does.

Should letter-sound correspondence be explicitly taught, or should learners be expected to infer letter-sound relationships from whole words? This subject has been debated. One side has won! The research evidence is overwhelming that for the vast majority of learners it is a big mistake not to explicitly teach letter-sound correspondence. That is, you somehow get the student to memorize that the a says ă and the b says buh, the c says kuh, the d says duh, and so forth. If you play your cards right, (and if you play my CD, or download my mp3 files, to be advertised more later) learning letter-sound correspondence can be fun.

Sounding and Blending Individual Words (Starting With Word Families)

The next stage is using the skills of phonemic awareness and letter-sound correspondence to sound out words. For example, you look at the word bat, say buh aah tuh, and then blend those sounds together to say bat.

In the seconds after you've sounded and blended *bat*, you've got memory traces in your head that make it especially easy to sound and blend *rat* and *sat* and *hat* and other close relatives of *bat* -- words in the same "word family." *Ram* and *hag* and *dab* and so forth are also in the same family as *bat*, only they aren't as close relatives. When you group words into these related sets or families, it's easier for the student to read them. So when we're talking about hierarchies of difficulty, it's easier to read "*mat sat hat fat pat*" than it is to read "*rip sat mob cull.*" So at the beginning, it's easier to read words with their family members present; as you gain more skill, you graduate to mixing them up and still being able to read them.

Sounding and blending words out loud gives practice in phonemic awareness (because you hear the sounds both separately and blended together) and in letter-sound correspondence (because you say the sounds each letter or letter combination makes). Thus doing this exercise as you learn to recognize words also strengthens the prior stages.

When you have done enough sounding and blending out loud, you are ready to practice recognizing words in a given word family without saying the individual sounds, but just looking at the word and reading it. This is the substage of gaining automaticity in word recognition.

When such automaticity has been gained with a wide variety of one syllable words, the learner is ready to start sounding and blending by syllables. Instead of saying aloud each phoneme and blending them together, the learner breaks the word into syllables (or uses a list in which this has been done for him), pronounces each syllable separately, and then blends them to say the whole word.

Reading Decodable Text

The last on our list of stages is reading decodable text. What is decodable text? It's a story or essay where the words actually mean something. "Decodable" means that the words in it follow the rules the student has learned so far. If the student has learned so far that e says ĕ, a says ă, c says kuh and h says huh, the word *each* is not decodable text. It becomes decodable when you've learned that ch says chuh and ea in lots of words says e. The more word families you've learned, and the more letter-sound correspondences you've learned (e.g. not just the 26 letters, but that tion says shun, ea says ee, etc.) the more text is decodable text for you.

Of course there's a difference between being able to call out the words when you read text, and being able to understand what those words mean, both individually and when put together in a certain syntax. How do you know when a learner has comprehended text? Test makers typically give a student some text to read and ask questions about it. Another way of assessing comprehension is asking the student to summarize what he remembers after reading a short passage.

Increasing Skills in All Former Steps

Some people feel a big rush to get to the text-reading stage, and feel reluctant to go back to previous stages once the student has gotten there. This is often a mistake. Yes, it's important that the student be exposed to writing that makes sense, in order to nurture and grow the interest in what books hold, but you can do this by reading to the student rather than requiring the student to read it himself. Meanwhile the student can spend a good bit of time doing exercises that will strengthen his ability to read text. It's much better to have a student succeed at the task of reading individual words or naming letter-sound correspondences or doing other "meaningless" exercises than it is to have the student struggle and be frustrated with reading text that makes sense.

Thus even after the student has learned to read simple text, it's very useful to continue to teach letter-sound correspondences, e.g. with letter combinations not initially learned; to continue to sound and blend many individual words in word families; to continue to work on listening comprehension; and even to continue to do phonemic awareness exercises until the student can do the hardest ones.

With enough repetition of these various tasks, there comes automaticity: the student doesn't have to devote such mental energy to figuring out what the words are, but can concentrate more on what the words mean.

Tailoring the Program to Different types of Learners

For young children, we can often start at the very beginning and take these stages in order. For older children or adolescents or adults, there is a need for tailoring.

Usually when an older child or adolescent or an adult is not reading well, despite a good bit of exposure to reading in school, there is a problem at the phonemic awareness or spatial awareness stage. It will be necessary to go back and do phonemic awareness or spatial awareness exercises, sometimes for a much longer time than with young children. The older the learner the more you can do away with the pictures that accompany these exercises. Usually with older learners there are also deficits in letter-sound correspondence, especially with the vowels. Older learners usually can benefit greatly from reading the words in word families. The content of the reading for practice can be tailored individually, with input from the learner.

Older learners can practice reading text, using children's stories, particularly if the older learner sees himself as practicing for reading those stories to children. Everyone should have the pleasure of reading to a young child, and this is one that older learners can get fairly early in their program.

The concepts in *Programmed Readings for Psychological Skills* have proved useful for adults. My hope is that most older learners, as well as younger ones, will experience most of these readings as appropriate for their age.

Stages for Psychological Skills

We went into some detail about stages of reading because of the great desire to choose activities that are not too hard, not too easy, but just at the right level of challenge for the student. But we also have to think about the student's psychological skills. Let's start first with the skill of sustaining attention to tasks.

Sustaining attention to tasks

At the beginning of your work, the student may be at any point on the range from very little skill at sustaining attention, to very great skill.

As you progress up from the lowest levels of attention skill, the learner becomes able to remain interested in longer and longer stories for a longer and longer time.

In the next stage, you can make a deal with the child, on the following terms. We'll spend a short time (3 minutes maybe for starters) on an activity the child is not initially interested in, and after completing that activity, the payoff is that we get to do the activity the child is interested in. In tutoring, this might translate into doing "exercises" for a few minutes and then the tutor's reading to the student.

In the next stage the same deal is able to be made, only the time in the "work" activity becomes longer, and the task becomes less of a novelty and more of a "get something accomplished" task. If you get to this stage, you're fully in business with the tutoring activities described in this manual.

Finally, the child becomes able to do work activities without one on one attention, but is able to do them alone or in a group. For example, the child is able to sit in a group and pay attention to a story, or sit at a desk and work on some written assignments. This is, of course, the degree of development in this skill that most school classrooms have to presuppose in order to run smoothly. (And, the fact that many children haven't attained this level of skill development is one of the reasons many classrooms don't run smoothly.)

If you explain to the learner that there is a progression in this ability, and that it is a very big deal to move up this progression, you help the learner understand why in the world someone would want to do something that is less entertaining when there are more entertaining things to do. You say things like, "So far I've just been reading stories to you, which is a very useful thing to do. But I'm thinking that you might be tough enough for the next stage, which is where you do some exercises before I read to you. If you can do this, this will really be a reason to celebrate, because the exercises really help you to learn to read."

At other times you say things like, "Every time you do one of these exercises, do you know what you are exercising? Not your muscles, but your ability to work! You're exercising what's called your work capacity. The more work you're able to do, the more you'll be able to succeed at whatever you try!

Self-Discipline and Compliance

The skill of self-discipline is the ability to work for a payoff that will not come right away. Delay of gratification the same thing as self-discipline. This skill is similar in many ways to that of sustaining attention to tasks, and the same stages that we mentioned for sustaining attention are relevant to thinking about it.

In the skill of compliance, many children start not just at ground zero, but in the negative regions. Ground zero would represent a child who only followed your commands and requests if he felt like it, and ignored them otherwise. The negative regions represent a child where your every request represents an opportunity to play the Frustrate the Authority Game. For such students, there is usually lots of hostility toward other authority figures in the child's life. This hostility gets projected upon whoever else happens to be in authority at the time.

The first positive stage of compliance occurs when you ask the child to do things that are intrinsically interesting and fun for the child, and the child complies with these requests. These are the sorts of requests where if you didn't ask the student to do them, he would ask you if he could do them! For tutoring, one such request often turns out to be, "Let's look at a book together, and I'll read it to you."

As the skill of compliance progresses to higher levels, the student is able to comply with your requests to do more and more self-discipline activities, more things that the student doesn't feel like doing, but can do for the sake of a future result. The student does this because he has come to trust you and because he knows that by complying with you, he is able to do more fun activities as well.

In tutoring, one of the ways that you teach compliance is simply by ending your session with the child if the child will not be reasonably cooperative and compliant. If your sessions contain enough fun activities and enough positive one-on-one attention, the child will be motivated toward cooperation by the desire not to have the session ended.

Handling Mistakes and Failures

The student who is most crippled by fear of failure will avoid trying to do any task that involves anything that can possibly be seen as a challenge or performance. This student will simply remain silent when asked academic questions.

The student who is a little less crippled will not remain silent, but will try all sorts of avoidance maneuvers to get out of the situation where her performance is being evaluated: physical complaints, disruptive behavior, and so forth.

Higher on this scale is the student who will cooperate with meeting challenges until he has one failure, and then wants to give up and quit.

Next higher is the student who can tolerate more than one failure, but still tends to quit or start doing avoidance maneuvers when he doesn't succeed nearly all the time.

Highest on this scale is the student who, when failing, tries to learn from his mistake, abstract the lesson so as to prepare him for the next attempt, and tenaciously keeps trying time after time until he succeeds, even if success takes a long time. Even before success comes, he feels good about his continuing efforts.

Let's think some about helping people progress along this scale.

When is avoiding trying because of a fear of failure rational and irrational? If someone untrained in brain surgery should somehow get the chance to try to remove a brain tumor, that person would do well to avoid trying because of fear of failure! Here there is something to lose, some danger, by trying and not succeeding. On the other hand, suppose a medical student has the opportunity to participate in a computer simulation of an operation. Now if there is fear of failure, it has to do with loss of face or embarrassment rather than actual harm to anyone. When trying and failing hurts no one, but simply allows the teacher to see where the learner is on the hierarchy, and allows the learner to find out what the limits on his current ability are, then avoiding trying because of fear of failure is irrational.

What harm is done by avoiding trying because of a fear of failure? Not working for improvement because of fear of failure is the cause of a huge portion of people's failures. A huge amount of failure at school is caused by students' avoiding tasks because they think they're no good at them and don't want to embarrass themselves. Most people could learn incredibly much more than they know if they just kept trying to learn, working at an appropriate level on the hierarchy of difficulty.

Why do people avoid trying because of fear of failure? Usually because someone has laughed at or teased or criticised them when they have tried and failed, and not when they haven't tried. The instructor should then try to instill the opposite attitude, that (except in cases like the brain surgery) you should feel good about trying, even if you fail. Why good feelings? Because even from failure you learn something that you can then use the next time. You never accomplish anything if you don't try.

How does the instructor instill this attitude in the learner? One way is by regulating approval and disapproval. You want to approve of the learner for trying, even when he failed, and you never want to disapprove of a learner if you think that he tried his best. If you see the learner gradually becoming more able to try things that he was scared to try before, give a lot of approval for this.

By advising a very low use of disapproval, are we saying that the instructor shouldn't tell the student that he got the wrong answer? No. The student needs informational feedback as to whether he did something correctly or not. By disapproval I'm talking about a disapproving tone of voice, or something that is designed to bring out shame in the student. If the student takes a guess at something he just can't get, the instructor might say, in a pleasant tone of voice, "OK! That was a hard one. You made a good try at it. The answer is ______. In a while you'll be able to get questions like that."

If you notice that the student gets frustrated and upset when he fails at something, it's usually a good idea to talk explicitly about the skill of handling mistakes and failures. You can say things like, "Just give it a good try, and if you don't succeed right away you've got nothing at all to feel bad about." or "Don't be ashamed if you miss some. The only thing to be ashamed about is if you give up before you even try." or "Don't be afraid to make a mistake. Making mistakes is how we learn."

Of course, it's easier for a learner to tolerate mistakes in individual tutoring than in group situations where mistakes may induce peers to try to humiliate the learner. If peers do humiliate other students for mistakes, then the first priority is to have lessons on why and how not to do this. The first priority is to instruct students in a code of conduct that forbids students from damaging others by deriding their mistakes.

With some students a tutor might enter into more of a dialogue about this problem, by saying, "Johnny, you know some people sometimes don't like to try things that look unfamiliar, because they're scared someone will laugh at them or tease them if they miss something. Do you ever feel this way?" If the student can talk about this, listen with rapt attention.

A tutor can use the power of "attribution," or "prophecy," in dealing with a problem like this. Attribution means that you attribute to the learner the ability to be fearless about trying things in the future. If you make a prophecy that the learner might be able to do this in the future, it could become a self-fulfilling one.

For example, the student misses something, and doesn't want to try any more. The tutor says, "OK, for now, let's go to something different. But let me tell you something important. Some day, probably not long from now, I'll bet you're going to be able to try hard problems and miss some of them and will be able to just keep on trying, without feeling bad at all. That's one of the things you'll learn from what we're doing together."

The tutor can use relabeling to help the student see overcoming this pattern of avoidance as a very desirable thing to do. You do this by talking about the ability to keep trying in terms of "being tough" and "being brave" and "being a winner" and other desirable traits. I.e. the student has the urge to quit in the middle of something, and the tutor says, "Come on, let's see if you can tough it out, and keep going all the way, even though it's hard." If the student is able to do it, the tutor can say things like "You did it! You got the urge to give up when the going got tough and you missed some, but you kept going anyway! That's being a winner! That's being brave."

Something else that may be a resource with learners with this problem is a song I recorded entitled "Here's How You Learn." (This can be found on the CD entitled *Spirit of Nonviolence*.) This song deals with this issue. The song advises, "Don't you worry if you're not perfect the first time. You weren't just born knowing how to do it well." You might want to sing it with the student. The story in *Illustrated Stories that Model Psychological Skills* called "The Boy Learns About Champions' Mistakes" also deals with this.

Another important way of dealing with this problem is to err on the side of having tasks be too easy rather than too hard, and to introduce new material more slowly rather than too fast. For the student with a great fear of failure, you should usually adjust the level of difficulty so that the student can be successful close to 100% of the time. Then you can stop and talk about the occasional failure and assess how well the student handled the lack of success.

Feeling Good About Successes

In order to have high achievement motivation, you need more than the skill of handling mistakes and failures. You also have to be able to feel good at the prospect of succeeding at meeting a challenge.

The student who is low in this skill seems to have a rather wooden, lifeless reaction when he gets something right or accomplishes something, even when the tutor approves and cheers. The student who is higher in this skill can feel good when the tutor approves and cheers, but not otherwise. The student who is highest on this dimension can feel good on his own, even without anyone else approving.

The student who is low in the skill of feeling good about successes is only able to feel good about the most major and complete successes, such as winning a tournament and getting a trophy. The student who is higher is able to feel good about more minor successes, such as winning a game. And the student who is highest on the scale is able to feel good about the elemental good moves or good decisions, even if the whole endeavor did not meet the traditional definition of success: for example, to feel good about some good moves made in a checkers game, even though the game was lost. Or, the student who is highest on this scale can feel good about the success in his doing better than his own usual performance, even though he still didn't do as well as someone else. Thus: even though I lost the checkers game, I still think it was one of the best games I've played, and I feel good about it.

One strategy that can't be beat for increasing the pleasure in success is for the student to develop a strong and close and positive relationship with the instructor, and for the instructor to take great pleasure in the student's successes.

Social Conversation

The bottom of the hierarchy for social converation is the person who can only sit passively and silently when someone tries to chat with him. Also occupying the bottom rung of the ladder is the person who is so busy in getting into everything, disrupting things, and getting distracted by one thing after another, that he can't carry on a conversation either.

Next higher on the ladder is the person who can interact in conversation only as long as there is some "thing" in the immediate environment that he and the other person can talk about. E.g. they have a box with a puzzle in it, and they say things like, "How do you get this box open?" "I think this is how you do it." "Wow, this looks hard." "I think this might go this way."

Higher on the scale is the student who is able to do some talking about things not actually present in the here and now. This student is able to talk about what happened in class a while ago, what happened over the week end, and so forth. But at this stage the student runs out of topics to talk and ask about very soon.

Higher still is the student who is able to think of things to talk about and ask about, without ever running out, but who for one reason or another isn't very pleasant for the other person to talk to, or doesn't enjoy the conversation much himself. Maybe the person monopolizes the conversation too much, or talks on and on about things that are dull to the other person.

Highest on our hierarchy is the person who can talk indefinitely with someone about things in the past, present, or future, in a way that is enjoyable and enriching for both people. This person can tell about his own experience, and can be a good listener, eliciting from the other person the other's experience.

One of the great things about tutoring is that you can practice this crucial skill at almost any point in the session. If the student wants to avoid practicing an academic skill by starting a conversation with you, you can usually go along with this in good conscience, because social conversation is so crucial. We have discussed before how listening and speaking are the basic foundations for reading and writing. In addition, if a person can participate in mutually enjoyable conversation, that person is set up for much more positive relations with people.

Kindness and Good Will

Perhaps the most important skill is kindness and good will, wanting to make other people happy, feeling good about making other people feel good.

The person who is most on the wrong end of the spectrum for this behavior actually gets a kick out of making people feel bad, takes pleasure from cruelty, is sadistic, and continues this behavior even when it is very self defeating.

A little higher on the scale for this skill is the person who can be nice to other people only when there is something tangible he wants to get out of the other person. For this person, kindness is purely exploitative.

Similarly tied to immediate external consequences is the person who can be kind primarily out of fear of punishment if he is unkind.

Higher on the scale is the person who is able to be kind, knowing that this way of acting makes it more likely that the other person will be kind and nice to him. The person is working for external consequences, but not just immediate ones – long term consequences for the relationship.

Highest on the scale is the person who takes pleasure in making someone else feel good, with or without any expectation of a consequence. This person finds that making the other feel good is a reinforcer in and of itself.

As a general rule, it is easier for a person to attain the higher stages of this scale if he has spent time in a close relationship with someone who operates toward him from the higher stages. Thus if the instructor can take pleasure directly in making the person feel good or in preparing the person for a better future, the person will get very meaningful and personal models of this skill. Most of the "modeling stories" available as adjuncts to this program are meant to model, among other things, the skill of taking pleasure in being kind to another person. But if you spend lots of time with the student, your own model will be at least as important. If your model is synchronous with the models in the stories, then the person will experience the two sets of models as strengthening each other.

Pleasure from Discovery

How much does the student enjoy learning? How curious is the learner? Some could argue that pleasure from discovery is the main goal of education. If education turns out people who love to learn, they will keep finding ways to do it somehow or other. If education produces people turned off to learning, no matter how much they know, they will soon be ignorant as their old knowledge becomes obsolete.

The person who is most deficient in this skill seems to want to run the other direction any time there is anything connected with learning offered to him. And when he is cajoled or forced to do learning activities, he looks and acts like he hates them, and reports that he hates them.

At the other end of the spectrum is the person who is very curious to read or hear things in books, loves browsing among nonfiction as well as fiction works, has a positive taste for educational films or videos, enjoys libraries, thinks the encyclopedia is interesting, and so forth. When this person is offered some learning enrichment activities, she feels privileged and excited.

Fortitude

Fortitude means the ability to put up with not getting what you want.

Lots of the activities described in this manual are exercises where you can get an answer right or wrong. Part of the drama of an exercise is the excitement from risking losing or getting a big setback. The learner with very low fortitude can't enjoy games because as soon as a loss or a setback happens, he feels such strong anger or upset that he can't continue. On the other end of the spectrum, the learner who is good at fortitude can handle such setbacks and losses without a great deal of negative emotion.

In learning sessions, a variety of different activities is available. It is frustrating for the learner when he can't do the one that he would most like to do at that moment. How does the learner handle that frustration? The learner at the low end of the scale gets so upset that he can't enjoy any of the other activities. The learner at the high end of the scale can handle such frustration well enough that he can go on and get some enjoyment out of his second or third or even his last choice.

Thus ends our explanation of various skill hierarchies. If you keep your eyes and ears open and watch what happens in teachers' relations with students, you see certain students being punished or teachers' being exasperated because the students have not progressed enough on one or several of these skills. As a result the student gets started in a vicious cycle of being frustrated by the authority and frustrating the authority back. If, on the other hand, you can recognize where the student is, and choose activities whereby the child can be successful given her current level of skill, you can have pleasant times with the child and start the child moving up the hierarchy.

Skills for the Instructor

The previous chapter dealt with skills we want to increase in the student. This one deals with the skills the instructor needs, in order to best help the student.

Let's summarize the main teaching skills with the following rating scale.

Rating Scale for Instructors

Rate the instructor's success on each of the following, on the following scale:

0=None
2=Very little
4=Some but not much
6=Pretty much
8=High
10=Very high

_____1. Friendliness. How much was the instructor very friendly and kind to the student?

_____2. Enthusiasm. How much was the intstructor enthusiastic, energetic, cheerful, and upbeat in general attitude?

_____3. Approval for the positive. How successfully did the instructor watch for the best things the student did, find some, and give very enthusiastic approval for them, within split seconds of when the student did the good things?

_____4. Avoiding unnecessary disapproval. How successfully did the instructor avoid giving unnecessary disapproval to the student?

_____5. Nonbossiness. How successfully did the instructor avoid being too bossy with the student?

_____6. Authority. How successfully did the instructor establish and continue the precedent that the instructor's directives are to be obeyed, that the instructor is to be treated with respect?

_____7. Responsiveness to conversation. How well did the instructor encourage conversation between the instructor and the student, particularly by being responsive to any conversational utterances the student made? (Responsive means follow-up questions, reflections, facilitations, follow-up statements, tracking and describing.)

_____8. Right level of difficulty. How well did the instructor choose activities at approximately the right level of difficulty for the student, and make the activities harder or easier depending on how the student did at them?

_____9. Right time on a task. How well did the instructor set a reasonable goals for time on each task for this student? How well did the instructor make the ends of tasks contingent on goal attainment and not on complaints or signs of boredom from the student?

_____10. Response to missed questions. If the student answered a question incorrectly, how well extent did the instructor give accurate feedback, modeling how you think in coming up with the right answer, instead of disapproving of the student, or continuing to request the answer from the student? Did the instructor sometimes reinforce trying, rather than getting the right answer?

_____11. Pacing of activities. How well did the instructor maintain a pace of the activities that was fast enough not to bore the student, but not so fast as to create a rushed atmosphere?

_____12. Response to undesirable behavior. How well did the instructor follow a reasonable decision tree in responding to undesirable behavior by the student? (Strategies to try: Ignore; calmly explain to the student what he should do, and why; end the session with expressed hopes of more cooperation next time.)

_____13. Mastery of activities. Did the instructor demonstrate full and smooth mastery of any activities that the instructor was leading? That is, how well did the instructor do each of the activities?

_____14. Avoiding arguing. Did the instructor avoid arguing with the student?

_____15. Differential reinforcement. Did the instructor show the student lots more attention, excitement, and interest when the student was doing something good than when the student was doing something neutral or undesirable?

_____16. Valuing work and achievement. How successfully did the instructor make comments that communicated the philosophy that work and achievement are good things?

_____17. Positive review. How competently did the instructor do a positive review at the end of the session?

****

Now let's go through these one by one.

Friendliness

Friendliness to the student is essential. Everything you say to the student should be courteous and polite and respectful. You may at times tell a student what he does not want to hear, but you should never use a tone of voice or set of words that belittles the student or is sarcastic or is hostile. This means never referring to anything about the student as "stupid"; never threatening the student; never raising the voice in anger at the student.

If you are assigned to a student who is difficult to work with, you should never give the student the impression you'd rather be teaching someone else instead of him. Remember that the student's job is not to entertain you. In teaching you take pleasure from helping the student come from where he is to where he can be. You act friendly to your student because that's your job as a tutor or teacher, not because the student is first nice to you. You must first be friendly to the student.

Enthusiasm

Item 2 has to do with assuming an enthusiastic attitude from the very beginning. Enthusiasm is a way of using your tone of voice in a way that says, "I'm full of energy! I'm excited about doing these things!" You can be nice, but if you're not also enthusiastic, the student is likely to get bored.

Most students like to arouse excitement in other people, especially their caretakers. I have a theory that the wish to get people excited is hard-wired into the brains of most children, because doing so helps them know that they will be noticed and won't be left to starve. Perhaps the children who have wanted to arouse emotion in their caretakers have been the ones who have been less neglected throughout centuries of evolution.

If you aren't excited and energetic and enthusiastic, a student will often try to get you excited. But the student may not know how to get you excited except by making you mad, frustrated, or exasperated. On the other hand, if you are so enthusiastic that you are having lots of positive emotions, such as joyousness, humor, fun, enthusiastic cooperation in activity, pride, nurturing feelings, and pleasure from accomplishment, then the student will enjoy the session more and won't need to bring out negative excitement from you.

People also imitate the emotional tone they experience coming to them. If they hear hostility or disapproval or exasperation coming toward them, they tend more to be hostile or disapproving back. If they hear joyous excitement, or calm patience, or gentle amusement coming toward them, they tend to reflect these positive emotions as well.

So if you want to be the best instructor, learn to keep yourself from getting excited about negative things, and get as excited as you can about positive things.

Approval for the Positive

Item 3 is Approval for the positive. This means that you watch for anything good that the student does, and take pleasure in it, and communicate that pleasure.

One obvious thing to celebrate and reinforce is the student's succeeding at a challenge. When you ask the student a question and the student gets it right, your job is to help the student feel good about his success. You do that by showing that you feel good about it.

But another very important good thing the student can do is to cooperate and try, even if he doesn't succeed. What if you've given the student a question that is so difficult that he can't get it, but he tries very hard? He's done his part, just as much as when he succeeded with an easier question. Your difficult question is the reason he didn't succeed, not the fact that he didn't try. He deserves approval for trying and cooperating and playing the Meet the Challenge Game.

If the student keeps paying attention to something for longer than before, that's worthy of celebration. That means the student is gradually lengthening his attention span. If you are reading to the student, and the student can listen to stories for 10 minutes whereas before he could only listen for 9 minutes, that's cause for celebration.

If the student wants to chat with you, even if on a different subject from the academic work, please consider the student's chatting something good, something to be approved of. Practice in putting thoughts into words and listening to words is a very important academic skill. Especially in tutoring sessions, there's always time to listen and talk. If the student is curious about something and asks you, that's not only chatting, but curiosity, which is doubly good. If you don't know the answer to a question the student asks, at least you can celebrate the student's coming up with the question.

If the student reports a time in which he helped someone or did some other positive act, that's another reason for approval.

As you learn more and more about psychological skills and positive examples of psychological skills, you can start seeing more and more of what the student does as an example of one psychological skill or another, and can take pleasure in it.

Your pleasure in what the student does is linked to the notion of "reinforcement." Reinforcement is something that rewards someone for what he or she just did, and thus makes the person more likely to do it again. Behavioral theory has taught for many years that "social reinforcement" including attention, approval, praise, and so forth are very important. For example: I give my best effort to answering a question, and someone whose approval I care about says, "That's great!" I feel good, and I want to give my best effort again.

Most writings on reinforcement have not emphasized a certain idea enough: for your reinforcement to be most meaningful, you have to feel some emotion. Suppose you say, "I'm really pleased that you did that," but you look and sound depressed and frustrated. Then what you say will probably not have much effect on the student, or will have a negative influence. On the other hand, if you really get a very large kick out of what the student did, almost anything you say is likely to reinforce the student's good behavior.

How do you psych yourself up to feel good about the student's accomplishments? I find that thinking certain things helps me be ready to feel good. I contemplate how many years the learner has ahead of her to use the skills she is learning, and I think about what an accomplishment it will be if I can impart a skill that the person will use well for the rest of her life. I think about the violence and hostility that prevails in the world, and think about how good it will be if the skills of kindness are strengthened in even one person. I think about how the emotions of early experiences tend to get called back by reminders from events throughout the rest of life, and thus reason that if I can have a learner experience some very pleasurable productive time, I am seeding memories that will help the learner to feel good throughout the remainder of a lifetime. I remember with pleasure some of the adults who were kind to me and had fun with me in my childhood, and I remember the feelings I had then; this makes me more sensitive to feeling good about happy productive things students do. I think about how much work I have to do in what I am doing with the learner, and therefore whenever a learner actually helps me by doing a task for me or by cooperating with my directions, I will feel a combination of relief and gratitude. I think about some of the times in childhood when I had childishly happy times, and I hope to be able to feel some of that child-level pleasure as well as the parental-level pleasure from being proud of the students' accomplishments. I think about how much reading and writing I've done in my life, and how much I've enjoyed these activities, and this makes me feel really good at the idea of teaching someone else to do them.

All this doesn't mean that you have to be at the pinnacle of happiness before you start teaching someone. However, if you are able to let the students lift you into high spirits, the activities will work much better.

What if the student is uncooperative? Part of being a good tutor or teacher is to figure out some activity in which you can enjoy the student. If there is only one activity that allows you to do that, then it's better to do only one activity than to have a bad time together trying and failing at other activities. You need to establish and practice the pattern of taking pleasure from the student. When both you and the student practice that pattern enough, it can spill over to other activities.

The approval you give for positive things the student does is often conveyed by your tone of voice. It's a good idea to practice communicating small and large approval in your tone of voice, and to feel the difference between those and a tone of no approval.

Avoiding Unnecessary Disapproval

Item 4 is avoiding unnecessary disapproval of the student. Disapproval includes such "No-No's" as saying, "You're stupid" or "You can't do anything right." Disapproval also includes saying "Why are you doing that?" in a disapproving tone of voice, or saying "No, that's not the right answer," in a disapproving tone, or grunting in a disapproving way over something the student did or said. Disapproval also includes saying, "Please stop doing that" in a firm tone, or "You know you're not supposed to do that" in a very reasonable and straightforward tone.

Sometimes disapproval is helpful and a good idea. Most people tend to overdo it. Some people are overly afraid of using it. A good rule is the 80% rule: try to give at least 4 times as much approval as disapproval.

When the student does something undesirable, the first impulse of most people is to disapprove. But there are other options that often work better: ignoring the undesirable behavior, explaining in a cheerful manner to the student what he is supposed to do, silently planning for shorter times on a particular task for the future, or ending a tutoring session for the day. When you give the learner a lot of disapproval, the learner tends to give it back to you, and to other people. Plus, the learner gets more pleasure from playing the Frustrate the Authority Game the more disapproval the authority person has given him.

Nonbossiness

Item 5 is nonbossiness. You want to avoid giving command after command in an unpleasant tone of voice. One of the main reasons why nonbossiness is an important value for instructors is that obedience is so important for the student. This sounds like a paradox, but it isn't. If you want to bring out disobedient behavior from your student, there's a pretty reliable way to do it: keep barking more and more orders and commands to the student in a bossy and mean voice. If you do this, any fear that your stern and mean voice strikes into the learner will quickly get desensitized. Many students will want to rebel against you and show you that you can't boss them around. And the more orders you give, the more opportunity you give the student to disobey. You want to give the student an experience of obeying 100% of your directions.

Nonbossiness does not mean that you are not an authority figure for the learner. You do want to set the climate that you expect the learner to obey you. But you want to cut down your commands to those so necessary and reasonable that obeying you is not a burden for the learner.

Authority

Even though it's important not to be too bossy, it's also important to establish a precedent of respect for authority in your sessions. One of the major skills the student needs to learn is self-discipline. Self-discipline is the ability to do things one doesn't feel like doing at the time, but which are the best things to do. One of the major ways that a student learns self-discipline is by obeying an authority figure who directs him to do something that might not be his first choice at the moment. By practicing obeying you in such circumstances, the student learns a skill that will later on help him to obey his own directives to himself. Disobeying authority figures is one of the worst habits a student can get into. One of the worst things you can do as an instructor is to give the student lots of directives that the student ignores or otherwise disobeys.

How do you act as an authority, sending the signals to the student that your commands are in no uncertain terms to be obeyed? You make it very clear when you are giving a command, and you distinguish that very clearly from a suggestion. When you are not giving a command, you feel free to clown around and play with the student and goof off. But when you give a command that must be obeyed, that you sense the student does not feel like obeying, your voice takes on a serious tone, so as to let the student know you are not playing around. When you give a command and the student disobeys, you let the student know that compliance is expected. You never take on a tone of voice that pleads with the student or begs him or haggles with him. When people do that, they give power to a rebellious person and reinforce rebelliousness.

Being an authority means being sensitive to, and using, various nonverbal and verbal ways of signalling that you are in charge. You are willing to go along with what the learner wants at times, or often, but that is because you choose to rather than because you have to.

You tell the student in a polite but firm tone what to do, and you avoid taking no for an answer. You don't back down once you make a command unless you decide you have made a real mistake by giving the command. You don't get yourself into binds by giving commands that you aren't prepared to stick with.

If you are a tutor, what are some options if the student is not cooperative? You can in a calm and serious voice communicate to the student that he is not meeting standards on cooperation. If the student continues not to meet those standards, you can talk this over with the parent and the child. You can listen to the student's point of view. You can speak to the student's parent and let that parent know that any session where the student does not cooperate will be terminated, and that the tutoring itself will be terminated if noncooperation is sustained. Make very sure that the cause for the noncooperation is not that you are giving tasks that are too hard or too easy, or that you are failing to reinforce the learner's completion of tasks. Consider cutting down the time of the sessions. Consider altering some aspect of the rewards contingent upon the learner's successes.

With very noncooperative students, you may need to think more about the hierarchy of difficulty for cooperation than the hierarchy of difficulty for reading. You may need to start at the very bottom of the hierarchy with respect to cooperation demands, and work your way upward. You may for example need to start with very small amounts of cooperation requested, followed by very desirable tangible or edible reinforcers. The challenges may need to start out very easy. Once you get cooperation with easy challenges, you are on your way.

Responsiveness to Conversation

Responsiveness is the opposite of bossiness. It means that when the student says something to you, you react in a way that makes the student glad he spoke up. Your reaction doesn't tell the student what to do; it just registers some pleasure over being able to hear what the student said, or checks to make sure you understood it right, or asks for some more information.

Here are some ways of being responsive to the student. One is called a facilitation. Suppose the student says, "I went to the museum yesterday," and you say any of the following:

Oh!
Is that right!
Humh!
Uh huh!
Hey!
Oh boy!
Yes?
Oh?
Wow!

Facilitations are little grunts that give the message, "I hear you, tell me more, keep going."

Another way to be responsive is to ask a follow-up question. If the student says, "I went to the museum yesterday," responses like these are follow-up questions:

Which museum was it?
How did you like it?
What did you see?
Who took you there?

These show interest in what the person is saying and a wish to hear more.

Another way to be responsive is with a reflection. Here you say back in your own words what you understood the person to be saying, so that you can check whether you understood it right. Suppose the student says, "Guess what, I did my homework every day, and I made the honor roll!" Here would be examples of reflections:

Wow, sounds like you have worked really hard!

You're feeling really proud, aren't you!

You tried really hard, and it paid off, didn't it?

Every single day. That must have taken a lot of self-discipline!

Reflections have also been called paraphrases, active listening, and checking out.

When you do reflections, you not only listen to the student's words, but also attend to the student's intonation, and state back to the person what you hear the person thinking and feeling. The reflection can sometimes be a question, and sometimes a statement. You restate what the person means, not just what the person says. For example, a reflection of "You're a pig!" would not be "You think that I'm a pig," but "It sounds like you're angry at me," or "It sounds like you're wanting to hurt my feelings," or "I was messy eating that last bite of food, and you caught me on it, didn't you?"

Here are some examples of reflections, in an imaginary conversation a student has with a tutor.

Student: Guess what, just a while ago I did some math problems with the other tutor, and I got them really easily.

Tutor: Wow, I'll bet you're proud about that!

Student: They're easy, they're no problem for me any more.

Tutor: You've got them knocked, huh?

Student: Yeah, but it's strange, the other day at school I got a bunch of them to do and just didn't do any of them. I hate doing them in school. My teacher thinks I can't do them.

Tutor: That's interesting to hear. You could do them in school, just like you do them here, but you hate doing them at school?

Student: Yeah. I don't know why. Maybe because I'm so mad at her for yelling at me all the time.

Tutor: So for that reason it just doesn't feel good to do math problems when she asks you to, huh?

Student: I feel like whatever she wants me to do, I'll just do something else. But I guess it really hurts me rather than hurting her.

Tutor: It seems to cause you more problems than it causes for your teacher?

Student: Yeah, because then I just do worse.

What are some reasons for using reflections? It is pleasurable for a person to know that he or she has been understood by another person, and reflections, perhaps more than any other communication, confirm such understanding. They provide an error-trapping method: any misunderstandings you communicate through reflections give the student a chance to say, "No, that's not what I meant," and to clarify. After you do an empathic reflection, the student is free to say whatever he wants next, so that the student feels a freedom in conversation, a feeling of not being directed; when the student is able to choose his own direction, he has more opportunity to home in on what he most wants to talk about. In order to do empathic reflections you have to concentrate on what the other person is communicating, rather than thinking up the next point you are going to make, as people often do in conversation. Finally, doing empathic reflections keeps people from using premature advice, criticism, commands, and other communications that often provoke defensiveness or stop communication.

Most people don't have strongly in their repertoires the ability to do "pure reflections." Most of the time when you ask people to make up reflections, they will give advice or encouragement or some other kind of direction. For example:

Student: I think I'm going to drop out of school as soon as I can. This whole business is just not for me.

Listener: Aw, you're too smart to do something like that. I know you can be successful. Keep up the spirit.

The problem is that the listener may not thoroughly enough understand where the student is coming from. It's necessary to do a lot of listening before giving advice. Contrast the above with the following:

Student: I think I'm going to drop out of school as soon as I can. This whole business is just not for me.

Listener: Oh? It's gotten so discouraging that you've got the urge to get away from the whole thing, huh?

This response simply restates and checks understanding, without giving any direction. The student is now free to tell more if he wants, or not if he doesn't want. It's difficult to argue with the reflection, whereas it's easy to argue with advice. It's good to practice until you have strongly in your repertoire the ability to do totally nondirective reflections. Of course you will not want to come out with a steady stream of reflections. But for those moments where they are just what your interaction needs, you want to be able to use them.

Here's a way to practice using reflections. Get someone to talk to you, or even read to you. Each time the person stops, make your reflection begin with one of the following prompts, and fill in the blank.

Prompts for Yourself to Do Reflections

So you're saying ________________?
What I hear you saying is ________________.
In other words, ______________?
So if I understand you right, _____________?
It sounds like ________________.
Are you saying that ______________?
You're saying that _____________?

****

Another way to be responsive is with a follow-up statement. Here you tell the student something about your own experience, something relevant to what the student just said. Suppose the student says, "I like getting exercise." Examples of follow-up statements would be things like:

Me too. I try to work out every day.

My favorite type of exercise is lifting weights.

I was riding an exercise bike the other day, so much that sweat was dripping off me.

If you master these responses, i.e.

facilitations
follow-up questions
reflections
follow-up statements

and if you do them frequently and enthusiastically, you will not only bring out conversation and encourage language development in your student; you will also have mastered listening skills that will be useful in almost every interaction you have with anybody!

Right Level of Difficulty

One of the main reasons why educational activities fail is that they are either too hard or too easy. Activities in the challenge zone, where they are not too hard, not too easy, but just the right degree of challenge, will be fun for the student.

You need to be skilled at observing a learner's reaction to an activity and seeing whether it is too hard or too easy. If the learner doesn't seem to be able to figure out how to do it, even when you've explained it well and demonstrated it yourself, the activity is probably too hard; if the learner gets it every single time and doesn't seem to feel particularly challenged by it or proud of his successes (even when he is proud at other times and thus demonstrates a capacity to feel proud of his successes) the activity is probably too easy.

A good rule of thumb is to rig the activity so that the learner can be successful on at least four-fifths of the attempts he makes at whatever he is being asked to do. For learners who are afraid of failure and insecure, the fraction of success at the beginning should be even higher, close to 100%.

Next, you need to know, for any given activity that you are doing, ways of making it harder and ways of making it easier. That way once you have perceived that the activity is too hard or too easy, you can very quickly adjust and get at the right level of difficulty, the "cutting edge" level of difficulty. For example, one reading activity is the "blending exercise," where you break words into the sounds that make them up and say them, and let the student guess the whole word. If the learner can't get "buh ă tuh er ee" (battery) then maybe that's too hard and it will be easier for the learner to get "buh at" (bat). Having simpler words, shorter words, and breaking them up into fewer parts makes the task easier. If you can automatically and quickly adjust any task to make it at the right level of challenge for the learner, you are a much better instructor than if you don't know how to do this.

Keep in mind one of the most well-kept secrets in education: an activity can be easy enough in the academic skill, but too hard in the psychological skill it demands. As an instructor you should be aware of which is the "rate-limiting factor." For example, a child can read the words in the individual word list easily enough, but the child can't sustain attention and use self-discipline to keep at the word lists very long. If this is the case you want to help the child become aware of this, to find a level of self-discipline and sustaining-attention challenge that the child can handle given current skill, and gradually move up the hierarchy of difficulty together. In this case you'd do this by gradually shooting for longer and longer time on task and greater concentration.

Right Time Devoted to Task

One of your jobs is to predict from past experience how much work capacity a student has with respect to a certain task, and to pick a point goal that may stretch the student's work capacity, but will not grossly exceed it. At the beginning, the times devoted to each task can be very small. Even a student with a very short attention span can get lots of useful work done if you have several different activities for the learner to do, and quit each one of them before the learner's attention span to that given activity is exceeded.

There are several types of "balance" to think about when you are trying to decide whether to quit one activity and start another. You want to keep a balance between learning new material and practicing with old material. The principle of balance between learning new material and practicing with old material is a result of the fact that there are at least two types of memory. Totally unfamiliar material gets stored in short term memory. If you keep loading more and more unfamiliar material into short term memory, the new material will crowd out, or interfere with, the material that you just loaded in. However, if you load a few bits of new information into short term memory, and then practice them over and over, they begin to get consolidated into longer term memory. Then you can load a few more bits of new information into short term memory, practice them, and then go back and practice the first ones again.

Have you ever experienced the unpleasant feeling of having so much information thrown at you that you can't remember any of it? Do an experiment. Imagine that something very important depends upon your doing the following task well. Please read each number in the following string once and try to remember them all (or have someone read them to you out loud):

7357205789823254629430586794652l
864978655

Now, see if you can skip the first 5 numbers and recite back the next 5 numbers. Can you remember the first 5, or the last 5? And how pleasant was the attempt to remember all these?

Now, look at the following string of numbers and try to remember them:

84532

Now can you recite back these five numbers?

If you're like most people, you could remember the five numbers when that was all you were asked to remember, but when you were bombarded with a lot more numbers to remember, you couldn't even recite a string of 5 numbers. The capacity of information to drive out other information from memory is referred to as interference. My effort at "teaching" you the additional numbers not only failed to teach those numbers to you; it drove out of your memory the ones you had already registered in your memory bank.

How sad it is when education is like this. The teacher and the student are working hard, but the additional information that is being thrown at the student is not only being forgotten, but also interfering with the retention of information that has previously been presented. And even sadder, the experience of trying to remember too much is producing very unpleasant feelings in the learner.

Suppose that when you are teaching a student to read, you try to teach him the letters and letter combinations for all of the approximately 40 sounds in the English language in one day. There will likely be lots of interference. (There were 40 numbers in the string you tried to remember above.) Suppose instead, that you go over four sounds, and then practice with these, until the student knows them cold; then introduce four more and practice a long time with these; then review the first 8; then add 4 more, and 4 more, and review the second 8, then review the first 16, and so forth. You will get better results the second way, for the same reason. We can call this technique "chunking." By chunking, we can store huge amounts of information in memory.

Different learners require different balances between practice of old material and introduction of new material. A very fast learner may be able to take in lots of new information relative to the practice of the old. A very slow learner may need huge amounts of drill with the old material relative to introduction of new material. You make the judgment of the best balance based on the learner's responses. If the student is catching on quickly and getting all the questions right, you can try moving in the direction of faster introduction of new material. If the student misses more questions, you move toward more practice with old material. Just as with finding the correct level of difficulty of the material based on the student's responses, you also find the correct rate of introduction of new material based on the student's responses.

There's another aspect of the learner that might make you want to change to a new activity: the learner's attention span, or "novelty-seeking" preference. For some learners, you may need to break up the activities into short bursts, because the learner gets bored with any given activity quickly. For some learners at the beginning of training with short attention spans you may find it best to do a given activity for no longer than 5 minutes at a stretch; for others (hopefully the same ones by the end of training) you can keep doing the same activity for an hour. Again, you want to meet the learner where he is, and try to gradually stretch out his attention span.

Another area of balance is that between sitting still and moving around. During tutoring some learners have been known to pace around while doing the activities. This is ok if it doesn't distract the learner from the task at hand. If the learner has been cooped up and made to be still for a long time before the session, and if the learner has to sit still during the session, the session is not as likely to be productive. Sometimes if you can work out a way for the student to have some exercise time before the session, the learner will do better in the session.

An Important Principle About Right Time Devoted To Task

Here's a very important principle. Knowing and following this principle can make the difference between a student who gradually grows in work capacity and a student who does not. So take careful note!

The principle is this: *make the ending of an activity contingent upon the completion of a preset goal, not upon the student's reaching a certain level of fatigue, boredom, or complaining.*

Here's an example of a tutor's not following this principle. The tutor and student start the sounding and blending exercise. After about 50 points, the student starts to complain, "When are we going to be done?"

The tutor says, "Oh, not a lot longer, keep going."

Then after a while the student says, "I want to stop. Come on. I've got to stop."

When the student has whined and complained enough, the tutor decides the student has had enough and stops.

What has happened here? The student, like all other human beings, gets fatigued from effort. The stopping of that effort is pleasant (relatively speaking) – it's a reinforcer. But what the student got reinforced for was feeling pain or discomfort from such effort and complaining about it. The discontinuation of effort has reinforced the discomfort. In the next lesson, the discomfort will be just as great, or greater.

Now consider a second scenario. Before starting, the tutor says, "How does your work capacity feel today?"

The student says, "Not too good. I didn't get much sleep last night."

The tutor says, "OK. Let's go for 200 sounding and blending points instead of 300. How does that sound?"

The student assents and they get going. Now periodically the student asks, "How many points so far," and the tutor answers. When they reach 200, they stop as planned.

Now what is being reinforced? Each time the student asks how many points and hears a higher number, effort is being reinforced. The pleasure of termination of the effort reinforces the achievement of the points, not the conjuring up of a certain level of discomfort.

If the student achieves a goal for a higher number of points than the student had achieved before, that is the occasion for much celebration. That should be interpreted to the student as another record broken on the way toward greater work capacity.

Response to Missed Questions

There are at least two incorrect ways to respond when a student misses a question. One way is to give unnecessary disapproval, such as by saying "No! Come on! You should know that's not right!"

The incorrect response is to keep prodding the student to answer the question when the student doesn't know it. For example:

Tutor: What's the next word?

Student: Wet?

Tutor: No, it looks like wet, but it has a different ending.

Student: I don't know.

Tutor: It doesn't have a tuh at the end.

Student: (silence.)

Tutor: It's something that people get onto with their computers.

Student: (Gets off task and goes over to look at something else in the room.)

Why is this such a bad way of responding? Because it's uncomfortable for the student not to know the answer, but the instructor won't let the student get off the spot. The instructor keeps pulling for an answer that the student just doesn't know. The student comes up with a way of escaping this unpleasant situation. This is a good way of turning the student off to the Meet the Challenge Game.

Here's what the instructor might have done instead.

Instructor: What's the next word?

Student: Wet?

Instructor: Almost! Listen to this clue: wuh eh buh.

Student: I don't know.

Instructor: The word is web. Can you say web?

Student: Web.

Instructor: Good!

Here the instructor got the student off the spot quickly by telling the student the right answer after only one clue. The instructor didn't keep trying to pull the answer out of the student.

Pacing of Activities

This means how fast or slow you go. Let's use the example of reading a book to a student. You can read slowly, and linger over every page to look at pictures and talk about them. Or you can read very quickly and tear through the book as quickly as you can, keeping the pages turning rapidly. Which is better? It depends on the individual student. If the student seems to have a short attention span and needs lots of rapidly changing stimulation in order to keep on task, you'd probably better have a very fast pace. But that same student may gradually learn to tolerate a slower pace and it can be very good for the student to learn to be more patient. You want to go fast enough that the student doesn't get bored, but slow enough that there's time to think, and think a lot. You come to the best compromise you can with any student in any given session. At the beginning, when in doubt, keep a fast pace so the student won't get bored.

Response to Undesirable Behavior

There are of course all sorts of undesirable behavior, and you don't respond to all of them in the same way.

Some instructors have thought that certain behavior is undesirable when it's actually very desirable. For example, when reading a story to the student, it's fine for the student to make comments or ask questions about the story in the middle of it rather than just sitting passively and listening. This talk by the student should actually be reinforced.

Other undesirable behavior is best responded to by just ignoring it. For example, the student groans and complains before every activity, even though the tutor knows that the student likes the activities and gets lots out of them. It's of course more desirable that the student have a cheerful attitude. But the tutor might do best just to ignore the groaning and complaining, and be especially attentive and responsive if the student starts an activity without groaning and complaining. Or suppose in a cooperative game, the tutor isn't able to get the answer, and the student says, "Ha ha ha, you didn't get it!" in a taunting tone. This is the sort of provocative utterance that tutors often do well to ignore, to pretend that they didn't hear, or to respond to with a little "humh" to acknowledge that you heard but are choosing not to respond to further. If you pay lots more attention to the nice talk than to the unfriendly talk, the nice talk will come out more and more.

For other undesirable behavior, the best thing to do is to move down the hierarchy of difficulty. For example, a student has very low work capacity. When a tutor tries to have a 15-minute-long sessions of sounding and blending, the student gets restless and uncooperative after about 5 minutes. The tutor might start with 5 minute sessions of sounding and blending held as frequently as possible, followed by a more pleasurable activity that reinforces the student's effort. Gradually the tutor can lengthen the time as the student's persistence and self-discipline skills are stretched.

For other undesirable behavior, the best thing to do is to explain to the student what to do and why, in a very nice tone of voice.

When the student is not cooperating ideally, it is desirable not to get yourself upset. It's the student's problem, not yours. You'll enjoy your job more if you let the student continue to own the problem. After enough time working with noncooperative children you can cultivate the skill of being appropriately sympathetic, compassionate, tough, firm, or whatever -- figuring out the best way to unlock the student's cooperation, without feeling very bad about it.

For other undesirable behavior, the best thing to do is to end the session. For example, a student is in a terrible mood and won't cooperate with any activity, doesn't want to talk, doesn't want to just sit and be connected, and doesn't want to have the session. Whenever the student's behavior is such that you can't have a good session, the way out is to have no session at all. If the student enjoys the sessions, then this will be an incentive for the student to cooperate in the future. If the student frequently refuses to cooperate, consider greatly reducing the time of the sessions. It's probably better to have cooperation for a five-minute session than uncooperation for a much longer session.

When a student misbehaves, avoid yelling in anger at the student. Excitement sometimes reinforces behavior, even when the excitement is negative; some students will find themselves doing more of the behavior that leads the instructor to yell.

Since the main negative consequence for misbehavior in individual tutoring sessions is the ending of the session, you will do well to 1) include some fun activities in the sessions, so that the student will have an incentive to want to come to them, and 2) save the more fun activities for the latter parts of the session and get the least fun parts over at the beginning. That way there's an incentive to stick it out to the end.

When the student misbehaves, you have to take into account what the student's past habits have been. Just as with academic skills, you want to celebrate progress up the hierarchy from whereever the student started out. If the student has behavior problems and starts out the sessions with a large amount of inappropriate or hostile talk, think in terms of gradually working upward in the skill of respectful talk. This will sometimes take a good deal of patient teaching, watching for positive examples, and celebration of those positive examples.

Mastery of Activities

If you are reading to the student, mastery means reading at the right speed, emphasizing the right words, speaking distinctly, portraying in your tone of voice the emotions the characters are feeling, and so forth. If you are doing the sounding and blending exercise, mastery means recording responses without having to slow down and think, reinforcing the student properly, giving clues properly, and so forth. If you are explaining and demonstrating how to do an exercise, mastery means explaining very clearly and giving a brief but clear demonstration. Most instructors can't do any of these things with sufficient expertise the first time they try. That means the key to this item is to practice the activities with someone else other than your student -- such as another instructor -- until you are very comfortable with them.

Avoiding Arguing with the Student

If you find yourself going back and forth with a student, saying "It is too" and "It is not," or "Yes I can" and "No you can't," you're usually not doing the job right. Remember that it takes two people to have an argument. The way to stop the student from arguing with you is simply to stop arguing yourself. If the student is misbehaving and he starts to argue with you about what to do, don't bet on being able to win the argument with him and have him say, "OK, you have persuaded me, I'll do what you say." It doesn't happen very often.

There's a difference between an unpleasant argument and a debate or discussion. Suppose the student wants to debate with you over whether it's better to be a reptile or a mammal, or whether it's possible to be in two places at the same time, or whether it's wrong to copy certain software, or whether time travel will ever be possible, or any other academic question. If the student and you can enjoy such debates, more power to you. Sometimes debating in this way is a great stimulus to thinking skills.

Differential Reinforcement

Reinforcement means that you respond to a student's behavior in a way that rewards it, and the word differential means that you reward some behavior more than others. If you pay more attention to some behaviors than others, you'll gradually (over the course of several days or weeks) start seeing more of the behavior you pay attention to. If you get more excited over some behavior, you'll probably start seeing more of that behavior. Attention and excitement are the two big reinforcers to think about when we think about differential reinforcement.

Major, life-changing improvements in students' behavior have been brought about when people have learned to use differential reinforcement. Your students will love to get your attention and interest and excitement, so give these to the desirable things they do and ignore a good fraction of the undesirable things.

Think about this: Everything a student does while in your presence can be placed on some scale of least desirable to most desirable behavior. Everything you do can be placed on a scale of how desirable it is to the student. Every second during your time with the student, you are being some degree of reinforcing, neutral, or punishing. Ideal use of differential reinforcement means that when the student's behavior gets better, you get more reinforcing, and when the student's behavior gets worse, you get less reinforcing (but not necessarily punishing). So many people do just the opposite. When the student is good they figure they can take a break and leave the student alone. When the student is bad they figure they'd better go and fix things, either by correcting the student (the attention from which can often be reinforcing) or by trying to give the student what he wants so as to appease him (which is almost always reinforcing).

Valuing Work and Achievement

The item on valuing work and achievement has to do with making, from time to time, brief comments that communicate to your student ideas such as these: making the world a better place is a great thing: learning and education will help you to improve the world; work and practice and effort are the key to education. Examples:

"If you keep on working like you did today, you're going to be reading some day well enough to pick up a book that tells you how to help people in any way you want, and learn how to do it, from reading the book!"

"Guess what! I know somebody who wrote something that got printed in the newspaper! It was about what the city should do!"

"That person is so hard working! I bet they're able to work for 2 hours straight without even stopping once."

"That was really something what she did, wasn't it? I bet she had to practice and work for a long time to be able to do that."

"Do you know what it takes to get able to do something like that? Work!"

"Look at these pictures. I bet the person who drew these had to do a lot of work to draw them like this, and even more work to learn how to do it."

"You just did some good work. The work you did is the same type of work that people do when they achieve great things. It takes lots of work, and you can achieve things."

"How do you think he got to be able to do that? Do you think he got able to do that by watching television, or what? ... Yes, I think so too! He did it by working at it!"

"When we started, you had a hard time reading these little words. Now you can read them easily, and you can also read lots harder words. That's what we call achieving something!"

***

By such comments, if your student likes you and trusts you, you can help indoctrinate your student into the work ethic, the idea that you can make things happen by consciously trying to make them happen rather than by waiting to get lucky.

Doing a Positive Review

Doing a positive review means that just before you end the session, you recount to your student some of the best things the student did during that session. These can be in the areas of academic achievement, cooperative behavior, or anything else. It doesn't take long; a minute is almost always sufficient. The purpose of the positive review is to make the student's positive behaviors stand out in his mind so that he will be more likely to do things like that in the future.

Example:

"I sure did like how today you were able to keep working until you'd gotten 200 points. That's the skill of sustaining attention."

"When you said to me today that it was fun to do these things with me, that was a compliment you gave me. That was kind of you to do that."

"You made me proud of you today when you wanted to do a game at the end and I told you we didn't have time. You didn't get upset, and you handled it well. That's called fortitude, and frustration tolerance."

Notice two things from these examples. First, the tutor is not talking about the student's general way of being in the session, but about a specific, concrete event, a very short story that arouses a particular mental image in the student's mind. You want the image to be a concrete one, so that the recounting of it lets the student practice that image in his mind one more time. Second, the tutor might take the opportunity to label what psychological skill the positive act is an example of. These are the labels discussed in most of my other writings.

****

Thus ends the discussion of the items on the checklist for sessions. Each item represents a lot to know and to do well.

I recommend self-monitoring, using this checklist. If you really contemplate what each item means, and recall what is entailed in doing each item well, you'll do some very productive thinking.

Reading Activities

Learning the Most Frequent Sounds of Letters, Yourself

I'm referring to this as a step for the instructor, not the student! Most instructors will need, at some point, to expend some work to learn to say the isolated sounds of letters, particularly the short vowel sounds. If you have already done this, fine; if not, here are some suggestions.

I made reference earlier to the sounds usually taught first for each letter. What are those sounds? For each of the vowels, it's the "short" vowel. For g and c it's the "hard" sound rather than the "soft" one. For q it's a kwuh, and for x it's ks. The first sound of each word pictured on the "alphabet page" is the most frequent sound the letter makes, except for the letter x. If you are not already thoroughly familiar with these sounds, listen to my "What the Letters Say" CD or mp3 files until you are thoroughly familiar with them. Pay particular attention to the short vowel sounds, since these are hardest for most people.

Why are these sounds taught first? They are the sounds used in the simplest three letter words that are close to the bottom of the hierarchy for the learner.

Unless you have taught reading before, you may have had little cause to think about the sounds that letters make, in isolation. But this is a very important piece of knowledge to have as a teacher of reading.

Practice looking at the 26 letters and saying the sound each letter makes. Do this enough that you know these automatically. I've used the following exercise for groups of instructors. Seat yourselves in a circle. As a group, say the sounds for each of the letters of the alphabet. Go around the circle and let each person say the sound that comes next in alphabetical sequence. If everyone knows the letter sounds well, you should be able to do this in under fifteen seconds.

You shouldn't count the student as wrong when the student names another sometimes-used sound for a certain letter. For example, if you ask the student what sound a vowel makes, say "Right!" if the student says either the short sound or the long sound. You can then tell the student that the letter also makes another sound, or that at present you are working on another sound the letter makes, and you can say that sound.

One of the letter sound songs instructs the student about blends such as ch, sh, ph, th, oy, etc. The sounding and blending exercise with words in word families is an important way to learn the sounds of letter combinations. As the student progresses to lists that introduce new sounds such as the sounds of these blends, you will read a caption upon going to the list that says something like, "In this list ch says chuh as in church."

Choosing Which Reading Activities To Do

There are listed in this chapter many reading activities. How do you find the right level, how do you choose which ones to do with the student? The notion of stages is meant to help you find the right level. Here are the stages listed again:

Oral Language Development and Interest in Books
Phonemic Awareness and Spatial Awareness
Letter-Sound Correspondence
Sounding and Blending Words from Word Families
Reading Decodable Text

The general strategy is to find challenges that the student can be successful at nearly all the time, and move upward from there. When the student encounters frustration or "just can't get it," think about moving downward on the hierarchy. When the student is successful and morale is high, gradually move upward on the hierarchy.

The student doesn't need to have mastered totally any one stage before taking on activities in the next. Requiring total mastery before moving up would actually impede the rate of progress. If the student can get to the point where she can successfully do the sounding and blending exercise with the word lists, she can continue to practice phonemic awareness and letter-sound correspondence, as well as word recognition through that activity. But if you run up against a brick wall imposed by lack of readiness for the activity you are trying, recognize that quickly and move downward.

Suppose that a student can't enjoy hearing good, easy, books read to him, the types of books you hope he will learn to read soon. If it's not pleasant to hear the books, the student is missing a very important source of motivation that will help him learn to decode those books himself. Cultivating the student's pleasure at hearing books read is a central task, one that should not be skipped. It sometimes involves starting with very short, attention-grabbing, richly illustrated books, and working the way up to longer and more complex ones. This task is aided by trial and error at seeing what books the individual learner can enjoy. It's also aided by reading with great enthusiasm and expressiveness and with lots of positive attention to the student – not just to the book.

If the student can't do most of the tasks on the Phonemic Awareness Test which is printed in this book, and especially if the student can't do the "blending exercise" easily, then phonemic awareness activities are indicated. If the student doesn't get nearly all correct on the spatial awareness test, the student needs to work on the spatial awareness exercises.

If the student doesn't know all 26 letter sounds (the Letter-Sound Test printed in this book is one way of assessing this), and if the student isn't able to say the sounds quickly (hopefully under 15 seconds) then teaching letter-sound correspondence is in order.

The level the student attains on the Phonetic Word Reading Test, included in this book, gives a clue about where to start in doing word list work.

The main way to figure out what are the right activities is to have clearly in mind a hierarchical series of tasks, and to move up or down them according to the daily feedback you get from observing the student's performance on these.

Here is the hierarchical series of tasks.

The Hierarchy of Challenges for Reading

Oral language development and interest in books.

There are 5 core oral language development exercises in this program.

1. First is conversation between student and tutor (with the tutor using the listening skills listed earlier, in the section on responsiveness).

2. Second is the tutor's reading picture books to the student. These include the "letter stories."

3. Third is the tutor's reading to the student while the student listens, without looking at illustrations.

4. Fourth is the student's retelling of the stories that have been read to him.

5. Fifth is the student's making up of stories while the tutor writes them down and reads them back.

6. Sixth is drilling on basic concepts and basic vocabulary that is useful for future activities.

For students with language problems that are not responsive to this level of intervention, there are many more activities beyond the scope of this program.

Phonemic Awareness and Spatial Awareness

The letter stories mentioned earlier are also a way of developing phonemic awareness. Our Phonemic Awareness Test has 20 levels. With these it is possible to move gradually up the hierarchy of difficulty in phonemic awareness. The following are very important phonemic awareness exercises:

1. the blending exercise, (figuring out a word given the component sounds)

2. the "which sound" exercise, (hearing and being able to say the first, last, or middle sound of a word)

3. the segmenting exercise (taking a word apart into its component sounds).

The blending exercise is essential to what goes on in sounding and blending while reading. The "which sound" exercise is crucial for learning letter-sound correspondence. And the segmenting exercise is fundamental to spelling.

In each of these exercises you may use pictures to make the exercises easier or more pleasant. Later in this book are "three phoneme word" pictures. These include words such as bib, hat, kiss, and so forth. There is another set of 26 pictures, whose beginning sounds match each letter of the alphabet, printed on the "alphabet page" in this book.

You can give phonemic awareness exercises without pictures. For many students, especially older ones, the pictures are not necessary.

Phonemic awareness is an auditory skill: you hear the different sounds that make up words. There is a visual skill that is also an important foundation for reading; I have called it spatial awareness. Central to spatial awareness is recognizing the differences between one figure and another, particularly between figures and their mirror images. A lower case d is the mirror image of a b; in most forms of print a lower case p is the mirror image of lower case q. Left-right distinctions are central to spatial awareness. When you can reliably and without a mental struggle distinguish between b and d and p and q, you have achieved a large milestone in spatial awareness. One of the distinguishing features of this program is a set of tasks that are designed to take the learner along the hierarchy of difficulty in spatial awareness. Here are some of the stages:

1. Telling whether pairs of arrows are pointing in the same direction or different directions.

2. Telling whether arrows on a page are pointing to the left or to the right.

3. Telling whether two very assymetrical pictures are the same or different; you use pairs of pictures, some of which represent identical images and some represent mirror images.

4. Telling whether pictures are the same or different when they are more nearly symmetrical.

5. Doing the same-different exercise with pairs of letters, some of which are identical and some of which are mirror images.

6. Learning to say which letter is at the left, the right, or the middle of a three-letter word; learning to say whether a given letter is at the left, right, or middle.

7. Looking at sets of three pictures, two of which are identical and one of which is the mirror image of the other two; finding the picture that is not like the others and saying whether it is on the right, on the left, or in the middle.

8. Doing the same as the previous step with sets of three letters.

9. Looking at b's and p's and d's and q's and saying whether the ball is on the right or left of the stick.

10. Looking at a series of b's, p's, d's, and q's and identifying them, by letter name or by sound.

Letter-Sound Correspondence

The letter stories mentioned earlier are meant to help with letter-sound correspondence as well as oral language development and phonemic awareness. In addition, there are other letter-sound correspondence exercises:

1. The instructor reads alphabet books to the learner. Sometimes the instructor says letter sounds rather than letter names.

2. The learner hears and learns to sing the letter sound songs included on "What the Letters Say."

3. The learner and tutor look together at the four-letter-pages. The learner points to or says the position of the letter that makes a certain sound given by the tutor.

4. The learner and tutor look at the four-letter-pages. The learner makes the sound of a letter when the tutor points to it or says its position.

5. The learner practices giving the sounds and letter names associated with the first letters of the three-phoneme words and the letters of the alphabet page.

6. After doing the which-sound exercise for ending sounds and middle sounds, the learner practices giving the sounds and letter names associated with the second and third letters of the three phoneme words.

7. The learner looks at printed letters in alphabetical order and in random order, and tells their sounds (as well as their names).

Word List Work

There are 4 major activities for this stage.

1. The student says each word in one of the "Words in Word Families" lists, immediately after the instructor says the individual sounds. (Instructor sounds, student blends.)

2. The instructor says the individual sounds in the word, and then the word; the student does the same thing immediately afterward. (Instructor sounds and blends; student sounds and blends.)

3. The student says the individual sounds in the word, and then the word, without having heard the instructor do this immediately before. (Student sounds and blends.)

4. The student reads the words without saying the separate sounds, and works to do so gradually more rapidly. (Student practices word-reading fluency.)

If all of these activities are hard for the student because the student is unfamiliar with the words, sometimes an easiest of all "activity 0" is a good idea: the student simply repeats the words after the instructor.

If the student isn't successful with activity 3 or 4 for any given word, the instructor drops to activity 1 or 2. If the student still is not successful, the instructor drops to activity 0.

When the student gets to a level of proficiency with one-syllable words, the student then can do exactly the same sounding and blending activities with polysyllabic words, only this time saying the sound of each syllable before blending, rather than the sound of each phoneme.

Reading and Comprehending "Decodable Text."

There are four main activities in this area:

1. The student reads to the instructor from text that is appropriate for the student's level.

2. The student and the instructor take turns reading to each other from text appropriate for the student's level.

3. The student and the tutor do the "reflections exercise" with text.

4. The student and the tutor discuss what they have read together.

The first volume on the hierarchy of difficulty is the *Primer* of Illustrated Modeling Stories. From here you can go to the beginning of the *Programmed Readings for Psychological Skills*, and go straight through that volume, from start to finish. Meanwhile you can also use the *Illustrated Stories That Model Psychological Skills*. A list of other supplemental books is included later in this book. The supplemental books are compiled so as model positive skills and to avoid celebration of violence or rudeness.

Now let's go through these activities in more detail.

Activities for Oral Language Development

Oral Language Development: Conversation Between Student and Instructor

If the child has no motivation to talk and listen, how can the child have motivation to read? Writing and reading are only ways of encoding and decoding talk. One of the key goals of early education is developing a child's interest in the miraculous thing called communication through spoken words; if that interest is there, the motive for reading will be greatly strengthened.

If you want to help a young child have a conversation, the key is modeling. You simply tell some about your own experience. If you want to bring out positive reports from the child, tell the child about good things you've done or nice things that people have done for you or things you have to celebrate. Don't engage in talk that celebrates violence or rudeness, no matter how subtly. It may take a while to raise your consciousness so that you are able to recognize the most subtle examples of this. Remember that the child's role is not to hear a confessional of your major faults and failings. Take seriously your possible status as a role model for the student, and expose the student to the most imitation-worthy of your own experience. This is not hypocrisy; it's being selective about what images you import into the student's memory.

Oral Language Development: Reading Picture Books to the Student

The illustrated stories that you read to the student include the illustrated modeling stories and the letter stories. The phrase "modeling stories" refers to the positive models of thought, feeling, and behavior that these stories try to present. Let's talk a little more about the letter stories.

Reading the Letter Stories

The "Letter Stories" are part of the larger set of "modeling stories." They have characters who are letters. The letters can speak normally to each other, but to human beings they can only speak their sounds; they communicate words by getting together and blending their sounds. They do acts of helping and rescuing by speaking words to people.

In this activity, an instructor simply reads the letter stories to the student. There is no drilling or question-answering.

In a way that is hopefully fun and playful for the student, the letter stories expose the student to the "fundamental idea" that reading occurs by sounding and blending, as each letter says his sound separately, and the letters then blend to form the word. The student also gets to hear the sounds that many of the letters make. Finally, since the communication of the word usually saves someone from a disaster, the student gets reminded that words and the ideas they communicate can be very important: figuring them out is not something that will be done purely to please a parent or teacher.

Tips on Reading the Letter Stories

When you are reading the letter stories, the sounds that the letters say are to some extent signalled by the story; for example d will say "duh" and b will say "buh." You want to say the sound the letter makes, tacking on as little extra sound as possible. I put "buh" and "duh" and so forth in the stories only because I couldn't think of a better way to signal the reader that he or she is supposed to make the b or d sound. But the less of an "uh" sound you can make, the better. You don't want to throw in a bunch of sounds that the student will then have to eliminate when the sounds blend together to make a word.

This same reminder goes with all the activities involving saying letter sounds. (The "uh" is referred to as a "schwa.")

The main rule is to say the sound that is in the word the letters will say. Thus if the word the letters will eventually make is "fire," the letter i will say a long i, and if the word the letters will eventually make is "sit," the letter i will say a short i.

Read the letter stories to the student as many times as the student wants to hear them. Hopefully this will be many times. If the student hears these over and over, the repetitions will give him a great head start on learning to read.

Oral Language Development: Reading Stories To the Student

In this activity, you simply read a story to the student. It's important to read very expressively.

This activity often comes at the end of the session, and is the student's reinforcement for doing the more self-disciplined work of the rest of the session.

Oral Language Development: The Student Retells Stories That Have Been Read

In this activity, you can ask the student to go back to the beginning of an illustrated story that you have just read. You ask the student to turn the pages and look at the pictures and tell you back the story. If the student can do this, you reinforce every single utterance in the student's retelling of the story.

Oral Language Development: The Student Dictates Stories

Here the student tells a story or an essay to the instructor, while the instructor writes it down (usually at a computer keyboard). Afterwards, the instructor reads it back to the student. As an extra touch, instructor might print out the story, draw a few quick illustrations, or let the student draw some illustrations. This can then be used as another illustrated story.

For the student who has trouble making up stories, there are two levels of help the tutor can give. The first is "Fill in the Blank." The second is "Multiple Choice."

For "Fill in the blank," the tutor says something like, "Let's make up a story together. I'll start it, and you fill in the blank. Once upon a time, long ago and far away, there lived a ... what? Can you fill in the blank?" If the student says "a boy," the tutor says "Good!" and then continues, "This boy's name was ... what was his name?" The tutor gradually gives the student more responsibility for the story, saying things like, "And then the next thing that happened was ... "

If the student is not ready for the level of storytelling demanded by "Fill in the Blank," the student might be ready for "Multiple Choice." Here the tutor says something like, "Let's make up a story together. I'll start it, and there are times that you get to pick what we put in. One time, there was ... a boy, a girl, an old man, a wolf, a bear, or an airplane?" Suppose the student says, "an old man." The tutor says, "Good choice! One day this old man decided he would do something. Was it going for a walk, calling a friend, sailing across the ocean, or riding a bear?"

If you do this activity please establish the ground rule that the stories will not have the characters doing violent things. If the student has the characters kill each other or blow each other up or something violent, then you say something like, "One thing that we're really interested in, in this project, is making up some stories that are nonviolent. Can you have them do something where they don't hurt each other?" If the student can't or doesn't want to, then you say something like, "It's something you learn to do as you get to be a better and better storyteller!" Try not to make the learner feel bad about his initial efforts of violent storytelling, but also try not to reinforce such stories. For example, don't print out and illustrate and send to the student the violent stories.

Bringing out stories in these ways that are fun for the learner is an art that requires quite a bit of practice to perfect. It's one of the harder ones in the list. Make sure you practice it thoroughly before doing it with a student.

One way of bringing out stories is to use a "fill in the blanks form." This helps the student learn to tell stories with a character, a complication, and a resolution, by prompting them with parts of the story, but leaving parts out. Here's an example of such a form.

Once upon a time there was a person whose name was ______. This person lived in ________________. One day the person decided to go to ____________. On the way, the person met someone else, who __________________.

A problem came up. It was that ______________________.

____________ wondered what to do about this problem. So ________ decided to ask somebody else for some advice. When ________ asked ________ what to do, ____________ said, "______________________."

Then something surprising happened. It was that ______________.

Finally the problem got solved. Here's how it got solved: ________________________.

After this, ______________ felt so __________ that ____________________.

The End

If the student is so shy or inhibited that she can't fill in the blanks, you can give multiple choices. You can also fill in any of blanks yourself to keep the story moving, especially the ones that call for a repetition of one of the character's names. The student may be surprised to learn that you can generate many different stories with this form. If you get tired of this one, you can generate new ones, or use the ones in Peggy Kaye's book, *Games for Writing*, from which this idea was taken.

Here is an even more important and useful way of generating some writings by the child himself. As you read the *Programmed Readings for Psychological Skills*, the child gradually gets very familiar with sixteen psychological skill groups. They are

productivity
joyousness
kindness
honesty
fortitude
good decisions
nonviolence
respectful talk
friendship-building
self-discipline
loyalty
conservation
self-care
compliance
positive fantasy rehearsal
courage.

In this exercise, you ask the child, "What have you done lately that you are glad you have done?" This is called the "celebrations exercise." You are looking for any examples of any positive behaviors of any sort, almost all of which can be classified into at least one of the above categories. You write down what the child tells you about his positive behavior, in a vignette just like those of the Stories that Model Sixteen Skills and Principles. You print this out and give it to the child, and let this be part of the reading that the child practices.

Some children will make up stories about great things they've done. Rather than chiding the student for being a liar, I find it works best to compliment the child's imaginative ability and to simply write the story as fiction.

Activities for Phonemic Awareness

Phonemic Awareness: The Blending Exercise

The blending exercise has several different formats, ranging from very easy to very hard. You want to start with the level that is best for the learner according to the the learner's performance on the blending exercises in the Phonemic Awareness Test.

The blending exercise is the most fundamental of all phonemic awareness exercises, because it mimics most closely what someone must do when putting sounds together while sounding out words, or taking words apart into sounds when spelling.

The Blending Exercise With Pictures

For this exercise you can use the pictures in the section of this book entitled "Three Phoneme Words, with Pictures." It is good to do this easiest level a good bit even if it seems easy for the student, for a couple of reasons: it establishes what the names of the pictures are, it gives the student lots of practice at hearing those sounds separately, and it prepares the student for doing the which-word and which-sound activity with these words.

To do this easiest version of the blending exercise, you ask the student to look at two of the pictures on a page. You tell the student what names these pictures go by. For example, you say, "The first picture is of a bag. The second picture is of a corn cob; we will call it a cob." For the young student, you might even ask the student to repeat these words to you, to make sure that the student can pronounce them right. "The first picture is of a bag: can you say bag? ... Good. The next picture is of a corn cob; can you say cob? ... Good." Then you say, "I'm going to take one of these words, and break it up into parts. You try to guess which one I'm thinking of. I'm thinking of the buh – ag. Can you guess which one I'm thinking of?" In this easiest stage you divide the word into just two parts.

In the next harder stage (but still a very easy one) you divide the word into its three phonemes. "The next picture is of a hen, and the next is of some gum. I'm thinking of the huh ĕ nn. Can you guess which one?"

The Blending Exercise With Verbal Clues

An exercise on the same level or perhaps a little harder level of difficulty as the blending exercise with pictures is the blending exercise with verbal cues. Here are some examples.

1. I'm thinking of something that means not little. It's buh ĭ guh. (big)

2. I'm thinking of something that a baseball player likes to get. It's to get a huh ĭ tuh. (hit).

3. I'm thinking of a place where they grind up flour. It's a muh ĭ ll. (mill)

4. I'm thinking of something that keeps it from being dark. It's the lll i tuh. (light)

5. I'm thinking of an animal that gives milk, that isn't a cow. It's a guh o tuh. (goat)

6. I'm thinking of another animal that makes a sound sort of like a goat. It's a sh ee puh. (sheep).

7. I'm thinking of a part of my body. It's my huh ĕ duh. (head)

8. I'm thinking of another part of my body. It's my chuh ĭ nnn. (chin)

9. I'm thinking of something you talk on. It's a fuh ō nnn. (phone)

10. I'm thinking of something someone wrote. It's a buh oo kuk. (book)

11. I'm thinking of something that holds things together. It's tuh ā puh. (tape)

12. I'm thinking of something that I wear on my foot. It's a ss ŏ kuh. (sock)

13. I'm thinking of something I use to spread peanut butter on bread. It's a nnn ī fff. (knife)

14. I'm thinking of something I don't like to get in my clothes. It's a rrr ĭ puh. (rip)

15. I'm thinking of a part of my body, and it's my buh ă kuh. (back)

When the student can do these comfortably, you can go up to longer words -- four phoneme words, and then five phoneme words.

4 phoneme words:

16. I'm thinking of part of my body, and it's my rr ĭ ss tuh. (wrist)

17. I'm thinking of something I work at, and it's a duh ĕ ss kuh. (desk)

18. I'm thinking of something I like to drink, and it's mm ĭ lll kuh. (milk)

19. I'm thinking of something I like to do, and it's to sss wuh ĭ mmm. (swim)

20. I'm thinking of a taste I like and it is sss wuh ē tuh. (sweet)

21. I'm thinking of something that is running water, and it's a kuh rr ē kuh. (creek)

22. I'm thinking of something you put into a computer, and it's a duh ĭ sss kuh. (disk)

23. I'm thinking of something you eat, and it's buh rr ĕ duh. (bread)

24. I'm thinking of something that plays music, and it's a buh ă nnn duh. (band)

25. I'm thinking of a piece of clothing I have, and it's my buh ĕ lll tuh. (belt)

26. I'm thinking of something that means a little bit wet. It's duh ă mmm puh. (damp)

5 phoneme words:

27. I'm thinking of something I have two of. They're my huh ă nnn duh zzz. (hands)

28. I'm thinking of a piece of metal that holds things together. It's called a kuh lll ă m puh. (clamp)

29. I'm thinking of something I do with my eyes. It's to buh lll ĭ n kuh. (blink)

30. I'm thinking of something useful that someone did to the floor. The person sss wuh ĕ puh tuh. (swept)

31. I'm thinking of a bad feeling people sometimes get in their belly. It's called a kuh rr ă mmm puh. (cramp)

32. I'm thinking of a part of a piece of bread. It's the kuh ruh ŭ sss tuh. (crust)

33. I'm thinking of something I like to do when I'm thirsty. I get a duh rrr ĭ nnn kuh. (drink)

34. I'm thinking of a man's name. The man was named fff rrr ă nnn kuh. (Frank)

35. I'm thinking of something a baby learns to do just before he learns to walk. He learns to ss tuh ă nnn duh. (stand)

36. I'm thinking of what you call it when you go uunh! It's called a guh rrr ŭ nnn tuh. (grunt)

37. I'm thinking of what you call it when someone plays a joke on someone. It's called a puh rrr ă nnn kuh. (prank)

38. I'm thinking of what you tell a computer to do when you want some words on paper. You tell it to puh rrr ĭ n tuh. (print)

39. I'm thinking of a time of year that is nice. It's the sss puh rrr ĭ nnn guh.

40. I'm thinking of something you might tie knots with. It's a sss tuh rrr ĭ nnn guh. (string)

41. I'm thinking what someone gets by lifting weights. He or she gets sss tuh rrr ŏ nnn guh. (strong)

42. I'm thinking about what you do when you believe someone is telling you the truth. It's called tuh rrr ŭ ssss tuh. (trust).

43. I'm thinking of a little animal that lives in the ocean, that people sometimes eat. It's a sh rrr ĭ mmm puh. (shrimp)

44. I'm thinking of what you make when you jump into a swimming pool. It's a sss puh lll ă sh. (splash)

45. I'm thinking of part of a tree. It's a buh rrr ă nnn ch. (branch)

46. Here's a sound that happens when you bite certain foods. kuh rrr ŭ nnn ch. (crunch)

47. Here's something that is a coiled up piece of metal: it's called a sss puh rr ĭ nnn guh. (spring)

48. Here's something that some people do when they're scared. It's to sss kuh rrr ē mmm. (scream)

49. Here's something that is sometimes on a door. It's a sss kuh rrr ē nnn. (screen)

50. Here's another word for a creek. It's a sss tuh rrr ē mmm. (stream)

Since the first edition of this book was written, I've been even more impressed than previously with how these blending exercises with sentence clues are a great way to develop phonemic awareness. Therefore, in a later section of this book, you'll find 587 more such sentences!

Phonemic Awareness: The Blending Exercise with Stories

In this activity, you take one of the modeling stories, and say to the student, "I'm going to read you a story. As I read it, I'm going to take some of the words apart, and see if you can blend them back together, to guess which word I'm reading. For example, if I were to say "Once upon a time there was a boy named Tuh-om," you would say "Tom." If I were to say, "Tom had a duh-og," you would say "dog." Do you understand?

Then you read the story from start to finish to the student, taking some of the words apart and letting the student put them back together. Don't forget to feel and show your pleasure when the student succeeds at this. Don't take so many words apart that you break up the continuity of the story. Choose easy or hard words according to the ability of the student. Break them down into few or many parts according to the ability of the student.

Phonemic Awareness: The Blending Exercise Without Clues

In this version of the blending exercise, you can get many more repetitions per minute in, because you aren't spending time on clues. You give one word after another, broken up into parts, and let the student put it back together for you. I recommend using the list of words in word families, so that you can prepare the student for sounding and blending those words later on. As you continue this exercise, you gradually build up speed, so that the learner is getting lots of practice repetitions per minute.

Phonemic Awareness: The Student Segments the Words

In this version, the student thinks of a word, breaks it into parts, and lets you put it back together. The job of the student is to break the word into the correct parts. This is the most difficult version of the blending exercise. This exercises the phonemic awareness skill for the student called "segmenting." This is particularly useful in learning to spell.

Phonemic Awareness: The "Which Word" or "Which Picture" Exercise

This exercise is meant to reinforce phonemic awareness skills. It helps the student to further isolate the sounds in words.

You can do this with the pictures in the section of this book entitled "Three Phoneme Words, with Pictures." You say something like, "I'm thinking of either the hen or the six. Let's see if you can guess which one. Here's your clue. I'm thinking of the one that starts with sss. Can you guess whether I'm thinking of the hhh-en or the sss-ix?" If the student can get the right answer at least 80% of the time, then you continue with this exercise without having to drop back on the hierarchy of difficulty.

If the student doesn't know the meaning of the word "starts," you explain it, making reference to the letter sound song "Ă As In Apple." You say, "The sound a word starts with is the one that you hear first. For example, apple starts with ă , bus starts with buh, cat starts with kuh, dog starts with duh."

If the student can do the blending exercise with pictures but can't do the which-picture exercise, there are some intermediate steps. In the first, you ask the student to say the word with the first sound split off. So this goes like this: "I want to see if you can say exactly what I say. Do you see the picture of the man? Please say man. That's good! Now please try to say it with the first sound split off, just like I say it: mmuh-an. Right!" The first intermediate exercise is simply repeating words with the first sound split off.

The second intermediate step is to show the student the two words on a page, and ask the student to repeat them after you with the first sound split off, and then ask the student which one starts with a certain sound. Like this: "Can you say mmmm-an? Good. Can you say buh-ell? Yes. Now guess which one I'm thinking of. I'm thinking of one with mmmm at the start. Do you think that's mmm-an or buh-ell?"

The third step is not to ask the student to repeat the word with with the first sound split off, but just to split it off yourself, just enough to emphasize it. Like this: "I'm thinking of either man or bell. I'm thinking of the one that starts with buh: is that mmm-an or buh-ell?" As this step progresses, you split it off less and less.

The fourth step is not to do any splitting off or emphasizing at all. You just say, "Between man and bell, which starts with buh?"

You can move along this progression with most students so that each stage is prepared for by the previous ones, and there's no stage that is extremely hard. If even the very first stage is frustrating for the student, go back and do the blending exercise with pictures more times.

In the next stage of difficulty, you don't use pictures, but just pick two words. You say, "I'm thinking of either a desk or a jar. Can you guess which? Here's your clue: it starts with juh."

After you have done the which-picture or which-word exercise for beginning sounds, you then go to something harder: you do the same steps, if necessary, for ending sounds. If necessary, you explain to the student what you mean by giving examples: "By the ending sound, I mean the one you hear last in the word. For dog, do-guh, guh is the ending sound. For cat, ca-tuh, tuh is the ending sound."

Then the hardest step is to do the same thing with the middle or vowel sound. You say, "The middle sound or the vowel sound is what you hear in the middle of these words. For dog, duh ŏ guh, the sound in the middle is ŏ . For cat, kuh ă tuh, the sound in the middle is ă ." You go through and do the same exercise for middle sounds as you did for beginning or ending sounds. For example: "Do you see on this page a man and a bell? Which one of those has an ă in the middle: is it man, or bell?"

Phonemic Awareness: The "Which Sound" Exercise

Here's what this exercise sounds like. Again, it's useful to use the three phoneme words with pictures.

"What do you see at the top of this page? Yes, a bat. Let's think about the word bat. Can you listen to the word bat, and tell me what sound you hear at the beginning, at the start of the word? Is it mmmm, or is it buh?"

Thus you give the student two choices to pick from. If this is too hard, you can make it easier by first emphasizing the first sound or splitting it off from the rest of the word, or asking the student to repeat after you when you do that.

When the student gets to the point where he can answer correctly when given two choices, you ask the student to tell you the answer without multiple choice. Thus the question format is simple: "What sound does bat start with?"

Notice that you are talking about sounds, not letters, in all these phonemic awareness exercises. If the student answers the question "What sound does man start with?" by saying "the letter M," you say to the student, "M is the name of the letter that word starts with, that's good. But what I want is the sound that it starts with, not the name of the letter. Is it mmmm, or guh?"

After doing this with the pictured words on the word pages, you can do it with other words, any you pick. Please do this exercise with the pictures on the alphabet page. To do this you direct the student's attention to the alphabet page, and you say things like, "Do you see the apple? Good. What does apple start with: is it ă or kuh?" When the student does the which-sound exercise for beginning sounds enough with the pictures on the alphabet page, the student is getting much readiness for learning letter-sound correspondence.

After you do this with beginning sounds, you go back to the three phoneme word pages and do this with ending sounds and middle sounds. Here's what this sounds like.

"Do you see the web on this page? Please listen to the ending sound in web. Does web end with buh, or with juh?" If the student can't get this, you make it easier by saying "We-buh. Does we-buh end with buh, or juh?"

When the student can answer these two-choice answers correctly, you can move to questions without multiple choice. For example: "Do you see the man? What sound does man end with?" Again, you want the sound, not the letter.

Finally you do the which-sound exercise for middle or vowel sounds, starting by splitting the word up and giving two choices. "Do you see the bat? Buh -- ă -- tuh. Tell me which sound you hear in the middle: is it ks, or is it ă ?" When the student gains facility at this, you stop splitting the word up, and you can also make the exercise harder by giving two choices that sound similar, such as ă and ĕ or ĕ and ĭ. When the student still is able to be successful nearly a hundred per cent of the time, you go to the which sound exercise for middle sounds without two choices. "Do you see the cup? What sound do you hear in the middle of cup?"

There are a good number of other phonemic awareness exercises that teachers have used. But if the student gets to the point of close to 100% success on the blending exercise, the which-picture or which-word exercise, and the which sound exercise, the skill of phonemic awareness is probably developed to the point where it is not the rate limiting step in starting to sound out words. The skill of phonemic awareness will be continue to be exercised greatly when you move to the exercise of sounding and blending words in word families.

Phonemic Awareness: The 20 Levels of the Phonemic Awareness Test

Another way of getting in mind the various phonemic awareness exercises described earlier is to think about the twenty levels of The Phonemic Awareness Test. This test presents phonemic awareness activities that range from the very easy (almost all children can be successful with Level 1) to fairly hard. This test is reprinted in the portion of this book entitled "Tests." Practice giving this test enough times that you are very familiar with the items on it. The hierarchy of difficulty with phonemic awareness exercises usually corresponds to the levels of this test. With some students you will need to go through each of the 20 types of exercises; with others you can skip some of them. (Some other students somehow show up with an ability to do all of them, before receiving any instruction at all!) You want to aim for a goal where the student can score close to 100% on the Phonemic Awareness Test. Below are the 20 levels that are tested in that test. Feel free to teach to the test. For maximum generalization, use different words than the specific ones in the test. It's helpful to look at the "Words in Word Families" list when coming up with examples for these exercises.

Level 1: Blending with two choices. Say: I'm going to break a word into the separate sounds that make that word. I want to see if you can put the sounds back together, and guess the word. For example, if I say duh ŏ guh, the word is dog. OK?

Example:

The word is either kite or goat. guh ō tuh. (goat)

Level 2: Blending without two choices. Say: Now I'm going to do the same thing, only without giving you two choices first.

Example: huh ă tuh (hat)

Level 3: Blending without two choices, 4 phonemes. Say: Here are some words with four sounds for you to put together.

Example:

mmm ĕ lll tuh (melt)

Level 4: Blending without two choices, 5 phonemes. Say: Here are some words with five sounds for you to put together.

Example:

buh lll ĕ sss tuh. (blessed)

Level 5: Saying first sound split off. Please leave a little silence between the beginning sound and the rest of the word. Say: Now I'm going to say some words, sometimes splitting the first sound off from the word. I want you to just repeat after me, and say exactly what I say, just like I say it.

Example:
Say jump. Now say juh-ump.

Level 6: Yes-no for beginning sounds. Say: Now listen to the first sound in the word, and tell me whether the word starts with that sound or not, yes or no. For example, if I ask you does net start with nnn, you'd say yes. If I ask does goat start with juh, you'd say no.

Example:
Does berry start with buh?

Level 7: Which sound for beginning sounds, two choices: Say, Now listen again for the beginning sound of the word, the sound the word starts with. For example, if I say does dog start with duh or sss, you say duh.

Example:

Does corn start with kuh or duh?

Level 8: Which sound for beginning sounds, no choices. Say: Now I'll say a word, and you tell me the sound it starts with.

Example:

What's the beginning sound for mouse?

Level 9: Same or different for beginning sounds. Say: I'll say two words, and ask you if they have the same beginning sound, or different beginning sounds. For example, if I give you dog and cat, you'd say different, because they have different beginnning sounds, duh and kuh. If I give you dog and dip, you'd say same, because they both start with duh.

Listen to the two words and tell me whether they have the same or different beginning sounds.

Examples:

win and watch (same)
jump and vat (different)

Level 10: Saying ending sound split off. Please leave a little silent space between the ending sound and the rest of the word. Say: Please repeat after me, and say exactly what I say.

Say book. Now say boo-kuh.

Level 11: Yes-no for ending sounds. Say: Now please listen to the ending sound of the word, the last sound you hear in the word. Say yes or no to the question I ask about the ending sound. For example, if I say, does dog end with guh, you'd say yes. If I ask, does dog end with puh, you say no.

Example: Does great end with tuh?

Level 12: Which sound for ending sounds, two choices. Say: Now please listen for the ending sound again, the sound the word ends with. Instead of saying yes or no, tell me the sound it ends with. So if I say, does dog end with guh or duh, you say guh.

Example:

Does band end with puh or duh?

Level 13: Which sound for ending sounds, no choices. Say: Now listen for the ending sound again. I'll say a word, and you tell me the sound it ends with.

Example: What's the ending sound for tack?

Level 14: Same and different for ending sounds. Say: Now I'll say two words, and ask you if they have the same ending sound, or different ending sounds. For example, if I give you dog and pot, you'd say different, because they have different ending sounds, guh and tuh. If I give you dog and pig, you'd say same, because they both end with guh.

Listen to the two words and tell me whether they have the same or different ending sounds.

Example: Whirl and for (different)

Level 15: Yes-no game for middle sounds. Tell me the sound you hear in the middle, the one called the vowel sound. For dog, the sound in the middle is ŏ . So if I say, for dog, is it ŏ ? you'd say yes. If I say, for dog, is it ee, you'd say no.

Example: for sit, is the middle sound ĭ?

Level 16: Which sound game for middle sounds, two choices. Say, keep listening for the middle sound, the vowel sound. Tell me which sound you hear in the middle. I'll say something like, for dog, is it ŏ or ee, and you'd say ŏ .

Example: for boat, is it o or ŏ ?

Level 17: Which sound game for middle sounds, no choices. Keep listening for the middle sound, the vowel sound. I'll say a word, and you tell me the vowel sound in the middle. So if I say dog, you just say ŏ.

Example: What's the middle or vowel sound for got?

Level 18: Segmenting, three phoneme words. I'll say a word, and you break it down into the first, middle, and last sound. Like if I say dog, you say duh ŏ guh.

Example: seed. (correct answer is sss e duh.)

Level 19: Segmenting, four phoneme words.

Please take each of these words apart into 4 sounds.

Example: tank (correct answer is tuh ă nnn kuh)

Level 20: Segmenting, five phoneme words.
Please take each of these words apart into 5 sounds.

Example: cracks. (correct answer is kuh rrr ă kuh sss)

Spatial Awareness Activities

Phonemic awareness is an auditory skill. But reading also involves visual skills: recognizing letters and letter patterns, and discriminating them from others that look similar.

Whoever made up the alphabet made the visual-spatial challenges especially hard for many learners by having a letter "b" that is the mirror image of the letter "d." Also "p" and "q" cause difficulty – perhaps a little less, because q is a more rarely used letter.

Sometimes just remembering to read letters from left to right is a problem. And remembering which way to write a 3 and an E and and S and so forth is hard at some stage for almost all learners.

An Entry Level Spatial Awareness Activity: Same or Different Directions of Arrows

The following activity is close to the bottom of the hierarchy of difficulty for some young or struggling learners. In this exercise, the learner looks at pairs of arrows and decides whether they are pointing in the same or a different direction.

For this exercise, you look at pairs of arrows (presented later in this book) that look, for example, like this:

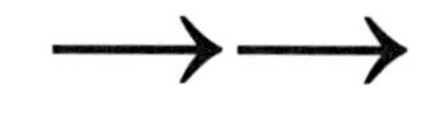

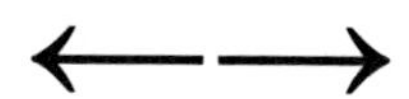

The question to the learner, for a given pair of arrows is, "Are these two arrows pointing in the same direction, or in different directions?" If the learner can't answer this, it could be that he doesn't know the meaning of same or different. You teach this concept by showing the learner pairs of identical or totally different pictures, to illustrate what same and different mean.

If, however, the student knows what same and different mean, but finds this exercise difficult, it could be that you can make it easier by explaining and demonstrating. You do this by pointing with your finger in the direction the arrow is going. You touch one arrow and say, "This arrow is pointing that way; it's pointing up." You touch the second arrow and say "This arrow is pointing that way too. It's pointing up, too." If the learner can not then answer correctly the question of whether the arrows are pointing in the same or different ways, then the learner probably does not understand the linguistic concepts involved.

Is the Arrow Pointing Left or Right?

In this activity, the learner looks at a set of arrows and for each, says whether it is pointing right or left. For example:

1. →

2. ←

The phrase "right away" is a useful mnemonic for this exercise, because the arrows that point to the right point away from the number of the exercise.

The Rest of the Spatial Awareness Hierarchy

Next on the spatial awareness hierarchy are more practices exercises in discriminating images from their mirror images. You can take learners along the hierarchy of difficulty in these exercises, and hopefully this will help them with "reversals."

The next set of exercises involve saying whether two pictures are the same or different. Sometimes the pictures are identical, and sometimes one is a mirror image of the other.

The next exercise involves doing the same thing with b and d pairs and p and q pairs.

The next asks the learner to decide which of three pictures is not like the others. Some part of the brain is responsible for distinguishing images from the same images rotated in space; these brain circuits get exercised by these tasks. If the student also has to give the answer by telling whether it's the picture on the left, the middle, or the right, then this gives exercise in distinguishing left from right.

The next exercise involves doing the same thing, only with triplets made of b's and d's. One of the three is not like the other two, and the learner says whether that odd man out is on the left, right, or middle.

Another spatial awareness exercise that can be done when the learner knows the names of the letters involves looking at three letter words, and telling the name of the letter, or the sound, that is on the left, in the middle, or on the right. Alternatively, the student can hear the name of a letter or a sound and tell whether it is on the left, middle or right. One might ask, how can the student practice spatial awareness in this way, if spatial awareness precedes letter-sound correspondence and this exercise requires that the student knows either the sounds or the names of the letters? This exercise reminds us that letter-sound correspondence can, and should, be trained at the same time as spatial awareness. The word "stage" is not meant to imply that one piece of learning must be complete before the next one begins.

The next step for teaching the difference between b and d is helping the learner see these letters as a combination of a "ball" and a "stick," and practicing saying whether the "ball" is on the right or the left of the "stick" when looking at these letters. To avoid getting the learner confused, please always ask this question in terms of where the ball is relative to the stick rather than where the stick is relative to the ball. That is, with b the ball is to the right of the stick, and with d the ball is to the left of the stick. In this task the learner looks at a bunch of b's and d's and practices saying "right" for the b's and "left" for the d's.

Next, the learner practices looking at b's and d's and actually saying whether they are b or d. For some learners it is helpful to remember the word "bright." In the word bright, the b stands for b and ball, and the rest of the word, right, reminds us that in b the ball is on the right. One of the letter sound songs on the recording *What the Letters Say* reminds us that "the ball's on the left with the d and the q" and "the ball's on the right with the b and the p."

Spatial awareness is a foundation skill for letter-sound correspondence. If you get into teaching letter-sound correspondence and the student has a lot of trouble, especially with b, p, d, and q, it's probably time to go back and do lots of spatial awareness practice.

Please see later chapters of this manual for the pictures used with the above-mentioned spatial awareness exercises.

Activities for Letter-Sound Correspondence

Letter-Sound Correspondence: The Letter Stories

The letter stories are meant to help with letter-sound correspondence as well as oral language development and phonemic awareness. Keep reading them as long as the student enjoys hearing them.

Letter-Sound Correspondence: Reading Alphabet Books

Part of the way that many students learn the names of the letters is by repeatedly hearing alphabet books read to them, perhaps by a parent at bedtime during early childhood. There are many alphabet books. This is a good activity for any young learner who hasn't learned to associate letters with letter names yet.

When you read alphabet books to the child, don't drill the child about them. Simply read the books to the child as many times as the child wants. If you want to try some game in which the child participates, for example by calling out the name of the letter when he sees it, do the game only if it is fun. You want to preserve a precedent for the child that being read to is a pleasure.

The way alphabet books are usually read, the student learns to associate the letter name with the symbol rather than the sound with the symbol. Thus the student learns to associate this symbol: B or b

with this letter name: "Bee."

But letter-sound correspondence means associating the B or b with the sound, "buh."

When you read the alphabet books, some of the time you can read them using the sound rather than the letter name. You want the student to learn both. To keep the student from getting confused, tell the student what you are going to do. "Last time I read this book with the letter names. This time, I'm going to use the letter sounds. These are the sounds the letters usually make when they are in a word."

Letter-Sound Correspondence: The Letter Sound Songs

A central part of this teaching program is the recording entitled "What the Letters Say." Play the letter sound songs often; if you are lucky the student will listen to them often on his own accord.

The alphabet page (which is printed later in this book) can be used with the letter sound songs. As the sounds are sung, the student can point to the appropriate letter or picture on the alphabet page.

You have my permission to take the alphabet page to a photocopy center, (or any place else with a copier capable of the task) and get the alphabet page blown up to a very large picture. If you're a classroom teacher, you'll want to tape this page onto the wall. The students can look at it while singing the songs, and one student can point to the letter or picture being sung.

The first letter sound song starts out like this:

"Bom bom bom ă as in apple, buh as in bus. kuh as in cat, duh as in dog."

The words apple, bus, cat, and dog and so forth correspond to the pictures on the alphabet page. So this song tells the student exactly what picture to point to.

Here's an exercise with the first song and the alphabet page: You sing or play the first song, and you say the sounds and let the student say or sing the names of the objects. You say, "Now let's do it another way. I'll start singing, but I'll leave out the picture, and you say it for us. For example, I'll say bom bom bom ă as in ... and you say apple. I'll say buh as in ... and you say bus. OK?" If the students can do this with you, this is greatly to be celebrated.

You should repeat this exercise several times. Ask a student to take his finger and point to the picture while he is naming it.

Perhaps next you go to the song, "This is what the letters say." This one says the sound of each letter five times in a row. The song starts out like this:

This is what the letters say, this is what the letters say, this is what the letters say, what the letters say.

ă , ă , ă ă ă
buh, buh, buh buh buh.
kuh, kuh, kuh kuh kuh
duh duh duh duh duh.

The first agenda, of course, is simply to let the students hear the song enough that they get it in mind. If you have a group of students, the simplest thing after that is simply to sing the song as a group. With an individual tutee, you can do an exercise in which you sing the sound twice and the tutee sings it the next three times. "This time let's do it together. I'll go ă , ă , and then you finish it by doing ă ă ă with me. I'll go buh, buh, and then you do buh buh buh with me, and we'll continue like that, to the end of the song."

When you have done this several times, you go to the next step: you sing the sound the first two times, and the student sings it by himself the next three times. So you sing ă , ă , and the student replies ă ă ă , and then you sing buh buh and the student replies buh buh buh, and so forth.

If the student can do these songs with you, then the student is probably ready to do the song entitled "The A says Ă."

The student sings along with you and points to the pictures. Once or twice during the song you check to see which picture the student is pointing to.

When the student has done this successfully, then you see if the student can fill in the sounds while you sing the letters. That is:

You: The a says...
Student: (says or sings) "ă "
You: and the b says
Student: buh
etc.

If the student enjoys the songs, you can spend a lot of time using the same techniques with the rest of the songs on the tape: singing them together, singing them by taking turns, singing them and checking where the student is pointing to. The blends song and the "balls and sticks" song don't correspond to the alphabet page at all.

If the student doesn't enjoy doing the songs in these ways, you may be able to cut these activities short and just ask the student to listen to the letter songs on his own time. The student will probably have to pay for that by doing more drilling activities, but it's better to do this than to have a bad time trying to do the songs with someone who doesn't want to do them.

Letter Sound Correspondence: The Four-Letter Pages

These pages, presented later in this book, have four letters on them, one each at the upper left, upper right, lower left, and lower right.

The tutor decides whether to take on all four sounds at once, or to start with two or three of them. Let's assume that the tutor starts with only two. Then the tutor would say, "This letter says buh. Can you say buh?" When the student says the sound, the tutor reinforces. Then the tutor does the same thing with the second sound. Then the tutor says, "I'm going to say a sound, and you point to the letter that makes that sound." Or, for the second type of activity, "I'm going to point to one of these letters, and you say the sound of the letter I point to, please." After drilling on the two letter sounds until they are easy and automatic (and this often takes only a minute or two) a third and then a fourth letter are added.

It's very important, while learning the letter sounds, to review cumulatively. That is, you don't just take on four new letters a day; you also review all the letters that have been learned in previous days. If the learner needs lots of review, you may forego taking on new letters on some days, so that the learner can work on becoming fluent and automatic with the letters already studied.

If you are doing tutoring by phone, rather than pointing at the letters or having the student point to them, you say the position, e.g. "upper left," "lower right," etc.

Letter Identification and Letter-Sound Correspondence: the Rabbit Exercise

This exercise is very simple. You write anywhere from three to ten letters on pieces of paper. (You can use upper case or lower case, depending on what trying to teach.) You call out the names of the letters (for letter identification) or the sounds of the letters (for letter-sound correspondence). The student "points" to the correct answer.

What makes this simple drill a fun game is that you write the letters very large on pieces of paper, put them onto the floor, and the student, who is the "rabbit," points to the correct letter by jumping onto it. The student tries to jump from one letter to the next in the minimum possible jumps. If there is an error, you stop and correct it. As the student jumps without error, you call out letters or sounds faster and faster. You see how fast the jumping can get. Even the most restless student will reach a point where he wants to sit down and rest.

The game is even more fun for the student when the instructor is the rabbit and the student gets to take on an additional job of fitness trainer for the instructor! If you want, you can play the game such that at some point the instructor will make a deliberate error to see if the student can catch it.

As in the use of the four-letter pages, the tutor is careful not to overload the student's working memory. The rabbit game is a good one for practicing the letter sounds once the student has gotten them into memory already using the four letter pages.

Letter Identification and Letter-Sound Correspondence: Same or Different for Letters

Suppose a student is having difficulty hanging onto memories of the letters' names or sounds. You want to give useful practice that will prepare the student for learning the letters, without bcing too frustrating for the student's current skill level. In other words, you are looking for an activity low on the hierarchy of difficulty.

Same and different for letters may be just what a particular student needs at a particular level. In this, you simply go to your word processor and make pairs of letters, like these:

a a

z h

j k

You use your hand to cover up all but one pair of letters. The question for the student is: are these two letters the same, or different.

What if this activity is still too difficult, for the young or struggling learner? Then you use pictures to teach and practice with the concepts of same and different. You go back to your word processor and use clip art to make pairs of pictures that are either identical or totally different. When the student is good at deciding whether the pictures are the same or different, he will be much more equipped to decide whether the letters are the same or different.

Letter Identification: Using the Alphabet Page

It's useful to know the names of the letters as well as their sounds. Letter identification is knowing that b is the letter "bee"; letter-sound correspondence is knowing that the b says buh. In telephone tutoring it's especially important for the student to know the names of the letters, since a telephone tutor can't readily point to the letters. The telephone tutor will be saying, "What sound does the w in that word make," rather than just pointing and saying "What sound does this letter make?"

You can use the alphabet page to in teaching the names of letters. You look at each picture, and connect it with the upper and lower case letters written above it.

Tutor: What's the next picture you see?
Student: A pencil.
Tutor: Good. Do you see the letters above it? The one on the left is upper

case p, and the one on the right is lower case p.

Once the tutor has told the student a few letters, the dialogue goes like this.

Tutor: Do you see the pencil?
Student: Yes.
Tutor: What letter is above the pencil?
Student: A p.
Tutor: Good! Now can you find the picture just to the left of that?
Student: The ostrich.
Tutor: Right, the ostrich! What letter is that above the ostrich?
Student: An o.
Tutor: Good!

Letter-Sound Correspondence: Using the Alphabet Page Pictures and the Three Phoneme Word Pictures

By the time you get to this activity, you have probably already used the three-phoneme word pictures and the alphabet page pictures for phonemic awareness exercises. So the learner has already practiced looking at the apple and saying that the beginning sound is ă , and so forth.

For this exercise, the picture is the same, and the answer to the question is the same, but the question is different. The question is not "What is the first sound in apple," but "Do you see that letter A above the picture of the apple? What sound does A make?" If the student doesn't know the answer, you say, "Here's a hint: it's the first sound in apple."

To use the three-phoneme word pictures to teach letter-sound correspondence, you do an activity that is very much like the "which sound" activity with these pictures and words. You say, "Do you see the picture of the bag? Do you see the word bag written beside it? Here's the letter b. What sound does b make at the beginning of the word bag?" Then: "Here's the letter a. What sound does a make in the middle of the word bag?" Then "Next is the letter g. What sound does g make at the end of the word bag?" Try to make sure the student looks at the letters while answering these questions. If the student is proficient at the which-sound exercise for beginning, middle, and ending sounds, this twist upon it should not be hard.

Letter-Sound Correspondence: Telling the Names and Sounds of Letters

You use for this activity the numbered lists of letters at the beginning of the "Words in Word Families" lists. There are four lists, for upper case and lower case letters in and out of alphabetical order. You ask the student to start at the beginning and say what the names of the letters are. You also ask the child to start at the beginning of each list and say the sound of each letter.

When the student does this activity, you let the student have the alphabet page nearby. That way if the student can't remember the sound of a letter, the student can look at the alphabet page and see that letter, and think of the first sound of the word pictured by the letter.

As I've mentioned before, it's important not to overload the learner's working memory. If your work with the four-letter pages has been very successful, the learner can look at all 26 of the lower case letters and say the sounds. For the upper case letters, you might start with just the first 4 letters. Then you do the next four. Then you review the first 8, and so on. Here's a possible schedule:

A B C D
E F G H
A B C D E F G H
I J K L
M N O P
I J K L M N O P
A B C D E F G H I J K L M N O P
Q R S T
U V W X
Q R S T U V W X Y Z
M N O P Q R S T U V W X Y Z

Then all letters.

But if the student has heard the letter-sound songs a lot and has done lots of the other exercises, you may not need a lot of repetitive drill.

You want to repeat this activity until the student can give the sounds quickly. When the child can say the sounds for each of the four lists, backwards and forwards, in 15 seconds or less per list, you have "arrived" where you need to be for letter-sound correspondence. For telephone tutors, if the learner can do the sounds quickly enough, you know that the learner couldn't be relying on the alphabet page, because it is time consuming to find the picture on the alphabet page.

Letter-Sound Correspondence: Mnemonic Sentences for Short Vowel Sounds

Some learners have special trouble reproducing the short vowel sounds. If you say, Please say ă ," the student will say "ŭ," and think he's gotten it right. This is an exercise to help those learners. You don't need to do it with most of them.

You ask the learner to repeat after you.

Aaah, forget it! (ă sound)
Eh? What did you say? (ĕ sound)
Ih! That doesn't taste good! (ĭ sound)
Ah! That does taste good! (ŏ sound)
Uh, I don't know. (ŭ sound)

In this exercise you should be an actor and portray the emotion that the sentence conveys, and encourage the student to do the same.

After the learner can repeat these sentences after you, you then see if the learner can repeat the first word in each sentence (with the same emotion portrayed) without the rest of the sentence. This is the same as repeating after you the sounds of the short vowels. Some learners will need lots of work on this task before they can recall the sound of a short vowel upon seeing it. The inability to remember such letter-sound correspondences without a lot of repetition characterizes a lot of folks with "dyslexia." But by repetitive work, most learners can become able to do the task that eluded them before!

Saying Letters, Given Sounds

The question for this activity is "What letter makes this sound?" You ask the student to review letter-sound correspondence in the other direction from that done in previous exercises. This exercise prepares the student for writing, where the student will go from the sound to the symbol rather than from the symbol to the sound.

Let the learner have the alphabet page in front of her. Say, "Can you find a letter that says wuh?" and ask the learner to tell you what letter it is. If the learner needs a hint, say the name of the picture on the alphabet page: "wuh as in watch."

After the learner has done this for a while, she can try it without the alphabet page present.

More Letter-Sound Correspondence from the lists of Words in Word Families

After you've done all the activities so far, does the student know all about phonics that he needs to know? Unfortunately not. If we had a totally phonetic language (such as Esperanto) the student would be able to figure out how to pronounce every word in the language from just learning the sounds of each of the letters. But English is more complicated. Sooner or later the student will need to learn the sounds of ch, sh, ph, all the long vowels (we've only done the short ones so far), tion, and various other combinations.

In this program, rather than attempting to master all the letter combinations at the beginning, the students start reading words after they have learned the first 26 sounds. Then you gradually introduce more letter-sound correspondences in the lists of words from word families, and the student gets to practice reading these words.

Sounding and Blending the Three Phoneme Words

By the time you get to this exercise, the student is thoroughly familiar with the three phoneme words with pictures, from the various phonemic awareness exercises that have been done with them. The student is now ready to start the exercise that will occupy a good deal of effort in this program: sounding and blending words. By sounding and blending words, I mean saying the individual sounds separately, and then blending those sounds to say the word.

I recommend taking a page of the three phoneme words with pictures and doing the four steps:

1. You sound, and the student blends.

2. You sound and blend, and the student repeats after you exactly.

3. The student sounds and blends.

4. The student looks at the words and reads them without sounding and blending.

Here's what these steps sound like.

1. "Let's look at this page. I'll say the sounds of the words, in order, and you blend them to say the word. For example, when I say buh ă guh, you say bag. OK?"
Instructor: buh ă guh.
Student: bag.
Instructor: Good! kuh ŏ buh.
Student: cob.

2. "Now listen as I sound and blend the word, and say exactly what I say. For example, when I say buh ă guh bag, you say buh ă guh bag right after me."
Instructor: buh ă guh bag.
Student: buh ă guh bag.
Instructor: Good! kuh ŏ buh cob.
Student: kuh ŏ buh cob.
Instructor: Right!

3. "Now let's hear you sound and blend each word, from the first to the last. In other words, just start with bag, and say buh ă guh bag, kuh ŏ buh cob, and keep going."
Student: buh ă guh bag.
Instructor: Good!
Student: kuh ŏ buh cob.
Instructor: Yes!

This step is often well repeated several times, until the student can do it easily and quickly.

4. "Now I'm going to put my hand over the pictures. Sound out the words in your head, but don't say the separate sounds. Just say the whole word. When you say it, I'll move my hand so you can see the picture."

Student: Bag.
Instructor: Yes! (Moves hand down to reveal picture of the bag.)
Student: Cob.
Instructor: Right! (Moves hand down to reveal picture of the cob.)

Sounding and Blending the Words in Word Families

When the student has been successful with sounding and blending the three-phoneme words with pictures, the student is ready to start into a major undertaking, one that is central to this program. This undertaking is to practice first sounding and blending and then fluently reading the lists of "Words in Word Families." (These lists are presented near the end of this book.)

Each word list focuses on one type of correspondence between sound and a letter or combination of letters. The following outline eliminates some of the detail in order to show the big picture of how the word lists are organized.

1. Short vowel words, mostly three phoneme words.
2. Consonant blends, still with short vowels
3. Th, qu, sh, ch.
4. Some sight words that don't follow the rules.
5. Vowel combinations: ai, ay, a_e, ee, ea, ie, i_e, ow, oa, oe, o_e, oo, ew, ue, u_e, ar, or, er, ir, ur, oy, oi, ou, aw, au, al, are, are, air, ear, wa.
6. Some more sight words, exceptions to the rules.
7. Some contractions.
8. Words with suffixes: er, ing, y, ies, ed.
9. Other combinations: le, c pronounced s, g pronounced j, s pronounced z, silent g, k, t, w, gh, l, h. Igh, eigh, ph, other pronunciations of ea, the sound of u as in put, ou as in young.
10. More suffixes: tion, cious, tious, cial, tur and ture, sure, ive, or, some, come, ance, ence.

Why Reading Lists of Words is A Good Thing

Why are words grouped with their "relatives" who are spelled and pronounced similarly in some way? When they are grouped like this, the learner can transfer learning from one word to the other, and the process is much more efficient. For example: although it's a shame that our crazy language has a long i sound made by igh, once you have learned this for the word bright, you can immediately transfer that learning so as to read fight, flight, fright, light, might, sigh, and so forth. It's much more efficient to learn the whole group than to learn each word separately.

Let me take a minute to explain why it is not a horrible thing to ask a learner to spend time reading word lists. I do this because there are some theorists who feel that it is dreadfully bad to ask the learner to read words separated from context and "meaning." Here's why these people are wrong!

First, our brains can only do so much at once. When we are starting to read, we can afford to spend some time concentrating fully on decoding the word, without allocating additional brain energy to thinking about what the word means. Why not spend some time focussing totally on how to sound out the words? When we gain more automaticity, more fluency, in calling out the word, we have more neural energy to divide our attention between figuring out what the words are, and understanding what they mean.

Some opponents of working on word lists also argue that reading indvidual words is not exciting, that it is of low stimulation, that it takes self-discipline, it's not entertaining. This is a major reason to do it! The developing learner needs to spend *some* time on self-discipline-requiring tasks, if the learner is ever to develop self-discipline. The learner who gradually increases his tolerance of drill and practice is a learner who is more likely to be a success at almost any venture. Compared with the learner who is raised with the idea that "You're not expected to do any learning task that isn't entertaining," the learner who can tolerate drill and practice is much less of a wimp!

This is not to say that reading instruction should *totally* focus on word lists, for long periods of time each day. But somewhere between five and thirty minutes a day on word lists will develop self-discipline and develop reading skills faster, for most readers.

Finally, direct research supports the notion that practice with words in word families is extremely useful in learning to decode words, especially for those who find reading difficult. This activity has taught some students with reading difficulties the skill of decoding well enough to make the rest of school infinitely more fun than it would have otherwise been. You want to have enough other fun activities that the student can tolerate the discipline of this one. You also want to teach the learner to value self-discipline.

There are certain students who can learn to read simply by reading more and more stories, just as there are some students who need no phonemic awareness practice and no spatial awareness exercise. There are students who can skip all sorts of steps. My purpose here is to include enough steps so that every learner can be successful. If certain children can skip steps and still be successful, that's fine!

Getting Nearly Errorless Performance in Reading Word Families

The instructor should insure that during this activity, the student experiences success on at least 80% of the "trials." A trial is defined as an occasion in which the student tries to do something. The instructor adheres to the 80% rule by keeping the task in the correct range of difficulty for where the learner is at this time.

But even more pleasant for the learner than 80% success is close to 100% success. This is possible for most learners, using the four steps outlined in a section above. Because these are so important, let's repeat them here.

0. "Activity 0" is for the instructor to say each word and let the learner repeat it after the instructor.

1. The tutor says, "Please look at the words, and the separate letters, while I say the separate sounds of the word. Then you blend the sounds to say the word. For example, if I say puh ă tuh, you say pat."

Instructor: buh ă tuh
Student: bat.
Instructor: That's it! kuh ă tuh.
Student: cat.
Instructor: You got it!

2. The tutor says, "Now I'm going to sound and blend each word, and you do it just as I've done it. You repeat after me. For example, if I say puh ă tuh pat, you say puh ă tuh pat right after me."

Instructor: buh ă tuh bat.
Student: buh ă tuh bat.
Instructor: Yes! kuh ă tuh cat.
Student: kuh ă tuh cat.
Instructor: Right!

3. The student says the separate sounds, and blends them together to say the word. This is the "regular" way of doing the sounding and blending exercise. Keep doing this until the student has sounded and blended all the words in the list, with all correct, at least twice. Some students should sound and blend all the words on the list many times more than this. Here's how this sounds:

Student: vuh ă tuh, vat.
Tutor: Good!
Student: fuh ă tuh fat.
Instructor: You got it!

4. The student reads the words without saying the separate sounds. At first the student may want to say the separate sounds to himself before saying the word. Gradually the student picks up speed. You aim for an eventual performance where the student can read the words in one second per word or less.

Adjusting the Level of Difficulty in Word List Work

There are two ways of going back down the hierarchy in response to the student's having difficulty: with a word, or with an entire list.

First, with any particular word, if the student is attempting activity 3 or 4, the instructor gives a hint by saying the individual sounds (activity 1) or by sounding and blending and asking the student to repeat (activity 2).

Second, if the student needs this sort of help on as many as 20% of the words in the list, then the instructor should move back to activity 1 or 2, and work on the whole list with one of these activities. After enough experience with activity 1 or 2, the student will be able to move up to activity 3 and be successful.

These steps can be combined with another method of adjusting the difficulty: you do the above steps with only a small subset of the list. This is especially useful for long lists. You can use the first 10 words, or if the student has trouble, only the first 5 words. You keep going over those until at least activities 1 through 3 are easy for the student. Then you do the same thing with another 5 or 10 words.

Thus you have two major ways of making the word reading activities easier, if you need them. With these two techniques, you should be able to follow the 80% rule without needing to abandon a given list once you've started it. Let's look at a concrete example of how this works.

Let's say that Johnny has gained enough skill in sounding and blending that the first time the student approaches a new list, all the instructor usually has to do is to read the direction for the new sound in that list. The student can take that knowledge and go with it. In that case, the student starts with step 3 and just sounds and blends, without going through steps 1 and 2.

On an occasional word, Johnny isn't successful right away; the instructor does the sounding for him on that word, and lets him do the blending.

If Johnny goes below the 80% success rate, the instructor may say, "Let's go through this list one time with activity 2. I'll sound and blend each word, and you do it right after I do it." The instructor sounds and blends each word, and the student repeats after the instructor.

If this is a really hard list, and Johnny still falls below the 80% criterion, the instructor picks out a set of only five words. They do activities 1 and 2 with just these 5 words. When Johnny has done activities 1 and 2 with this set of words several times, then activity 3 (where Johnny sounds and blends) is very likely to be successful. After mastery of these five words, they take on five more, and five more.

What if the words are so unfamiliar that Johnny has difficulty with activities 1 and 2? Then the instructor goes to "activity 0," simply saying the word and have Johnny repeat it. Once the word has come out of the student's mouth, it's easier for the student to blend it when the instructor sounds it

The Decay Curve, and Frequency of Reviewing

. In a given session, you may work your way up to what appears to be a level of mastery of a list. But a big question remains: how will the student perform on that list tomorrow? For some very rarely seen "dyslexic" students, the memory decay curve seems very steep, so that it soon appears as if you are starting all over again. For most students there will be some decay in memory and skill but not much.

Here's an important principle: learning is much easier when you review soon enough after learning that memory decay has not progressed very far. To put this another way, it's much easier and faster to bump your memory from 90% to 100% than to wait until the memory has more completely decayed and start all over, going from say 10%

to 100%. Ideally, you want to review before the per cent retention dips significantly. It takes lots less work to keep retention high than to let it go way down and raise it up over and over.

The implication of this is that the steeper a given student's memory decay curve, the sooner review should take place. For some "dyslexic" students with steep decay curves, review of previously mastered lists should take place very frequently.

Keeping Track of Points In Word List Work

Reading individual words does not carry the intrinsic rewards present in reading interesting text. I've found that keeping track of "points" with word reading practice is a good way of making the activity more fun. It's also a good way of measuring the increases in the learner's attention span over time.

A good way of keeping up with points is to use a "tally counter" that can be bought in many office supply or sporting stores or over the Internet. The low tech way of keeping track is to use a pencil and paper and tally marks. I have given one point for each correct answer the student gives, with or without assistance. The only exception to this is that if the student both sounds and blends correctly in activity 3, I give 2 points.

Tones of Voice In Reinforcing Success

The most important reinforcers for success in word reading are not points, but the tones of your voice. Make the reinforcement in your tone of voice follow within a split second after the learner has responded. If you delay it, you reduce the effectiveness of your reinforcement. Say "Right," or "Good," or "Umh humh," or "Golf is right," or something like that. If there is a list that the student masters, which previously was difficult, comment on this. "Wow! You did that whole list, so fluently! Do you remember when it was so hard?" If there is a hard challenge, set the stage for it, especially when you anticipate that the student might meet it. "This next list is going to be hard. It involves the short e sound, that's been the hardest one for you so far. Let's see if you can do it." Then, when the learner does it successfully, "Wow! You did it! You conquered the short e list!"

Responses to Wrong Answers

When the learner misses the word, give an assist only by saying the sounds separately (activity 1) or modeling how to sound and blend (activity 2), or by just telling the word and asking the student to repeat it (activity 0). Don't give clues of any of the following sorts:

"It's a game that people play out on a big course."

"You had this one yesterday, remember?"

"Look at the vowel sound."

"No. Think. You're not thinking."

"I know you know how to do this."

Why not give responses to wrong answers other than moving down to activity 1 or 2? When the learner gets a wrong answer you want to avoid prolonging the learner's discomfort by repeatedly asking the learner a question that he clearly does not know the answer to. You don't want to embarrass him by giving many hints and having him still not be able to get it. You want the hints to involve the thought process of sounding and blending, not that of remembering when the word was last seen or guessing the word from clues not involving reading.

There's another advantage in responding to wrong answers in a very standardized way. For most learners this type of response is quite comfortable, but not reinforcing. The standardization and sameness of the response to wrong answers keeps the stimulus-seeking learner from unconsciously trying to get a break in monotony by producing wrong answers. Geting varied responses out of you can be reinforcing. So make the responses to right answers varied, and responses to wrong answers standardized.

Above all, don't keep repeating a question that the learner doesn't know the answer to. Don't keep expecting a learner to answer when the learner has already communicated that he's stumped. This way of teaching is unpleasant, tends to produce resistance in the learner to trying to meet the challenge at all, induces fear of failure, spurs avoidance responses, and wastes time. If the learner doesn't know the answer, give one very informative hint if you want, and then tell the learner what the answer is and move on.

It's different in a situation where the learner really can figure it out if he just persists longer. Here what you need to do is not to give hints, but to say something like, "This is a situation where I think you can figure it out if you keep persisting, but I'm not sure. I'm going to keep quiet a bit and let you keep at it. Even if you can't get it, you can still practice your skills of persistence. Tell me when you want me to tell you the answer and move on." Whether or not the learner gets the right answer, reinforce the learner for spending some time persisting. For example: "Even though you didn't figure it out, you spent some time persisting on it, and that's important! Good for you!"

In the sounding and blending exercise, comment with enthusiasm as the learner passes milestones: each 100 points, the first 1000 points, etc.

It will often help the student's developing mathematical ability if you make a running commentary on how many points the student has gotten. In this way the student will get a gut feeling for how long it takes to get a hundred points; she will get a gut feeling that it takes about twice as long to get two hundred points, and that it takes about ten times as long to get a hundred as it takes to get ten, and so forth. The tutor simply makes statements like, "You're already up to 300 points!" "Only 100 more points till you've got 1000!" and so forth.

Reading word lists is a very important activity. Once the learner gets to the stage where he can do this activity, do it every session, unless there is a very good reason for it not to. In a research project I did, we found about a one grade level increase in reading ability for every 6000 repetitions of sounding and blending.

When the Student Reads the Word But Can't Say the Sounds Separately

The sounding and blending exercise is not just to drill the learner in reading the words in the lists. It's to drill the learner in saying the sounds, separately, and then blending them together to read the word. Don't skip this step. Some learners have memorized whole words and are able to use these memory traces to call out the beginning words. You want the learner to use a mental process that links sounds to letters and letter combinations, and the best way to make sure this happens is to do the sounding and blending exercise.

If in activity 3, the student says the word, but doesn't say the separate sounds, prompt the student to say the separate sounds. Say something like, "Could I hear 3 separate sounds, please." Or, "Each sound separately, then blend them please." If in response to this prompt the student can't say the separate sounds, then sound and blend and ask the student to repeat after you (activity 2). If the student frequently fails to say the separate sounds in words, the phonemic awareness tasks need to be practiced more.

Teaching the Student the Value of Self-Discipline

Some learners will react to certain exercises by saying, "This isn't fun, I don't want to do this." Before you even get to this point, explain to the learner something very important: there is a reason to do things other than that they are entertaining. You also do things because they produce good results, not just because they are fun. In our entertainment-oriented culture, some learners, even older ones, do not realize this. From the very beginning, when you explain the exercises, you should explain that there will come a time when the learner will not "feel like" doing an exercise. But that's the point, you explain, where the learner gets to practice something very important: self-discipline skills. Self-discipline means being tough and brave enough to do something, because it makes something good happen, even if you don't feel like doing it. Being wimpy means that you can't get yourself to do anything you don't feel like doing. Getting yourself to practice sounding and blending even when you don't feel like doing it is a very self-disciplined thing to do. It shows that you are tough.

There are many people who are failures in life because they haven't learned to take pride in getting themselves to do what they don't feel like doing. They haven't learned to resist temptation. The more you can make rational decisions about what to do rather than being ruled by what you feel like doing, the more you have inner strength.

The person who is luckiest of all is the person who, having decided what is best to do, is able not only to get himself to do it, but to find things to enjoy about it. For example, the person who needs to lose weight and who exercises every day but hates it is better off than the person who doesn't exercise at all; the person who finds a way to enjoy exercising is best off of the three.

You want to search for the words that the student will understand, and gradually explain these concepts to the student. Probably several short speeches will be more effective than one long speech. The second major section of *Programmed Readings* is about self-discipline; the students may benefit from hearing this section read to them at the beginning of their instruction.

If the student can become convinced of the value of self-discipline, and can have, in your reading course, the first-hand experience of successfully using self-discipline to become an expert reader, something wonderful has happened.

Of course, teaching the student about self-discipline doesn't relieve you of the responsibility of picking the correct place on the hierarchy of difficulty for all the demands you make on the student's self-discipline. You have to pick a length of time on task for a given learner that the learner has a chance for success at. For some students with very short attention spans, just 3 minutes of working on word lists will be sufficient at the beginning of the learning process. The priority at the beginning is establishing a pattern of success, establishing the precedent that the student can do what you ask him to do. Only when that precedent is set do you gradually rachet up the level of expectations. Eventually, you want to work up to the point where the student is getting 400 word list points and 600 or more text reading points per lesson.

Activities for Reading Text

Reading Text: The Modeling Stories

This is the stage of the reading process where the student actually gets to read something that means something, e.g. stories.

Some reading teachers are in a rush to get to the point where the student can read meaningful material as opposed to reading word lists, on the theory that if the student doesn't do this, the student won't realize what reading is all about, i.e. getting meaning from words rather than just calling them out. But in the rush to have students read stories early, the stories are sometimes made pretty devoid of meaning. It's hard to construct great literature from sentences such as "Sam sat on a mat."

The other problem with reading text too early is that the student sometimes has to devote so much energy to decoding the words that there isn't working memory space left over to appreciate what they mean and what's going on in the story.

The philosophy of this program is to help the student enjoy literature and the meaning of words by reading to the learner, as long as necessary, so that the learner experiences with great comfort the whole point of what reading is for. In early sessions, the student works on reading word lists and gets more and more automaticity with this, and hears stories read to get more and more automaticity in the listening comprehension proccss. When reading words is fairly automatic and making meaning from spoken language is also fairly automatic, then the learner is ready to read text in a way that is pleasant and not a big jump up on the hierarchy of difficulty.

Another principle of this program is that stories should model positive ways of thinking, feeling, and behaving. Especially for young children, stories should in large part avoid modeling very negative patterns. By showing the reader how to handle situations well, the story works at two things at once: reading skill development and character development.

The hierarchy of difficulty for the text used in this program is simple: the first volume is the *Illustrated Modeling Stories, Primer*, which is printed in this book. You start by reading the stories to the student, as many times as the student is interested in hearing them. That way the student has the memory traces of the stories, as well as sounding and blending skills, to make it easier to read the words. That way it is more likely that the first experience with story reading will be a positive one. You can read each story immediately before the student reads it. When the student masters the *Primer*, the student is ready for work in either or both of two sets of materials: the unillustrated stories in *Programmed Readings for Psychological Skills*, and the *Illustrated Stories that Model Psychological Skills.* When the student has mastered the readings in all of these two volumes, the student has probably reached at least the average level achieved by most third or fourth graders in the United States. In addition, the student has been exposed to lots of examples of positive skills and lots of useful concepts on psychological skills.

At the same time, of course, you can read any supplemental books you want. Be sure to pick books easy enough not to frustrate the learner. If a book you pick turns out too hard for the learner to read, read the book to her. Come back to it later when she is ready to read it herself.

It is often fun to take turns reading books, with an instructor reading one page (or one paragraph, or one vignette) and the student reading the next. This is especially useful in telephone tutoring, when it's nice to get frequent confirmation that the other person is still at the other end of the line!

It's surprisingly easy with a tally counter to count the number of words the student reads from text. You click once for each word, and the counter gives you a running total. For many students, text-reading points are much easier to get than any other type. One of the main goals of this program is that the learner gets the ability to get very large numbers of text-reading points quickly, say 500-1000 points per sitting. When the student can do this and can understand what he has read, we have achieved a great goal!

Ways of Adhering to the 80% Rule for Text Reading

The 80% rule applies to text reading just as it applies to the reading of word lists: we want the student to be able to read successfully at least 80% of all the words in a given passage.

There are two important ways of making it easier for the student to read any given story. One is to read the story to the student just before the student tries to read it. That way the memory traces assist the student in reading. The second way is to read again stories that the student has already read before. You keep returning to familiar stories so as to increase the fluency and automaticity of reading. You want the student to experience the pleasure of reading without struggling to decode each word.

As an example: the first day you might do the first three stories. The next day you might do two new ones, and two of the old ones. On subsequent days you might do one new one, and four old ones. You gradually build up until the student can read 10 new ones each session – but the buildup is very gradual.

If a student can't read a word during text reading, just read the word yourself quickly so that you can move on. You don't want the student to spend a lot of time trying to decipher one word while text reading. Spending time in this way bogs things down; the student forgets what the passage is about.

Using the Readability Ratings in Word Processors

You can get a fairly useful "readability" rating by using a word processor such as *Microsoft Word.* Click on "Tools" and then select "Options," then "Spelling and Grammar," then "show readability statistics," and then "OK." This turns on the readability statistics measurer if it was not on. Then type in a sample of the text you want to measure. Select it. Then, click Tools, then Spelling and Grammar. When the checking is done, you may see a display which includes "Flesch-Kincaid Grade Level" (where 0.0 is easiest) and "Flesch Reading Ease" (where 100 is easiest. (On the other hand, if the program is having a bad day, it may not feel like giving you these statistics!)

Comprehension Practice with the Programmed Readings

Our preferred format for using *Programmed Readings* is for the tutor and student to take turns reading sections, for the student to answer all the comprehension questions, and for the tutor to give lots of approval when the student reads well and answers questions correctly.

How does the student know the answer to the question? At the beginning, you have to read to the student the list of 16 skills and principles and get these words familiar in the student's mind. When the student deliberates, you might help out by referring to the initial list and reading the brief statement that defines each of the skills and principles. Or, you can at the beginning, answer the question yourself and explain why you answered it this way.

The Reflections Exercise

The second major format for doing the *Programmed Readings* (or any other text reading) is used for those students where a major goal is language development and comprehension. In this format, you do the "reflections exercise." Here's how you do it. You take turns reading a vignette (in the *Programmed Readings*) or a paragraph (in any other book). Whoever did not read does a "reflection" of what the other person read, by saying the words "So you're saying ______" or "In other words ______" or "What I hear you saying is ______" and filling in the blank with a brief paraphrase of the story. The tutor can if desired give feedback on the accuracy of the student's reflection. This exercise gives lots of practice at listening for main ideas and restating them in your own words. This is a skill that is of paramount importance. This format puts some stress on the student's patience skills and concentration skills. This, of course, is the best way to grow those skills. But you may not want to do this when such a task is too high on the hierarchy for a particular student.

Here's how the reflections exercise sounds with a couple of passages from *Programmed Readings*.

Tutor: OK, is is my turn to read?
Student: Yes.
Tutor: Ann was at school. At talk time, the boys and girls got to talk. They said what they thought.

Ron said a wrong thing. Ann got the urge to say, "Ron, you don't know a thing." But then Ann thought, "Why make Ron feel bad?" So Ann said, "I have a different idea." She told what she thought.

Ron did not mind this. Ann was glad she had not been rude to Ron.

respectful talk (not being rude) or compliance?

Student: respectful talk.
Tutor: Right! Ready to do a reflection?
Student: What I hear you saying is that when Ron said something wrong at school, Ann got the urge to put him down but she didn't. She just told her different idea instead, and she was glad she didn't hurt his feelings.
Tutor: Good! OK, your turn to read.
Student: Biff was very strong. Biff was very fast. Lunk said to Biff, "I'll fight you. You can't win."

Lots of kids said, "Get him Biff. Show Lunk he's wrong."

Biff said to Lunk, "Why should I hurt you? Why should you hurt me? That would be dumb."

Lunk said, "You are just scared."

Biff said, "You can think what you will."

The kids were sad. Biff said to them, "To watch a fight should not be fun for you."

The kids knew Biff was right.

nonviolence or productivity?

Student: nonviolence.
Tutor: Right. Now it's my turn to do a reflection. In other words, Lunk challenged Biff to a fight, and even though Biff could have beat him up, and even though a bunch of kids wanted to see him fight, he refused to fight. He told the kids they shouldn't want to entertain themselves by watching a fight.
***

In more advanced stages of work, you can do a variation on the reflections exercise, in which the student reads the vignette or paragraph silently, then does a reflection in his own words. Doing this with passages that the student has already read before is a good way to build up fluency in silent reading.

If a student reads the entire book of *Programmed Readings for Psychological Skills*, doing the reflections exercise, the student will be well practiced in both decoding and comprehension skills, as well as with concepts that should assist greatly in psychological skills. If you get the opportunity to provide this experience for a student, don't pass it up!

Reading Text: Discussing The Reading

You want to model for the learner how to take an interest in the text rather than just calling out the words. Accordingly, it's good to make a comment or two about what you've read or what you're reading, to show the learner how to generate ideas about stories. Here are some examples of several types of comments.

What-If Questions:

He was lucky that the other boy said "Yes" so quickly when he was nice to him. I wonder what he would have done if the other boy had been really shy, and just turned his head in the other direction?

I think he already knew the man and the dog. Do you think he should have given a piece of his hamburger to a dog if he didn't know the owner and the dog?

Questions about Motives:

I wonder why Ronko was trying to bug Bill like that. Maybe Ronko was bored and wanted some excitement.

Good Decision or Not:

I think that it was a good decision when Rusty decided to give the boy a swimming lesson rather than to get really mad at the boys who were teasing him.

I don't think the dog's owner made a good decision by letting the dog run loose at that place. Do you?

Example of :

They did some examples of good decision-making together, didn't they? I guess that's what the author is thinking that this story is an example of.

How a person felt or thought:

Do you think that Alex felt scared? He might have been scared that Ronko would be mad at him.

I'll bet that Jerry felt proud of himself for saving that boy.

Some people might have felt mad that the people didn't thank him, but it looks like Mack didn't care about that, doesn't it.

I wonder if Mack worried that somebody would think he was trying to kidnap the little girl.

That reminds me of:

That reminds me of a time that I helped someone who had gotten lost.

That reminds me of having to hold still and be very quiet when I played hide-and-seek.

That reminds me of a house in my neighborhood when I was a child that I used to pretend was a haunted house.

****

If the learner picks up on these comments and chats about them, fine. If the learner starts to imitate these after a while and starts to talk about the stories, the tutor can reinforce this by very enthusiastic listening.

Reading Text: Reading Modeling Stories to A Younger Child

One of the main payoffs of learning to read is that you get to make the world a better place by reading stories to young children! Once the student has mastered a number of the illustrated modeling stories, (meaning: the student can read them with expression and drama, and not just call the words) then try to engineer it that the student reads the stories to a younger child.

Many older learners will want to be able to read stories to younger children. Unless the older learner has no desire to do this at all, you can harness this motive and actually consider the older reader's reading the modeling stories as a practice for reading them to children. In this way you can get around the problem of the modeling stories' being too juvenile for the older reader. The older reader is not reading the stories for his own entertainment, but to practice helping someone else.

Recycling Through Earlier Stages

Speaking of various stages of reading development doesn't mean that the learner has to master totally one stage before going on to the next. Likewise, when you move to a higher stage, you can keep reviewing the lower ones. Particularly, once the student can read some decodable text, it's still good to progress through the "Words in Word Families." As you do this, more and more text becomes decodable.

The work on maintaining interest in books should be kept up by doing lots of reading to or with the learner, perhaps taking turns on alternate pages or paragraphs, or letting the learner relax and listen to you read. Don't be so driven that you feel the learner has to do some reading every time you experience a book together. On the other hand, taking turns reading to each other is a fun activity for people of all ages, including adults.

Do All Students Need All These Activities?

The answer to this is simple: No. In fact, some students learn to read without doing *any* of them, except for text-reading. This program has so many activities because it tries to supply a task at the right level of difficulty for any learner, and tasks that go up in small increments of difficulty for those who need this.

Many students do not need to be taught phonemic awareness or spatial awareness – it seems that these skills develop, without special training, at or before the time for the child to learn to read. Yet for others, these skills simply do not develop without lots of work. A wonderful breakthough in reading instruction is the discovery that certain types of work, along a hierarchy similar to those described here, will develop these skills.

For another example, many learners do not need to spend time sounding and blending words by syllables. But for many others, this activity done for not a particularly huge quantity of time will lift their reading fluency by leaps and bounds. For this reason, this book contains many pages of words broken into syllables for those who can use them.

Fortunately, making the judgment calls about which students need which activities is not difficult in individual tutoring. When in doubt, the tutor can simply try a given activity. If the student does it easily and fluently, not much time has been lost. If it's difficult, more time needs to be spent either on it or on one of the activities below it. If the tutor is very familiar with the hierarchy and very willing to experiment, the activities at just the right level can be found.

Points and Tangible Reinforcers

What is the Point of Points?

Why keep track of points as the student learns? For those doing research in the area of reading teaching, keeping track of points allows us to answer a very important question: how much of a certain type of work does it take for a certain amount of progress? How many phonemic awareness points does it take, for various children, before the child has mastered the phonemic awareness exercises? How many sounding and blending points does it take for the child to move up a grade level on tests of decoding skill? These are questions that are answerable only if we keep track of these points.

The second reason for keeping track of points is to help motivate the learner. If you are asked to sound and blend word after word, with no sense of direction or going anywhere, the tediousness of the task can start to become oppressive. On the other hand, if you are setting out on a journey and making progress, knowing that you are aiming toward various milestones of points, the quality of the experience can be totally transformed.

Without a doubt it takes self-discipline to continue to sound and blend one word after another. Your social reinforcement (Good! Right! Yes!) after every right answer helps the child to continue this task. But also, it is good for the child to find that by sustained effort, he can achieve other more distant goals.

The Logistics of Points and Rewards

Suppose a child wants a baseball glove, or a subscription to a magazine. The child also wants to cooperate with doing lots of sounding and blending exercises. One option is for the child to get the magazine or glove for free, and to do the sounding and blending exercises with nothing but social reinforcement. But I believe that it is a very positive experience for a child to set his or her sights on a goal, and to work diligently, day after day, until that goal is attained. Experiences of this sort are part of the basic building blocks in the development of self-discipline. I believe that it is good to set up contingent reinforcement, such that the child gets the magazine or the glove when he has accumulated, say, 5000 sounding and blending points.

For some very unmotivated learners, rewards every 5000 points are not sufficient. It is best for some to have a reward after every session in which the point criterion (e.g. 100 or 200 points) were met. For some children we can rig up a system where the child gets a piece of candy if he meets the criterion. Or, the child gets about 10 calories worth of candy for each 100 points that he earns.

Money and the permission to spend it are powerful reinforcers. These can be made contingent upon points.

There's a catch in the use of tangible reinforcers. It's that the parent has to withhold whatever the reinforcer is, unless the child meets the criterion. If the child, for example, can get all the candy he wants any time, it is pointless to promise the child candy contingent upon a certain performance. If the child is in an environment where he gets all the material goods he wants at any time, material rewards will not be reinforcing. If the child gets a big allowance, the child will not be motivated to work for money. There needs to be some deprivation in order for anything to be reinforcing.

The use of junk food as a reinforcer, if it is done with the cooperation of the learner, gradually helps the learner learn to withhold junk food from himself when he has not earned it, and to give it to himself when he has earned it. Learning to exert conscious control over your intake of junk food is a self-discipline accomplishment that many people never reach.

Another type of reward that can be made contingent upon the attainment of point milestones is special outings or trips. Most children request things that are not necessities of life from their parents, and often their parents say "Yes." I encourage parents to say, "Yes, when you get the next multiple of 5000 points." In this simple way noncontingent reinforcement is changed into contingent reinforcement. The child is given another reason to look forward to getting the next 5000 points.

For children who already have enough -- or too much – material wealth, an option is to gradually educate the child about what is done by various charitable organizations, and to let the child get points toward being able to make a donation to an organization whose cause the child supports. One of the problems with tangible reinforcers is that what we work for, we tend to value more highly; it's good for a program to capitalize on the motivating power of junk food and material possessions, but ultimately it's great if the child develops a wish to make the world a better place as well as a wish to eat and spend. Working for the right to give charitable gifts is a great way to harness the fact that reinforcers often become more valued when we work for them.

Many people are afraid of contingent reinforcement, especially with food reinforcers. My reading of the research evidence and my direct experience with this leads me to think that the risks of contingent reinforcement are greatly overestimated, and the benefits are greatly underestimated, by most people.

We can think of a hierarchy for contingent reinforcement programs.

Near the bottom, the learner collaborates because because very desired reinforcers are withheld and delivered contingently; the learner would steal the reinforcers if he could. As the learner goes up the hierarchy, he comes to understand that the reinforcers are withheld for a reason, and can comply with the rule against stealing them. Gradually the learner becomes able to keep track of points and to know which reinforcers are due at what time. Finally, the learner becomes able to self-monitor, withhold reinforcers from himself, and deliver reinforcers contingent upon points, without the help of any other person. Very few people ever reach the degree of self-discipline of this highest stage; if the learners you work with can reach it, you have accomplished something very important indeed.

Summary of Types of Points

What are reasonable ways to assign points to various activities? For phonemic awareness activities, you can give one point for each correct answer to exercises like those in the Phonemic Awareness Test: the blending exercise, the which-sound exercise, the segmenting exercise, etc.

For spatial awareness, you can give one point for each correct answer to the *Exercises for Spatial Awareness*.

For letter-sound correspondence, you can give one point for each correct answer to the question, "What sound does that letter make," or "What letter makes this sound," or the easier exercises leading up to these.

For the work with reading lists of words, you give one point per word for activity 1 (saying the word after you say the separate sounds); one point per word for activity 2 (sounding and blending the word immediately after you sound and blend it); two points per word for activity 3 (student sounds and blends on his own) and one point per word for activity 4 (student reads words without saying separate sounds). If the student tries to sound and blend a word but fails, and the instructor hints by activity 1 or 2, give 1 point if the student gets the right answer after the hint.

For text reading, you give one point for each word read in stories.

For the purposes of reinforcement, all the points add up to one total. If you are curious about how many points yield how much progress, you will want to keep these point totals separate.

Especially For Classroom Teachers

Most of the activities described in this book can be done with groups of children as well as individuals. Teachers, you have my permission to photocopy any of the pages from this book onto overhead transparencies or slides, and project them on the wall for your group. Or you can enlarge them and tape them on the wall.

The Wall Chart and the Letter Sound Songs

The alphabet page is included in this book; it also comes with the CD, "What the Letters Say." You can enlarge a copy and tape it up on the classroom wall. Now you're ready for various activities with the letter sound songs.

Point and Sing Along

Put on the "What the Letters Say" CD, and play the first track, Ă as in Apple. Use a pointer to point to each picture as it is sung about in this song, and you sing along with the song. When the song says a sound, you point to the letter, and when it says a word, you point to the picture of that word. For example, when it says "buh as in bus," you point to the letter B as you sing *buh*, and you point to the picture of the bus on the word *bus*. You might even prance or dance around while doing so. Do you think you will have your students' rapt attention while this goes on?

Say to the students, "Now we're going to play it again. I want everyone to start to sing along, and I want to get someone else to use the pointer. Who wants to use it?" At the beginning, you can help the student who is using the pointer by pointing with your finger, and letting the student follow along with the pointer.

You can make getting up in front of the room and using the pointer a bigger deal by congratulating the pointer or clapping for him. You can make pointing a prized role for students.

After the students have gotten the hang of how to point along with the music on the first song, you go to the next ones. Even learners who are shaky on letter identification can rise to the occasion and keep up with matching the sung letters with those they see on the alphabet page, if they have a good sense of rhythm, since the transitions from one letter to the next are in rhythm with the lines of the song.

Gradually you progress through the various songs. For the vowels song and the blends song, you'll need to write the vowels and blends on the blackboard.

By repetition, you teach the students to sing the songs along with you. I hope that you and your students can spend many happy hours singing the letter songs together. If you do so, you will find that the students have learned a great deal about letter-sound correspondence through this activity.

The Students Make Up Their Own Version of "Ă As in Apple."

After the students are very familiar with this song, they make up their own words to substitute into the song. For example, instead of "Ă as in apple, buh as in bus. Kuh as in cat, duh as in dog," the students might come up with "Ă as in Adam's apple, buh as in boing boing. Kuh as in cool, duh as in dude. Ĕ as in eggs for breakfast, fuh as in forget about it..."

There are, as always, several different ways to do this. You can divide the students into groups, and let each group think of the words for two or three sounds. You can let the students think of words individually. You can go around and listen to the words before the students sing the new version, to make sure the sounds are right. That way you keep any student from feeling embarrassed. When the song is sung, the student or the group who thought up the word sings it out. After you do this a few times, the students can start to remember the new words and sing them along. When you get tired of the new words, people can make up another set. This can be a fun activity for the classroom, and can give lots of practice on letter-sound correspondence and phonemic awareness.

The Dance and Freeze Activity with the Letter Sound Songs

You can play various games with the letter sound songs. The more the students hear these songs in the context of games and fun, the less tedious will be their learning of letter-sound correspondence.

One good musical game is "dance and freeze." It's a good one for the psychological skill of impulse control, or self-discipline. You explain that when the music comes on, everyone can get up and dance around. (That means you, any teacher aides, and any other adults in the room!) But when the music stops, everyone is to hold perfectly still until the music starts back up again. (Except for the person who will be pushing the pause button of the CD player.) Getting to push the pause button of the CD player is a good prize for a student.

Phonemic Awareness Exercises With the Group

You will probably have students for whom phonemic awareness is already mastered, and you will have some others that need to start at the very beginning. How can you do group activities that accomodate them all?

The students who have not mastered phonemic awareness will gain a lot if they can just listen to the questions and answers given by the other students. In addition, you can give various types of phonemic awareness exercises to the group, and vary the difficulty according to whom you plan to call on.

For example, in doing the blending exercise, you break the word "ostrich" down into 6 phonemes and say them separately, and call upon one of the faster-progressing students to guess the word. Then you break the word "cat" into "kuh" and "at" and also ask one of the faster students to guess the word, so that you won't set a discernible pattern that the slower students get the easy ones. But later on, after the more slowly progressing students have had the benefit of hearing the game, you start calling on them for the easier ones.

Then you can introduce a twist into the game. You whisper into the ear of one of the faster progressing students, "Say buh ă guh." The student says the separate sounds, and you call on another student to guess. Once the faster students have gotten the hang of this, you whisper, "Say the separate sounds in the word hand." The faster students are now doing the segmenting activity, a harder phonemic awareness exercise, while the slower students are getting good practice with the blending exercise. In order not to stigmatize the slower ones, you can whisper into their ears, "Say tuh ă guh," an easier direction to follow than "Say the separate sounds of the word tag." But since you're whispering, you aren't broadcasting the fact that students are getting different directions.

The Blending Exercise with Students' Names

Instead of random words, you can have an exercise where you say the students' names split up into their separate phonemes. When the students have gotten good enough at the blending and segmenting exercises, you can play the following game: one student says the name of another student, with the sounds split apart. You call on someone to guess whose name was called. Then the student whose name was called is the next one to say someone else's name, with the sounds split apart. There is a feeling of power that comes from getting to choose the next object of attention, and this can make blending and segmenting more fun than just thinking of random words.

Unison Response With the Blending Exercise with Stories

You read a story to the children, (for example one of the illustrated modeling stories, with the pictures projected on the wall.) Every once in a while instead of saying a word, you say the separate sounds. When you point to the class, everyone together blends the word, and you resume reading.

A Magic Trick with Phonemic Awareness

This book includes pictures (with the accompanying printed words) for easily picturable three-phoneme words, such as doll and bag and so forth. I recommend enlarging any of the first nine of these pages taping them up on the wall. For these pages, no two words have the same beginning, ending, or middle sounds.

Before you can do the magic trick, the children need to practice several phonemic awareness exercises. Here they are:

First you do the blending exercise with pictures. You walk over to a certain page, and you say the separate sounds of the word. Then the children tell you which of the pictures you are referring to.

Next you practice the which-word exercise. You say, which word on this page begins with wuh? Which word begins with tuh?

Then you practice the which-sound exercise with two choices. Which sound does wig start with, is it wuh or tuh? When the children get good at this, you progress to the which-sound exercise without choices. Which sound does pencil start with?

Once the children are good at these, you can graduate to the phonemic awareness exercise that you will use in in the magic trick. Let's say you are looking at your page taped onto the wall with wig, bag, doll, hill, and pin on it. You say, "I'm thinking of a word that starts with the same sound that *water* starts with. What sound does water start with? Ok, good. Which of these words starts with wuh? After the children are used to this, you can leave out the intermediate step. Which of these starts with the same sound as hopping? Which starts with the same sound as demonstrate? Which starts with the same sound as particular?

As a final step, you do this exercise with nonsense words. Which starts with the same sound as pahrooka-meechonga?

When the children are good at this exercise, you are ready to do the magic trick. To clue them for any of the words for any of the pictures you have on the wall, you stand near that picture and say some "magic words." They simply listen for the sound that your magic word starts with, and look for the picture on the poster that begins with the same sound. That is the mystery word.

Finally, you make a deck of cards, by photocopying the "three phoneme words with pictures" (presented in this book) and cutting up those pages so that each has one word (and picture of that word) on it.

Now you practice doing the trick. You get a student to play the part of the "visitor." You announce to the visitor that this is a magic mind reading trick. You show the visitor a cut out picture of any of the words you have posted on the wall. The visitor is to pick a card, any card, and show it to you, but not to the students. Then you will concentrate very hard on that picture, and the students are going to read your mind and tell which card it is.

After you see the card, you wander around the room, dramatically, and you utter the magic words, like "Par ooka meechonga, acres and fairs, send this picture from my mind to theirs!" The students miraculously tell which card was picked. How do they do it? The students look to the poster on the wall that is closest to where you are when you say those magic words. They find the word on the poster that starts with the same sound as your magic word. For example, you stand near a poster with bat, sun, ten, pig, and mop on it, and as soon as the students hear the magic words "Par ooka meechonga," they know the answer is pig.

You can call on one student to say what is in the picture, or you can all have them answer in unison. To get real drama, you have the first two say something about the picture, as if they are picking up mind signals. For example: the first child says, "I'm getting that it's an animal." The second says, "I'm getting that it has legs and no wings." The third says, "Could you beam it just a little stronger? OK, I see it clearly now -- it's a pig!"

Once they have practiced, you ask one of your fellow teachers (or your principal, or the janitor, or a parent, or an older child, or your spouse...) to come in and see the magic trick. (If necessary you might clue the visitor that their role in the drama is to alternate between skepticism and amazement.) The students guess the identity of the card, and the visitor is incredulous. "That was just lucky," the visitor says. "You could never do it again in a million years." And so forth. A visitor who is a good actor, who can alternate between doubting skepticism and startled astonishment, can make this really fun for the kids.

The purpose of this is to give the students one more source of pleasure in their power to identify words by sounds. It is like magic, so magic tricks are appropriate.

Word List Work

You can work with the "Words in Word Families" lists with your class. Feel free to photocopy the pages of word lists onto overhead transparency film and project these words onto a screen or onto the wall. Or you can use the low-tech method of copying the words onto a blackboard, or getting a student to do so.

Suppose, as is always the case, you have some children who are faster learners, and others who are slower? How can you do this exercise with the whole group? Here's how:

1. You get the faster learners to sound and blend the words at the beginning, without having heard anyone else do so. This gives them a challenge.

2. After all your students have heard all the words sounded and blended, it is now easier for the slower learners to sound and blend. But they still may not be ready. It is easier for them to blend, given the sounds. So you go into a phase where you call on one student to sound. Then you call on another student to blend, having heard the first student say the separate sounds. The students who blend can sometimes be the faster learners, so the students picked to blend will not be stigmatized. But the slower learners can get their tastes of success by blending after someone else has sounded. If necessary, you can repeat the sounds that the sounder has said, doing a better job of cluing the blender.

3. You can call upon one faster-learning student to sound and blend a word. Then you can call upon a slower-learning student to sound and blend the same word immediately afterward. Thus the faster student is doing what we've called activity 3, while the slower learning student is doing activity 2. All are participating successfully, but activity 3 is more challenging than activity 2.

4. After the students have heard the words sounded and blended several times, the students who learn more slowly may be ready to do the sounding as well as the blending.

A Magic Trick With Reading Three Phoneme Words

Once the students have learned to read the three phoneme words, you can do another magic trick. Now you tape the words on the "three phoneme word" pages up on the wall, only this time without the accompanying pictures. So for example, you have one page with bat, sun, ten, pig, and mop on it, another with bag, cob, hen, gum, and six on it, and so forth. You hand the visitor the same set of cards you made for the previous magic trick. You ask the visitor to "Pick a card, any card." The visitor is to show the card to you but not to the students. You wander around the room and put your hand up to your forehead to beam the word to your students. When you say, "Ready, say," they all chant the word!

This trick is good to do when the visitor has been let in on how you did the previous one. Now the visitor might act out the part of a smug insider who knows how the trick is done, who is now dramatically astonished when you can do it without saying magic words.

How do the students know the word? In your wandering, you wander close to one of the lists. The list you stand closest to is the one they are to read the word from. When you touch your forehead, you touch it with a certain number of fingers; that number is the number of the word in the list. Thus if you touch your forehead with three fingers, they are to read the 3rd word on the list, counting from the top.

A different way to clue the students, (to keep the visitors mystified) is that when you send the image to them with your mind, you say the word "Send" several times. The number of the word in the list is the number of times you say the word "Send." So if you very dramatically say, "Send! Send! Send! Send!" the students know to read the fourth word on the list you are closest to. If you don't put your fingers on your forehead, they are to count the word send. That way the visitor can't figure out how the signal is sent, because it isn't sent the same way each time. If you want to make sure the students get the right number, you can use both the number of fingers on the forehead *and* the number of times you say "Send." That way you have a double-check.

Reading to Younger Students

When the students have begun to be able to read stories, such as those in the Illustrated Modeling Stories, Primer, you can have them start practicing for reading to younger students. One of them plays the part of the younger student, and one of them plays the part of the reader. The reader's job is not only to read the words correctly, but to remember to hold the book so the younger student can see the pictures, and to read very expressively.

If there actually are younger students in the building where you teach, then your students can visit them and read to them. If there are not younger students there, then the students can take the stories home and read them to younger siblings or neighbors. They can then report in class whether the younger child enjoyed them.

Teaching Older Students to Tutor Younger Ones

Here is my opinion of one of the most useful programs a school can start. Take this manual and give it to older students. Teach them the contents of it, thoroughly. Then have them practice the tutoring exercises with each other. When they have reached the criterion of being able to do the exercises extremely well, and when they can rate highly on all the items of the skills for instructors' checklist, they get to start doing individual tutoring with younger children. Teachers help them know which activities are at the challenge zone for the particular child they are working with. In doing this they learn interpersonal skills, teaching skills, and experience the tremendous psychological benefits of actually doing something very useful for another person.

In my vision of the ideal school, students would spend a part of their day from about fourth grade up either in practicing tutoring activities, reading about how to be a good tutor, tutoring, training younger tutors, and/or supervising younger tutors. If we could turn out graduating classes full of students who are excellent at these activities, we would also turn out

classes of excellent parents, good
friends, and good business managers --
a monumental accomplishment.

If You're Running a Tutoring Program

There are many reading tutoring programs which lack what I think of as the key ingredients. Those key ingredients are as follows:

1. There is systematic selection of tutors. At a minimum, the tutor should be entering into the activity because of a real desire to help someone, and not under coercion. The tutor should have a track record of behaving responsibly and kindly. And the tutor should be able to read well enough, and to pronounce the individual sounds of letters well enough, to teach someone else.

2. The program uses a systematic curriculum (possibilities include this one).

3. Tutors are trained "to criterion" using role-playing: that is, they keep observing models, practicing, and getting feedback until they can do proficiently the exercises they will be doing with their tutee.

The training of tutors also includes interpersonal skills, such as the tones of approval exercise and being a good listener. Tutors should be thoroughly familiar with the technique of going down the hierarchy and back up again when the learner is experiencing frustration.

4. Students are pretested, to determine both where the student should begin in the curriculum, and how much improvement later has been made.

5. There is at least some "process monitoring," or evaluating what goes on in the tutoring. At a minimum, this consists of keeping track of how often sessions take place and what their approximate durations are, and how satisfied the student is with what is going on, and whether the student likes the tutor. Are the "appointmentology" skills of both tutor and student adequate for success? (At least 80% of scheduled sessions should be kept.)

More intense process monitoring consists of sessions actually frequently observed and rated, as for example by the rating scale given in the chapter on skills for the tutor. The person doing the rating can be a supervisor, a peer who is also a tutor, or the tutor him/herself. The process monitoring is fed back to the tutor so that this feedback may be used for quality improvement.

One of the key elements of expert tutoring is *pleasant interaction.* Are tones of approval commonplace? Is much celebration going on? Tutoring should be a joyous activity for both the student and the tutor.

6. There is opportunity for tutors to consult with a supervisor or peer supervisors when problems arise, or to share what works well for the purpose of quality improvement. Tutors devote

at least some time to thinking and communicating about how the program is delivered, rather than devoting 100% of the time to delivering it.

7. There is periodic outcome monitoring, throughout the program, as for example by the tests included in this book. These may be administered by the tutor him/herself, or by someone else in the program. Another outcome to monitor is the student's answer to the question: "On a scale of 0 to 10, where 0 is hate it and 10 is love it, how much do you now like to read?"

8. There is some post-intervention outcome monitoring, using the tests included in this book or others.

9. The data on how much students improve over time are analyzed and studied, for the sake of quality improvement. Any innovations or modifications in the program are studied for their effects on measured outcomes.

10. I recommend testing the program in the following way, if you are working with elementary school aged students. You measure an age or grade level in reading at the beginning of the program and compute, for each student, the number of years of reading progress in reading the student has made per year of education so far. Then with the tests done during and after tutoring, you compute the number of years of reading progress per year of tutoring. You average these results for all the children in your program, and discuss them and (probably) celebrate them greatly!

These elements enable a tutoring program to have "structure." Structured programs are in marked contrast to those in which tutors and tutees are paired up and exhorted to "go to it," without either of them knowing exactly what the agenda is and what the desired outcomes are.

I believe that the skills of tutoring overlap so greatly with the skills of other human interactions that tutoring skills should be taught universally as a routine portion of education. I hope that by studying this book carefully, tutors of widely varying ages and situations can learn to experience the full success possible through this wonderful activity.

For Telephone Tutors

For the last several years I have been directing a program investigating the feasibility of telephone tutoring in reading. Many educators dismiss this possibility out of hand. But I can now give a good reason not to dismiss it: for most of the learners we've tried it with, it works, and works very well!

If tutoring in reading can be delivered effectively by telephone, this vastly increases the availability of tutoring as a force for good. It means that almost anyone who has access to a phone can be tutored, and anyone with adequate skills can be a tutor, regardless of where they live. It means that transportation difficulties should not preclude the giving or receiving of tutoring. It means that when a student or a tutor moves, the relationship does not have to be disrupted – the only question is "What day do I call the new number?" It means that well-educated and skilled tutors can reach those in need of more education every single day. It means that people who want to do good for others can do it without having to drive or get driven to those people.

I believe that in a better world that may evolve, telephone tutoring will be very widely used, and the possibilities for good are very exciting.

What changes in this program need to be made if you are doing it over the telephone rather than face to face with the learner? The answer, for most learners -- especially those who know the meaning of rows and columns and page numbers and left and right etc. -- is that surprisingly few changes need to be made. For the most part, the tutor simply calls the student at the appointed time, makes sure that they both have on hand the same materials, and they do the same activities they would do as if they were face to face.

A major disadvantage of telephone tutoring is that it is not possible to point to things. It is not possible to say, "What's that letter," and point to the letter with your finger. And in telephone tutoring it's hard to do the "rabbit exercise" with the child!

But the corresponding advantage of telephone tutoring is that the learner gets used to processing all the directions via words. Instead of pointing, the tutor says something like, "Now can you turn the page? What picture do you see on the next page? Hey, we're on the same page! How about the letter above that picture – do you know what it is? You got it!"

It takes a little longer to give all the directions in words, but I think it is very good for the learner, especially when learning to read. Reading involves decoding words. Giving and receiving directions over the phone makes it necessary to communicate in the same units that in which writing and reading communicate – words.

Let's talk about some of the very few special accomodations necessary for telephone tutoring.

Some Sine Qua Nons of Telephone Tutoring

The learner must have the attention span required to stay on the phone with you for at least a few minutes. If the learner has the ability to pay attention to hearing a very short story or two read in a very enthusiastic voice over the phone, then you are in business and can progress up from there. If the learner hasn't reached the stage where he can even stay on the phone with you without running off and doing something else, telephone tutoring is impossible.

You will want to speak to the parent or caretaker fairly often to make sure that the stimulus environment is as close to ideal as possible. What is the ideal environment? One where there are four walls and a closed door, a telephone, and the particular materials that the student needs to do the work with you. There is no television on, no siblings interrupting, no toys, electronic or otherwise, in the child's hand. If the parent is not able to furnish an environment that is free enough of distractions that the learner can attend to you, telephone tutoring is impossible.

The most important condition for the existence of telephone tutoring is that the student is at home and ready to work at the time of the telephone tutoring appointment. This is the obstacle that most often prevents telephone tutoring from working: the family life is simply too unpredictable for to permit appointments' being kept with any regularity. If regular appointments can be kept, almost all learners can eventually benefit from telephone tutoring.

The Importance of Tone of Voice

When you are face to face with a child, you can convey emotions of enthusiasm and approval and excitement by your facial expressions, by your movements, by touching the child, and by your tone of voice. In telephone tutoring, you must rely totally on your tone of voice. For this reason, it's important to be able to speak very expressively if you are involved in telephone tutoring.

When reading to a student over the phone, it is of key importance to read with a great deal of expression in the voice. This is a skill worthy of a great deal of attention and practice.

When the student answers a question correctly or when you want for any other reason to convey enthusiasm and approval, think in terms of a higher volume, higher pitch, greater range of notes from lowest to highest, and faster tempo. These are the musical qualities of your voice that will reach the student's emotional centers.

Oral Language Development: Reading Picture Books

How much does a student have to know already, in order to participate in telephone tutoring? If a child can listen to a picture book, turn the page when you say to, and name many of the common objects seen in picture books for young children, it's possible to work your way up from there.

In the picture book reading activity, you and the student both have your copy of the book. You read to the student, while the student turns the pages and looks at the pictures for his copy. For young children, the adult who is at home with the child will usually have to help by getting the right picture book for you and getting at the right starting page, if you are not starting at the beginning.

This activity is somewhat similar to one that many preschool children can do successfully, wherein they listen to tape recorded books and turn the pages when there is a certain signal. At the beginning you will have to signal fairly obtrusively, and check often to see if the student is on the right page. You can check whether the student is on the right page or not by asking him to describe what he sees on that page. For example:

Tutor: "Please turn the page now. What do you see in the picture?"
Student: A train, with smoke coming out the top.
Tutor: Good, we're on the same page!

As time goes by and you and the student get used to telephone readings, you can eliminate most of the checking and just say very quickly, "turning the page" when the page turns.

If you use alphabet books part of the time with the young learner, you can gradually start teaching the alphabet and the letter sounds to the young learner. This is easiest with books that are the simplest: with one picture and one letter per page.

Oral Language Development: Learning Vocabulary and Basic Concepts

There are several concepts very useful for the student who is being tutored over the telephone, so that the student can get "on the same page" and at the right place on the page with you. These are as follows:

1. next: next page, picture next to that one
2. turn back a page
3. top and bottom
4. the meanings of the words pictured in the "three phoneme words, with pictures"
5. the meaning of the pictures on the alphabet page

6. page numbers: how to turn to a certain page number in a book.
7. row and column
8. left and right
9. the letter at the beginning, middle, and end of a three letter word
10. the lower and upper case letters

Many students will have learned all these before telephone tutoring, and it will be easy to "get on the same page," and to direct the student to the same place on the page that you are looking at.

If the student doesn't know all these things at the beginning, you can use the ones the student does know to orient the student enough to teach the ones the student does not know.

For example: if the child knows most of the three-phoneme words pictured in this book, you can look at those pages with the child. You can identify the picture at the top, the picture under that, the picture under that, and so forth, and become clear on the names of all the pictures. You can point out that the letters to the left of the picture spell those words. You can point out that the letters are to the left of the picture, and the picture is to the right of the letters. Then you can look at the next picture and the next printed word, and ask the student which is on the left, or on the right, the letters or the picture. If the student is far enough along in letter recognition, you can see if the student can name those letters. You can point out, or ask the student, which of the letters is farthest left, farthest right, and in the middle. You can teach the child that the letter farthest left is at the beginning of the word, that the letter farthest right is at the end of the word, and the letter in the middle is in the middle of the word.

When teaching these concepts, first tell the child clearly, then check to see if the child understood. For example: "Do you see the picture of the bag? The word bag is to the left of it. Do you see the letter b, on the left side of that word? We say that is at the beginning of the word. Do you see the letter a? It's in the middle, and the letter g is at the end of the word. OK? Let's see if you remember. What's the letter at the beginning of the word bag? What's the letter in the middle? What's the letter at the end?

For another example: if the child knows the meanings of the words on the alphabet page, you can ask the child to find the apple on that page. When the child has found it, you can point out that it is in the top row of pictures. You can say that the apple is at the far left of the page. Then you can ask the child to find the bus. You can point out that the bus is next to the apple, and just to the right of the apple. You can ask the child, "What do you see next to the bus, just to the right of the bus?" If the child is able to answer, "The cat," you know the question is not too difficult. When you get to the foot on the alphabet page, you can say, "The foot is the last picture in the top row. Let's go down one row, and look back at the left side of that row. Do you see a picture of a guitar?" Then if you ask, "What picture do you see just to the right of the guitar," and the child answers, "a hat," you greatly celebrate. You are able to stay together on the alphabet page.

Games That Can Be Done Over the Phone

Sometimes it's nice to take a break from the work of reading instruction and play some games, especially with children. Here are some games that help with development of language skills and/or thinking skills.

Password. In this game, one person thinks of a word to be guessed by the other. Then that person gives the other person clues by saying other words. For example, if the password to be guessed is "food," you might give clues like "eat," "groceries," "meal," "edible," etc. This game exercises skills of searching through your vocabulary for the right word, and thus is good for verbal fluency.

Twenty Questions. One person thinks of something to be guessed by the other. The other person asks yes or no questions and tries to home in on the answer. (You can go over 20 questions if you want.) You should start with general questions like "Is it living?" and then move to a little less general life "Is it a person?" and thence down to more specific ones like "Is it someone you know?" "Is it I?" The ability to start with a wide focus and home in o answer is an important mental sk

Tic tac toe. You both get pencil and paper, and make a three by three grid, and number the cells from one to nine, going from left to right on the top, then middle, then bottom rows. Thus the upper left cell is 1, the middle left cell is 4, and the bottom left cell is 7. If player 1 moves first to a corner, and player 2 moves second anywhere else but the center, player 1 should be able to force a win. It's a useful thinking exercise to figure out how to do this consistently.

Mastermind. This game is marketed in a commercial version, but you can also do it with numbers. It's a great exercise in logic. You can alter certain features of the game to make it harder or easier. You can make it hard enough to challenge the logical thinking skills of anyone. One person thinks of a goal number, 4 digits long, where each digit can be from 0 to 5. Thus there are 6 possible digits for each of 4 possible positions. The challenge of the codebreaker is to figure out what the 4 numbers are. The codebreaker does this by making a guess of any 4 digits. The codemaker then writes down 2 numbers. The first tells how many digits in the codebreaker's guess are the right number in the right position. The second number tells how many digits in the codebreaker's guess are the right number in the wrong position. Then the codebreaker guesses again, and the codemaker responds again. The codebreaker keeps going until she can guess the correct numbers using the codebreaker's information. If this is too hard, you can make it easier! Just have the permissible digits be 0 to 4 or 0 to 3, or fewer, rather than 0 to 5. Or you can have only 3, or only 2 digits.

This game should not be attempted without each player having pencil and paper in front of him and knowing how to use it!

Hangman. In this game one person thinks of a word or phrase, and the other tries to guess it. The person who thinks of the word tells how many letters there are in each of the words, and the guesser writes down a blank for each letter. Then the guesser guesses letters, one at a time, and the other person answers by saying the letter is not in it, or else by telling where the letter is: e.g. "the 3rd letter in the 2nd word and the 6th letter in the 3rd word." Traditionally, each time there is a letter guessed that is not in the phrase, the guesser comes one step closer to losing, with another part of a scaffold and a person being drawn; the person gets hung if the word or phrase is not guessed soon enough, thus the name of the game. (The way my family plays this, the person in the drawing seems to keep getting more and more parts with more wrong answers, so that he never winds up getting hung.)

The Shaping Game. Shaping is reinforcing someone for getting closer and closer to a goal. The principle of shaping runs through everything that is done with students. You want to give recognition to the learner, not just when the performance is perfect, but when the learner improves. The phrase "rewarding improvement" means about the same thing as shaping.

The shaping game is a way for people to practice using shaping. Here are the rules for the telephone version of the shaping game:

1. There are two people. The "shaper" thinks of some imaginary behavior for the "shapee" to do, in imagination.
2. The object of the game for the shaper to give clues so that the shapee can do that behavior in imagination.
3. The object of the game for the shapee is to do that behavior in imagination.
4. The shapee begins the game by doing things in imagination like walking around, going different places, seeing things, eating, drinking, sleeping, and so forth.
5. The shaper can give clues only by approving of things that the shapee has already done. For example, the shaper can say things like, "I like it that you are going outside," or "I'm glad you're looking up in the sky," or "Thank you for jumping up."
6. Criticism or suggestions or commands are against the rules; approval only is permitted.

The shaping game is, I think, a fairly profound analogy to various intrapsychic and interpersonal tasks. The things that people find hard in this game are just the things that are hard for them in dealing with other people. Sometimes in the game, it's hard for someone not to criticize the shapee; the same way, in real life, it's hard sometimes to withhold criticism. Sometimes in the game, its hard to give approval before the person does exactly what he was supposed to do; the same way, in real life, it's sometimes hard to give someone approval for the baby steps along the way toward the goal. The game thus gives practice in the skills of self-reinforcement, of using positive reinforcement with others, of communicating appreciation to others, and of sustaining attention to tasks. It also requires picking up on social cues.

The telephone version of this game is fairly hard. You can make it easier at first by restricting the range of possible things. For example, you can say, "It's something most people do in the evening before going to bed," and have the answer be "Brush your teeth." Or you can have it be a household chore, and have the answer be making up a bed. Or you can have it be a certain type of exercise, and have the answer be "Go running."

List of Reading Activities

Oral Language Development:

Conversation Between Student and Tutor
Reading picture books to the student (including the illustrated modeling stories)
Reading the Letter Stories
Reading Unillustrated Stories
The Student Retells Stories That Have Been Read
The Student Dictates Stories
Learning Vocabulary and Basic Concepts
Oral Language Drills

Turn the pages and name the pictures

Next page or back a page, what do you see

What do you see on top? (or bottom; or where is the ___, on top or bottom?)

What do you see on the left? Where is the ___, on left or right?

Which is on top, the letter or the picture?

What letter is at the beginning, middle, end?

What sound is at the beginning, middle, end?

Phonemic Awareness

1. Blending with two choices.
2. Blending without two choices, 3 phonemes.
3. Blending without two choices, 4 phonemes
4. Blending without two choices, 5 phonemes.
5. Saying first sound split off.
6. Yes-no for beginning sounds.
7. Which sound for beginning sounds, two choices.
8. Which sound for beginning sounds, no choices.
9. Same or different for beginning sounds.
10. Saying ending sound split off.
11. Yes-no for ending sounds.
12. Which sound for ending sounds, two choices.
13. Which sound for ending sounds, no choices.
14. Same and different for ending sounds.
15. Yes-no for middle sounds.
16. Which sound for middle sounds, two choices.
17. Which sound for middle sounds, no choices.
18. Segmenting, three phoneme words.
19. Segmenting, four phoneme words.
20. Segmenting, five phoneme words.

Spatial Awareness

Same or different for pictures of objects, people, or animals

Same or different for directions of arrows
Same or different for identical or mirror-image pictures
Same or different for b-d, p-q pairs.
Naming the letter or sound on the left, right, or middle for three letter words (appropriate if the child has already learned the names of the letters and/or letter-sound correspondence)
Looking at three letter words and, given a letter or sound, saying whether it is on the left, the right, or the middle. (appropriate if the child has already learned the names of the letters and/or letter-sound correspondence.
Looking at three pictures and saying which is not like the other two: the one on the right, the left, or the middle.
Looking at triplets of b and d or p and q and saying which of the three is not like the other two.
Looking at letters b, d, p, and q, and telling whether the ball is on the left or right of the stick.
Looking at the letters b, d, p, and q and saying the name of the letter or the sound it makes.

Letter-Sound Correspondence

Reading the Letter Stories to the Students
Reading Alphabet Books
Listening to the letter sound songs
Singing along with and pointing along with the letter sound songs
The Rabbit Exercise
Using the Alphabet Page Pictures and the Three Phoneme Word Pictures for letter identification
Using the Alphabet Page Pictures and the Three Phoneme Word Pictures for letter-sound correspondence
Giving sounds for the middle and ending letters in three phoneme words
Telling the names and sounds of letters in alphabetical order
Telling the names and sounds of letters in random order
Mnemonic sentences for short vowel sounds
Saying letters, given sounds
More letter-sound practice with the lists of Words in Word Families

Word List Work

Activities 1-4 with Words in Word Families:
1. Instructor sounds (says the sounds of the word separately); student blends (says the word).
2. Student sounds and blends each word immediately after hearing the instructor do so.
3. Student sounds and blends each word without hearing a model just beforehand.
4. Student reads the words without saying the separate sounds.

If necessary, you can precede these with "activity 0": Say each word, and the student simply repeats the word after you.

When the student is fluent at sounding and blending by phonemes and reading one-syllable words of all sorts, use the same steps for sounding and blending polysyllabic words by syllables.

Reading Text

The Modeling Stories: *Illustrated Modeling Stories, Primer*, *Programmed Readings for Psychological Skills*, *Illustrated Modeling Stories*
The Reflections Exercise (especially with the *Programmed Readings*)
Discussing The Reading
Reading Modeling Stories to A Younger Child
Reading the supplemental books, tutor reading to student
Reading the supplemental books, tutor and student taking turns

A Dozen Skills for Instructors

This is obviously not an exhaustive list. But these are some of the skills that the instructor should be able to do easily, before starting with the first student.

1. Be able to read stories with a very expressive and dramatic tone.
2. Be able to have a good chat with the student, with an enthusiastic tone of voice, some appropriate telling about your own experience, and lots of reflections, follow-up questions, and facilitations.
3. Be able to do accurate and empathic reflections.
4. Be able to speak any phrase with whatever degree of approval and enthusiasm in the tone of voice is desired – neutral, small to moderate approval, large approval.
5. For any activity in this program, explain how you would go “down the hierarchy of difficulty” if you started the activity and it proved too hard for the student. What alternative activity could you go to?
6. Be able to say, accurately and quickly, the most frequent sounds of the 26 letters.
7. Be able to look at the list of words in word families, and the 20 levels of the Phonemic Awareness Test, and make up sample questions for each level, like those in the Phonemic Awareness Test.
8. Be able to do the blending exercise, the which-word exercise, the which-sound exercise, and activities 1 through 4 using the three-phoneme words with pictures.
9. Be able to say the answers to the spatial awareness exercises quickly and accurately.
10. Be able to look at the lists of Words in Word families, and rapidly sound and blend the words in any list.
11. Be able to do activities 0 through 4 with the lists of Words in Word Families, with someone role-playing the part of a student.
12. Be able to use the tally counter to keep track of points with each of the various sorts of exercises for which points are recorded. Get used to using a stopwatch or a watch that displays seconds, to time performances on saying letter sounds or reading lists of words.

Tests

If you are doing research on your reading program that you want to submit for publication, you'll probably want to use some commercially available tests to measure the outcome of your work. For Phonemic Awareness, the TOPA (Test of Phonological Awareness) and the CTOPP (Comprehensive Test of Phonological Processing) are thorough tests. The Slosson Oral Reading Test is a well-designed measure of word decoding. The Woodcock Reading Mastery Test has several different sections; one of these I find particulary useful is the Word Attack subtest. This asks the reader to pronounce letter combinations that are not real words, thus measuring decoding skill independent of word memory. The Test of Word Reading Efficiency has two sections, one a list of real words, and one a list of nonwords, to be read as fast as possible; the whole test can be done in under five minutes.

For reading comprehension, my favorite is the reading comprehension subtests of the Wide Range Achievement Test -- Expanded. This is very similar to the achievement tests that many students in elementary through middle school take yearly. Such school achievement tests, too, can be very useful in researching the outcome of your program. The Terra Nova, the California Achievement Test, the Iowa Test of Basic Skills, and the Stanford Achievement Test are some of these.

Another major resource for reading comprehension tests can be found by searching on the Internet for "released tests" and the name of a state, to find the state achievement tests given in recent years. The tests of the state of Texas, called the TAKS, are particularly useful, because if you look carefully on the Texas Education Agency web site, you can find data allowing you to infer the percentile score for each raw score. Type "released tests TAKS" into your search engine on the internet.

Once learners reach middle school and have gotten to be quite competent in reading, a great way to test reading comprehension is by giving a released version of the ACT, (a college entrance exam that's the chief competitor of the SAT). The book entitled *The Real ACT Prep Guide* (ACT Publications, Iowa City, Iowa) contain previous tests and tables that allow you to compute percentiles for how your students perform in comparison to college-bound juniors and seniors. If your tutoring program is turning out really high achievement, you can measure it by such an advanced level test.

The tests that follow are meant partly to decide on placement in this curriculum: where should we begin work with a given student? But also, in expert tutoring, "placement" decisions occur not just at the beginning, but throughout the course of the venture. These tests, given periodically, can be a supplement to the student's performance in the everyday exercises, to tell you where in this curriculum the student should be working: phonemic awareness, spatial awareness, letter-sound correspondence, sounding and blending words by phoneme or syllable, and/or reading text. If the student can't get all or almost all correct on the Phonemic Awareness Test and the Spatial Awareness Test, keep working on these skills by doing the exercises on those skills. How the student does on these two tests will also give you important information on how high in the hierarchy for each of these skills you should be working. When the student is good at these skills, learning letter-sound correspondence should be much easier. Keep working on letter-sound correspondence exercises until the student can get all items of the letter-sound test correct, and can rattle off the answers quickly. With a good score on all these tests, the student is ready for Word List Work. The words in the Phonetic Word Reading Test are a subset of the Words in Word Families list; how far the student gets on the test roughly correlates with where the student is in the word list work. Once the student can quickly read all the words on the Phonetic Word Reading Test, and Part 1 of Words in Word Families, the student is ready to start sounding and blending by syllables rather than phonemes. When the student can fluently read all the words to be sounded and blended by syllables, and can read the polysyllabic words in the Burt, Schonell, and the Unfamiliar Words Test, the student is ready to graduate from drills, and to practice reading by reading text from then on. If the student fluently reads and does the "reflections exercise" with *Manual for Tutors and Teachers of Reading*, the student is about ready to become a tutor!

Phonemic Awareness Test

There are several tests of phonemic awareness on the market; almost all of them are quite expensive and are scrupulously guarded from consumers such as tutors or teachers, so that the validity of the test will not be spoiled. The Phonemic Awareness Test is one that I constructed. It does not have norms; it can't place a child on a percentile rank. But it is extremely useful for teaching phonemic awareness. The tasks on the test are ordered in approximate level of difficulty. Give the test to the student and see what is hard and what is easy. Then in teaching, start with tasks that are just under the level where the student first starts to have difficulty, and work your way up. Replace the words in the test with similar words for learning exercises. Keep going until the student can do all the tasks on this test.

Here is the test.

Level 1: Blending with two choices. Say: I'm going to break a word into the separate sounds that make that word. I want to see if you can put the sounds back together, and guess the word. For example, if I say duh ŏ guh, the word is dog. OK?

_____1. The word is either cat or ball. buh aw ll. (ball)
_____2. The word is either run or pal. rrr ŭ nnn. (run)
_____3. The word is either net or bag. buh ă guh. (bag)
_____4. The word is either goat or pig. puh ĭ guh. (pig)
_____5. The word is either kite or doll. kuh i tuh. (kite)

If the testee misses 3 or more of level 1, skip to level 5.

Level 2: Blending without two choices. Say: Now I'm going to do the same thing, only without giving you two choices first.

_____6. nn ă puh. (nap)
_____7. buh ĕ lll. (bell)
_____8. lll ĭ puh. (lip)
_____9. mmm ŏ puh. (mop)
_____10. rrr ŭ buh. (rub)

If the testee misses as many as 3 of level 2, skip to level 5.

Level 3: Blending without two choices, 4 phonemes. Say: Here are some words with four sounds for you to put together.

______11. huh ă nnn duh (hand)
______12. duh ĕ sss kuh (desk)
______13. sss lll ĭ kuh (slick)
______14. kuh lll ŏ th (cloth)
______15. lll ŭ nnn ch (lunch)

If the testee misses as many as 3 of level 3, skip to level 5.

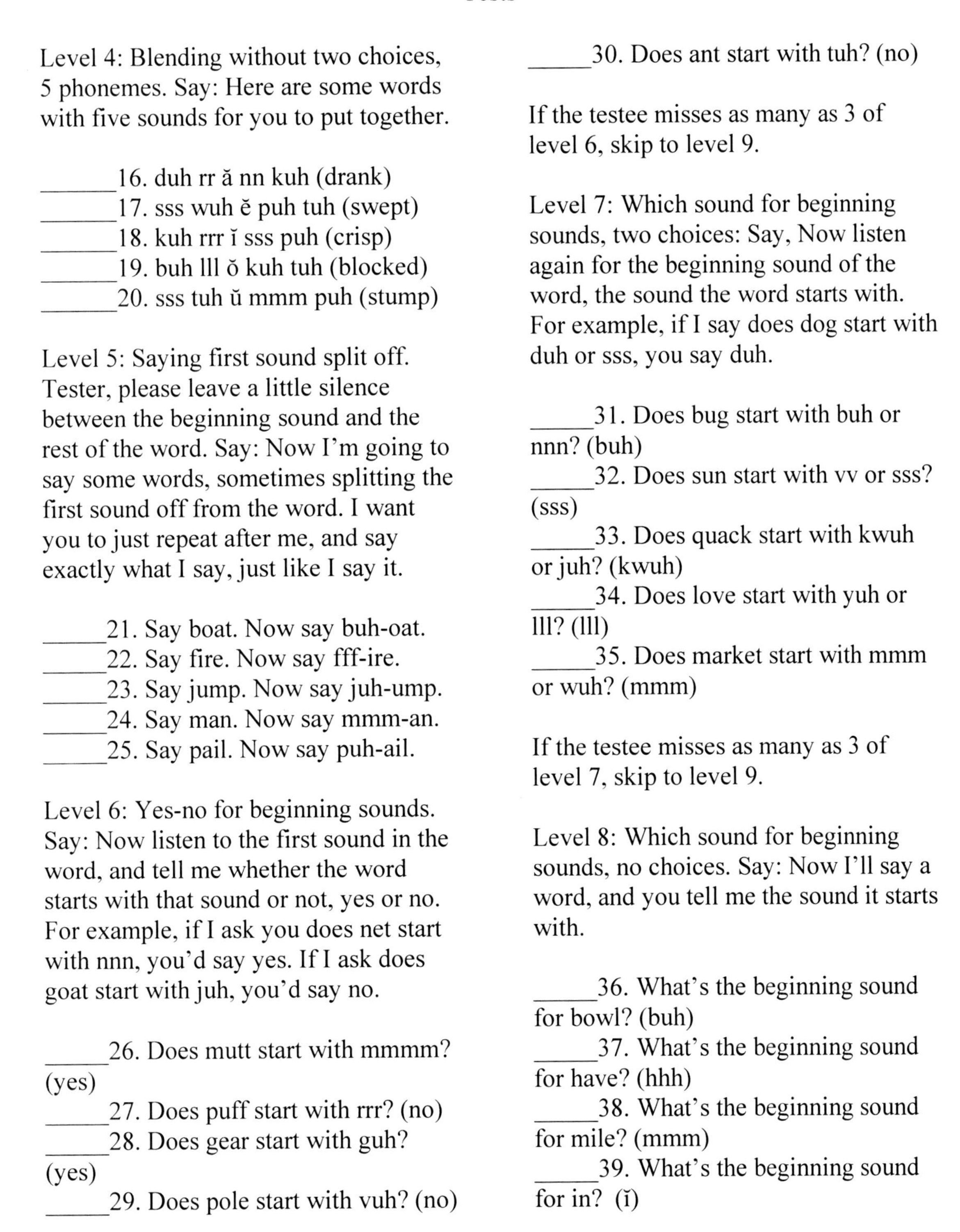

Level 4: Blending without two choices, 5 phonemes. Say: Here are some words with five sounds for you to put together.

______16. duh rr ă nn kuh (drank)
______17. sss wuh ĕ puh tuh (swept)
______18. kuh rrr ĭ sss puh (crisp)
______19. buh lll ŏ kuh tuh (blocked)
______20. sss tuh ŭ mmm puh (stump)

Level 5: Saying first sound split off. Tester, please leave a little silence between the beginning sound and the rest of the word. Say: Now I'm going to say some words, sometimes splitting the first sound off from the word. I want you to just repeat after me, and say exactly what I say, just like I say it.

_____21. Say boat. Now say buh-oat.
_____22. Say fire. Now say fff-ire.
_____23. Say jump. Now say juh-ump.
_____24. Say man. Now say mmm-an.
_____25. Say pail. Now say puh-ail.

Level 6: Yes-no for beginning sounds. Say: Now listen to the first sound in the word, and tell me whether the word starts with that sound or not, yes or no. For example, if I ask you does net start with nnn, you'd say yes. If I ask does goat start with juh, you'd say no.

_____26. Does mutt start with mmmm? (yes)
_____27. Does puff start with rrr? (no)
_____28. Does gear start with guh? (yes)
_____29. Does pole start with vuh? (no)
_____30. Does ant start with tuh? (no)

If the testee misses as many as 3 of level 6, skip to level 9.

Level 7: Which sound for beginning sounds, two choices: Say, Now listen again for the beginning sound of the word, the sound the word starts with. For example, if I say does dog start with duh or sss, you say duh.

_____31. Does bug start with buh or nnn? (buh)
_____32. Does sun start with vv or sss? (sss)
_____33. Does quack start with kwuh or juh? (kwuh)
_____34. Does love start with yuh or lll? (lll)
_____35. Does market start with mmm or wuh? (mmm)

If the testee misses as many as 3 of level 7, skip to level 9.

Level 8: Which sound for beginning sounds, no choices. Say: Now I'll say a word, and you tell me the sound it starts with.

_____36. What's the beginning sound for bowl? (buh)
_____37. What's the beginning sound for have? (hhh)
_____38. What's the beginning sound for mile? (mmm)
_____39. What's the beginning sound for in? (ĭ)

_____40. What's the beginning sound for walk? (wuh)

Level 9: Same or different for beginning sounds. Say: I'll say two words, and ask you if they have the same beginning sound, or different beginning sounds. For example, if I give you dog and cat, you'd say different, because they have different beginnning sounds, duh and kuh. If I give you dog and dip, you'd say same, because they both start with duh.

Listen to the two words and tell me whether they have the same or different beginning sounds.

_____41. fun and file (same)
_____42. boat and heart (different)
_____43. nail and noon (same)
_____44. yam and wet (different)
_____45. on and uncle (different)

Level 10: Saying ending sound split off. Tester, please leave a little silent space between the ending sound and the rest of the word. Say: Please repeat after me, and say exactly what I say.

_____46. Say net. Now say ne-tuh.
_____47. Say cub. Now say cu-buh.
_____48. Say hip. Now say hi-puh.
_____49. Say log. Now say lo-guh.
_____50. Say hill. Now say hi-ll.

Level 11: Yes-no for ending sounds. Say: Now please listen to the ending sound of the word, the last sound you hear in the word. Say yes or no to the question I ask about the ending sound. For example, if I say, does dog end with guh, you'd say yes. If I ask, does dog end with puh, you say no.

_____51. Does muff end with fff? (yes)
_____52. Does sick end with chuh? (no)
_____53. Does peg end with rrr? (no)
_____54. Does tire end with rrr? (yes)
_____55. Does mouse end with juh? (no)

If the testee misses as many as 3 of level 11, skip to level 14.

Level 12: Which sound for ending sounds, two choices. Say: Now please listen for the ending sound again, the sound the word ends with. Instead of saying yes or no, tell me the sound it ends with. So if I say, does dog end with guh or duh, you say guh.

_____56. Does goat end with tuh or mmm? (tuh)
_____57. Does miss end with vvv or sss? (sss)
_____58. Does life end with fff or tuh? (fff)
_____59. Does soap end with duh or puh? (puh)
_____60. Does walk end with kuh or lll? (kuh)

If the testee misses as many as 3 of level 12, skip to level 14.

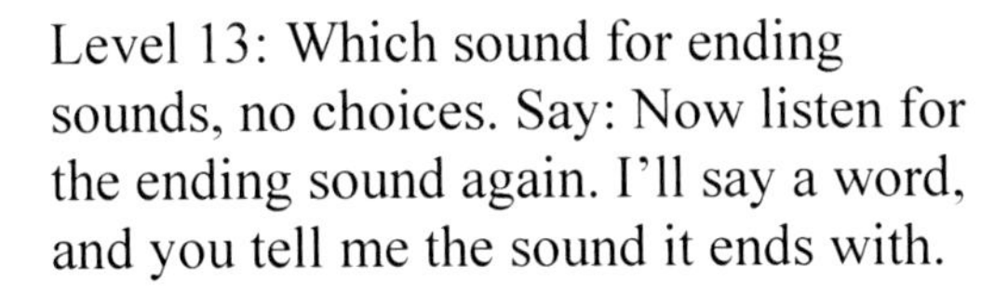
Level 13: Which sound for ending sounds, no choices. Say: Now listen for the ending sound again. I'll say a word, and you tell me the sound it ends with.

_____61. What's the ending sound for goat? (tuh)
_____62. What's the ending sound for van? (nnn)
_____63. What's the ending sound for mop? (puh)
_____64. What's the ending sound for tough? (fff)
_____65. What's the ending sound for flow? (o)

Level 14: Same and different for ending sounds. Say: Now I'll say two words, and ask you if they have the same ending sound, or different ending sounds. For example, if I give you dog and pot, you'd say different, because they have different beginnning sounds, guh and tuh. If I give you dog and pig, you'd say same, because they both end with guh.

Listen to the two words and tell me whether they have the same or different ending sounds.

_____66. float and mat (same)
_____67. cramp and pop (same)
_____68. list and kit (same)
_____69. some and love (different)
_____70. girl and fur (different)

Level 15: Yes-no game for middle sounds. Tell me the sound you hear in the middle, the one called the vowel sound. For dog, the sound in the middle is ŏ. So if I say, for dog, is it ŏ? you'd say yes. If I say, for dog, is it ee, you'd say no.

_____71. For jazz, is the middle sound oo? (no)
_____72. For rack, is the middle sound ă? (yes)
_____73. For kite, is the middle sound ŭ? (no)
_____74. For rich, is the middle sound ĭ? (yes)
_____75. For goat, is the middle sound o? (yes)

If the testee misses as many as 3 of level 15, skip to level 18.

Level 16: Which sound game for middle sounds, two choices. Say, keep listening for the middle sound, the vowel sound. Tell me which sound you hear in the middle. I'll say something like, for dog, is it ŏ or ee, and you'd say ŏ.

_____76.For lap, is it ă or ĭ? (ă)
_____77. For bun, is it o or ŭ? (ŭ)
_____78. For nip, is it a or ĭ? (ĭ)
_____79. For set, is it ĕ or u? (ĕ)
_____80. For hot, is it ŏ or a? (ŏ)

If the testee misses as many as 3 of level 16, skip to level 18.

Level 17: Which sound game for middle sounds, no choices. Keep listening for the middle sound, the vowel sound. I'll say a word, and you tell me the vowel sound in the middle. So if I say dog, you just say ŏ.

_____81. pan (ă)
_____82. gum (ŭ)
_____83. top (ŏ)
_____84. him (ĭ)
_____85. let (ĕ)

Level 18: Segmenting, three phoneme words. I'll say a word, and you break it down into the first, middle, and last sound. Like if I say dog, you say duh ŏ guh.

_____86. bad (answer should be buh ă duh)
_____87. rip (answer should be rr ĭ puh)
_____88. rob (answer should be rr ŏ buh)
_____89. pet (answer should be puh ĕ tuh)
_____90. hug (answer should be hhh ŭ guh)

If the testee misses as many as 3 of level 18, end the test here.

Level 19: Segmenting, four phoneme words.

Please take each of these words apart into 4 sounds. (After the first word only, you can give feedback and remind the testee that you need 4 sounds.)

______91. bank (answer should be buh ă nn kuh)
______92. sent (answer should be sss ĕ nn tuh)
______93. think (answer should be thuh ĭ nn kuh)
______94. pond (answer should be puh ŏ nn duh)
______95. pump (answer should be puh ŭ mm puh)

If the testee misses as many as 3 of level 19, end the test here.

Level 20: Segmenting, five phoneme words.

Now please take each of these words apart into 5 sounds. (After the first word only you can give feedback and remind the testee that you need 5 sounds.)

______96. planned (answer should be puh ll ă nn duh)
______97. crest (answer should be kuh rr ĕ ss tuh)

______98. blink (answer should be buh ll ĭ nn kuh)
______99. stopped (answer should be sss tuh ŏ puh tuh or duh)
______100. grunt (answer should be guh rr ŭ nn tuh)

Count all skipped items as 0. Give 1 point for each correct.

Total correct: ________________

Spatial Awareness Test

This is another test where we are aiming for 100% correct after sufficient practice with the exercises for spatial awareness that are given in this book. You can test repeatedly with this test to see how the student is progressing toward this goal. If the student has not learned the names or sounds of the letters other than b, p, d, and q, do part 1 only.

Part 1: b, d, p, and q

Say to the testee: Please look at the list of letters on this page. Each letter is either b, d, p, or q. These are the hardest letters for most people to tell apart. Please start with number 1, and say what letter it is. Then continue along the list. Say the number, so that I'll know for sure which one you're answering. So here's what someone would sound like, doing this: they would be saying something like "Number 46, b. Number 47, d. Number 48, b." Only of course you start with number 1. Do you understand? OK, start with number 1 and say what each letter is.

(If the testee would prefer to say the sound of the letter rather than the name of the letter, it is fine for the testee to say "buh duh puh and quuh" in this test rather than bee, dee, pee, and kew.)

Here are the directions for the second part, and an answer sheet for the tester to use.

Say to the testee: This next part is a test of telling right from left. You see a bunch of words, in a list. All you have to do is to tell me the letter that is on the far left of the word or the far right of the word. This is the same as the first letter or the last letter in the word. For example, next to the zero, do you see the letters h, o, t? If I were to ask, what letter is farthest left in that word, you would say h. If I were to ask, what letter is farthest right, you would say t. OK? Now let's start with number 1.

(As you ask these, you don't read the word; you just say "Number ____, what letter is farthest ____."

Tester looks at this list to ask questions and record answers. Testee looks at the larger list printed two pages from this.

1. coat (What letter is farthest left?)

____

2. miss (What letter is farthest right?)

____

3. sill (What letter is farthest right?)

____

4. jump (What letter is farthest left?)

______

5. much (What letter is farthest right?)

______

6. cram (What letter is farthest right?)

______

7. fare (What letter is farthest left?)

______

8. gone (What letter is farthest left?)

______

9. vest (What letter is farthest left?)

______

10. flax (What letter is farthest right?)

______

11. grow (What letter is farthest right?)

______

12. rope (What letter is farthest left?)

______

13. life (What letter is farthest right?)

______

14. know (What letter is farthest left?)

______

15. shin (What letter is farthest right?)

______

16. flat (What letter is farthest right?)

______

17. into (What letter is farthest left?)

______

18. yell (What letter is farthest left?)

______

19. tofu (What letter is farthest right?)

______

20. oval (What letter is farthest left?)

______

21. aunt (What letter is farthest left?)

______

22. jazz (What letter is farthest right?)

______

Number correct out of these 22_________

Number correct on b,d,p,q test

____

Total number correct on spatial awareness test:___________

Spatial Awareness Test, Part 1

________ total correct of b,d,p,q test

1. b
2. d
3. p
4. p
5. d
6. b
7. q
8. b
9. q
10. p
11. d
12. q
13. b
14. b
15. q
16. d
17. p
18. b
19. q
20. d
21. p
22. p
23. d
24. b
25. q
26. q
27. p
28. d

Spatial Awareness Test, Part 2.

Left and right side of a word

0. hot

1. coat
2. miss
3. sill
4. jump
5. much

6. cram
7. fare
8. gone
9. vest
10. flax

11. grow
12. rope
13. life
14. know
15. shin

16. flat
17. into
18. yell
19. tofu
20. oval
21. aunt
22. jazz

Letter-Sound Test

In this test we present the student with letters and ask the student to give one sound that the letter makes. We are not looking for the letter name, but the sound. Thus for z we do not want "zee," but we want zzzzz.

To introduce this test we say, "You'll see a list of letters. Look at each one of them and say the sound that the letter makes. I'm not talking about the names of letters like double-you and vee and cue. By sounds of letters I'm talking about things like sssss and buh and mmm and zzzz."

For vowels, count the sound correct if the student can name the short vowel sound, with or without the long sound in addition. So if the student tells the long vowel sound, say, "Right! and what other sound does this letter make?"

For c and g, count the "hard" sound as correct, with or without the soft sound. So if the testee says sss for c, say, "Right! And what other sound does this letter make?" Use the same prompt if the testee says the juh sound for g.

Continue with this until the testee has attempted all 26 letters. If the testee has missed 5 letters in a row and seems frustrated, just ask the testee to look at the list and say the sounds of any letters the testee does know or want to guess. Count the unattempted ones as incorrect. Give one point for each correct sound.

If the testee gives ALL answers right for the letter sounds, then ask the testee to say the sounds one more time, this time as fast as possible. Use a stopwatch to time how fast the testee said the sounds correctly.

Respond with liberal approval and excitement when the student gets an answer right.

For this test we are aiming for a score of 100% correct. We then aim for the 26 letter sounds to be named in 15 seconds or less.

****

Number correct:____________

If all were correct, say: "You got all of them correct. Now I want to see how quickly you can give me those correct sounds. Please go down the list a second time and say the correct sounds quickly."

Seconds for the timed second trial:___________________

1. m
2. z
3. t
4. r
5. q
6. w
7. v
8. x
9. l
10. n
11. a
12. p
13. b
14. i
15. c
16. o
17. k
18. j
19. u
20. d
21. e
22. f
23. h
24. g
25. s
26. y

Five Tests of Decoding Skill

On the following pages you will find five tests of word decoding. I recommend using these tests often throughout the course of tutoring, (after the student has graduated from phonemic awareness, spatial awareness, and letter-sound correspondence training) so that there are "no surprises" at the end of tutoring when the student gets post-intervention testing. In addition, the progress on these tests provides a morale boost; lack of progress on them raises a red flag that something is not right. For example, if a learner is working on word decoding but making no progress, it could be that the learner needs to go back and become more fluent in one of the earlier stages.

The Phonetic Word Reading Test

The first, the Phonetic Word Reading Test, is a "curriculum based test" for this curriculum: the words in this test are simply a subset of the Words in Word Families. I created this test partly because many other tests of word identification start with words that are not the easiest words for beginning readers. Many tests begin with "easy" words like *you* and *to* and *said* and so forth, which may seem simple, but which don't follow the first rules of letter-sound correspondence that students learn.

I assigned rough grade levels to the Phonetic Word Reading Test by performing a multiple regression to predict the grade level in a group of children who took both the Phonetic Word Reading Test and the Word Identification subscale of the Woodcock Test of Reading Mastery.

The Burt Word Reading Test

The Burt Word Reading Test is in the public domain, and has been used for many years in the UK. It yields an age equivalent; this score may or may not correspond to what someone "should" do at a certain age. But if one is able to make a certain number of "years" of progress in a lot less than that length of time (which is what we would expect for people who use this book's techniques diligently), there is cause for great celebration!

The Schonell Reading Test

The Schonell is another public domain test of word decoding that has been used primarily in the UK. The method of obtaining a rough age equivalent is as follows: the "reading age" equals 5 plus one tenth of the number of words read correctly. That translates that if someone gets no words correct, the reading age is 5, and the reading age increases one year for every 10 additional words read correctly, up to age 15, where total mastery of these words is expected (but probably not usually obtained). Despite the fact that the age equivalents should be taken with some suspicion: if the learner works for a year and improves the score by a good many more than 10 words, celebration is in order.

The Unfamiliar Word Test

This test, with four forms, is a "homemade" test mean to measure the same ability as tests of reading nonsense words, such as the "word attack" subscale of the Woodcock Reading Mastery Test. Such tests are perhaps the purest measure of decoding skill, because the learner usually has never seen the particular combinations of letters in the words, or pseudowords, on the test. Thus memory of particular words doesn't help the learner on this sort of test.

The words on the Unfamiliar Word Test look very much like the letter combinations on pseudoword tests. However, believe it or not, each word on this test is one I found in at least one dictionary; they are real English words! They are words that are used very infrequently.

There are no age or grade equivalents associated with the Unfamiliar Word Tests at this point. The most useful measure with this test is simply the percent correct. It's good to keep training until the learner can give a reasonable pronunciation of all the words on form A and B, and then see how much the learner's skill generalizes to the words on form C and D.

Directions for Administering the Five Tests of Decoding Skill

Each of the five above-mentioned tests are word lists, divided (by line skips) into groups of five. For each of them, start at the beginning, and ask the student to read each word. Use praise and encouragement liberally, both for getting words right and for trying them. Let the student know it's fine to say "I don't know" for any word. Keep going until the student misses all five words in one of the groups of five. Total up the number of words the student has read correctly. This is the raw score for each test.

The tester may make a copy of the test page to use as an answer sheet, or may make or copy the generic answer sheet presented later.

The Phonetic Word Reading Test

1. bat
2. ban
3. tap
4. lag
5. sad

6. jam
7. tab
8. nap
9. pet
10. leg

11. bit
12. sin
13. nod
14. hog
15. fun

16. tub
17. can
18. kid
19. pick
20. lock

21. land
22. test
23. rests
24. jumps
25. next

26. winks
27. plump
28. blend
29. crust
30. strap

31. this
32. that
33. thick
34. thrill
35. quill

36. quack
37. whip
38. whet
39. rush
40. shell

41. pinch
42. chest
43. said
44. they
45. steal

46. free
47. broom

48. roof
49. foot
50. wood

51. yard
52. sharp
53. storm
54. north
55. clerk

56. firm
57. point
58. hoist
59. sound
60. gown

61. jaw
62. haul
63. malt
64. aim
65. lay

66. blind
67. dried
68. blown
69. loan
70. blue

71. stew

72. cape
73. rate
74. care
75. snare

76. shine
77. file
78. cope
79. tone
80. duke

81. brute
82. unfit
83. locket
84. again
85. laugh

86. slipper
87. peddler
88. dipping
89. fading
90. party

91. carries
92. shouted
93. seated
94. robbed
95. hitched

96. bathing
97. bother
98. hobble
99. mangle
100. place

101. truce
102. dodge
103. urgent
104. pause
105. noise

106. knob
107. gnat
108. hour
109. daughter
110. sigh

111. sleigh
112. phrase
113. phone
114. enough
115. roughly

116. bread
117. dreaded
118. learn
119. steak
120. field

121. belief
122. bullet
123. awful
124. marvelous
125. touch

126. water
127. watch
128. station
129. delicious
130. traitor

131. active
132. influence
133. handsome
134. innocence
135. exclaiming

The number of words the student got correct (in the left column) corresponds to the approximate grade level (in the right column). The first digit in the grade level score refers to the grade, and the second refers to the fraction of a year's progress made toward the next grade level. So 0.9 is the average level after nine-tenths of the kindergarten year is complete; 2.3 is the average level after three tenths of the second grade year is complete, and so forth.

score	grade level
0	Below 0.9
1	0.9
2	0.9
3	1.0
4	1.0
5	1.0
6	1.0
7	1.1
8	1.1
9	1.1
10	1.1
11	1.2
12	1.2
13	1.2
14	1.2
15	1.3
16	1.3
17	1.3
18	1.3
19	1.4
20	1.4
21	1.4
22	1.4
23	1.5
24	1.5
25	1.5
26	1.5
27	1.6
28	1.6
29	1.6
30	1.6
31	1.7
32	1.7
33	1.7
34	1.8
35	1.8
36	1.8
37	1.8
38	1.9
39	1.9
40	1.9
41	1.9
42	2.0
43	2.0
44	2.0
45	2.0
46	2.1
47	2.1
48	2.1
49	2.1
50	2.2
51	2.2
52	2.2
53	2.2
54	2.3
55	2.3
56	2.3
57	2.3
58	2.4
59	2.4
60	2.4
61	2.4

62	2.5
63	2.5
64	2.5
65	2.5
66	2.6
67	2.6
68	2.6
69	2.6
70	2.7
71	2.7
72	2.7
73	2.7
74	2.8
75	2.8
76	2.8
77	2.8
78	2.9
79	2.9
80	2.9
81	2.9
82	3.0
83	3.0
84	3.0
85	3.0
86	3.1
87	3.1
88	3.1
89	3.1
90	3.2
91	3.2
92	3.2
93	3.2
94	3.3
95	3.3
96	3.3
97	3.3
98	3.4
99	3.4
100	3.4
101	3.4
102	3.5
103	3.5
104	3.5
105	3.5
106	3.6
107	3.6
108	3.6
109	3.6
110	3.7
111	3.7
112	3.7
113	3.7
114	3.8
115	3.8
116	3.8
117	3.9
118	3.9
119	3.9
120	3.9
121	or above: 4th grade level or above

raw score:_________

grade level:________

The Burt Word Reading Test

1. to
2. is
3. up
4. he
5. at

6. for
7. my
8. sun
9. one
10. of

11. big
12. some
13. his
14. or
15. an

16. went
17. boys
18. that
19. girl
20. water

21. just
22. day
23. wet
24. pot
25. things

26. no
27. told
28. love
29. now
30. sad

31. nurse
32. carry
33. quickly
34. village
35. scramble

36. journey
37. terror
38. return
39. twisted
40. shelves

41. beware
42. explorer
43. known
44. projecting
45. tongue

46. serious
47. domineer
48. obtain
49. belief
50. luncheon

51. emergency
52. events
53. steadiness
54. nourishment
55. fringe

56. formulate
57. scarcely
58. universal
59. commenced
60. overwhelmed

61. circumstances
62. destiny
63. urge
64. laborers
65. exhausted

66. trudging
67. refrigerator
68. melodrama
69. encyclopedia
70. apprehend

71. motionless
72. ultimate
73. atmosphere
74. reputation
75. binocular

76. economy
77. theory
78. humanity
79. philosopher
80. contemptuous

81. autobiography
82. excessively
83. champagne
84. terminology
85. perambulating

86. efficiency
87. unique
88. perpetual
89. mercenary
90. glycerine

91. influential
92. atrocious
93. fatigue
94. exorbitant
95. physician

96. microscopical
97. contagion
98. renown
99. hypocritical
100. fallacious

101. phlegmatic
102. melancholy
103. palpable
104. eccentricity
105. constitutionally

106. alienate
107. phthisis
108. poignancy
109. ingratiating
110. subtlety

Reading Age for Burt Word Reading Test, as a Function of Raw Score
Reading age is in years and months.

Raw	R. Age
0-1	<5-3
2	5-3
3	5-3
4	5-4
5	5-5
6	5-5
7	5-6
8	5-6
9	5-7
10	5-7
11	5-8
12	5-9
13	5-9
14	5-10
15	5-11
16	5-11
17	6-0
18	6-1
19	6-1
20	6-2
21	6-2
22	6-3
23	6-4
24	6-5
25	6-5
26	6-6
27	6-7
28	6-8
29	6-8
30	6-9
31	6-9
32	6-10
33	6-11
34	7-0
35	7-1
36	7-2
37	7-3
38	7-4
39	7-5
40	7-5
41	7-6
42	7-7
43	7-8
44	7-9
45	7-10
46	7-11
47	8-0
48	8-1
49	8-2
50	8-3
51	8-4
52	8-5
53	8-6
54	8-7
55	8-8
56	8-9
57	8-10
58	9-0
59	9-1
60	9-2
61	9-3
62	9-4
63	9-6
64	9-7
65	9-8
66	9-9
67	9-10
68	10-0
69	10-1
70	10-2
71	10-3
72	10-4
73	10-6
74	10-7
75	10-9
76	10-10
77	10-11
78	11-0
79	11-1
80	11-3
81	11-4
82	11-5
83	11-6
84	11-7
85	11-9
86	11-10
87	11-11
88	12-0
89	12-1
90	12-3
91	12-4
92	12-5
93	12-6
94	12-7
95	12-9
96	12-10
97	12-11
98	13-0
99	13-1
100	13-3
101	13-4
102	13-6
103	13-6
104	13-7
105	13-9
106	13-10
107	13-11
108	14-0
109	14-1
110	14-3

The Schonell Reading Test

1. tree
2. little
3. milk
4. egg
5. book

6. school
7. sit
8. frog
9. playing
10. bun

11. flower
12. road
13. clock
14. train
15. light

16. picture
17. think
18. summer
19. people
20. something

21. dream
22. downstairs
23. biscuit
24. shepherd
25. thirsty

26. crowd
27. sandwich
28. beginning
29. postage
30. island

31. saucer
32. angel
33. ceiling
34. appeared
35. gnome

36. canary
37. attractive
38. imagine
39. nephew
40. gradually

41. smolder
42. applaud
43. disposal
44. nourished
45. diseased

46. university
47. orchestra
48. knowledge
49. audience
50. situated

51. physics
52. campaign
53. choir
54. intercede
55. fascinate

56. forfeit
57. siege
58. recent
59. plausible
60. prophecy

61. colonel
62. soloist
63. systematic
64. slovenly
65. classification

66. genuine
67. institution
68. pivot
69. conscience
70. heroic

71. pneumonia
72. preliminary
73. antique
74. susceptible
75. enigma

76. oblivion
77. scintillate
78. satirical

79. sabre
80. beguile

81. terrestrial
82. belligerent
83. adamant
84. sepulchre
85. statistics

86. miscellaneous
87. procrastinate
88. tyrannical
89. evangelical
90. grotesque

91. ineradicable
92. judicature
93. preferential
94. homonym
95. fictitious

96. rescind
97. metamorphosis
98. somnambulist
99. bibliography
100. idiosyncrasy

The Unfamiliar Word Test, Form A

1. fid
2. guff
3. fen
4. gam
5. dap

6. jinn
7. scud
8. tench
9. thrum
10. tosh

11. trug
12. scrim
13. scop
14. pish
15. quod

16. gelt
17. grig
18. pash
19. whap
20. strath

21. snick
22. crump
23. yelk
24. clunch
25. vetch

26. bice
27. bouse
28. chert
29. bine
30. crone

31. gules
32. foy
33. glaive
34. gloze
35. grange

36. harl
37. kail
38. leet
39. plew
40. scarp

41. scree
42. skeen
43. sloe
44. smalt
45. nerts

46. spode
47. strafe
48. quern
49. thrave
50. shoon

51. yare
52. yean
53. vair
54. speel
55. jurel

56. kegling
57. kebbie
58. indult
59. inhume
60. gantline

61. costive
62. imbrue
63. inarch
64. selvage
65. tholepin

66. retuse
67. poundal
68. suffixal
69. interlap
70. lenify

71. janiform
72. vermian
73. thurifer
74. neurula
75. nidificate

76. sequacity
77. invigilate
78. bentonitic
79. gutteralize
80. macadamizing

The Unfamiliar Word Test, Form B

1. zek
2. ret
3. dib
4. kep
5. zax

6. fop
7. simp
8. grum
9. thrip
10. tilth

11. tret
12. twang
13. feck
14. palp
15. hist

16. vang
17. frons
18. grot
19. calx
20. mump

21. yegg
22. shog
23. scup
24. strass
25. strick

26. berm
27. blain
28. brome
29. cloy
30. coif

31. prow
32. firth
33. gar
34. glede
35. oast

36. grue
37. roil
38. keeve
39. marl
40. poon

41. soave
42. ope
43. skirl
44. sloid
45. smew

46. spalled
47. ribes
48. quid
49. strow
50. woad

51. wraith
52. maw
53. urb
54. spile
55. jinker

56. dotter
57. unhood
58. afreet
59. mooting
60. portance

61. corbie
62. guttle
63. osmics
64. evzone
65. suttee

66. twattle
67. qualmish
68. crustose
69. denary
70. deontic

71. monocarp
72. sulcation
73. indigoid
74. docetic
75. esurient

76. provenience
77. revanchism
78. presentative
79. tenebrific
80. rheometric

The Unfamiliar Word Test, Form C

1. nib
2. guv
3. gan
4. kab
5. vas

6. tup
7. gamp
8. squeg
9. snell
10. mulct

11. strop
12. comp
13. skulk
14. pish
15. slunk

16. fletch
17. quitch
18. tipt
19. sprit
20. dross

21. sprat
22. flet
23. sprent
24. plasm
25. flitch

26. erst
27. smew
28. stipe
29. bine
30. neve

31. caul
32. swatch
33. dace
34. pleach
35. fain

36. stope
37. prawn
38. gurge
39. herse
40. bort

41. bonze
42. quire
43. auld
44. virl
45. tierce

46. dree
47. dite
48. skeer
49. shrive
50. goaf

51. scrouge
52. dray
53. gnar
54. dene
55. incult

56. daglock
57. curlew
58. bantling
59. keelage
60. shaslik

61. stertor
62. shealing
63. formate
64. endite
65. degust

66. steenbok
67. trappous
68. haverel
69. diorite
70. biotope

71. legator
72. sudation
73. vetivert
74. proximo
75. sympodia

76. misericord
77. holozoic
78. homosporous
79. navicular
80. schistosomiasis

The Unfamiliar Word Test, Form D

1. gid
2. lev
3. dom
4. nub
5. dag

6. lop
7. spiv
8. snash
9. haft
10. plash

11. veld
12. rusk
13. guck
14. scup
15. hist

16. whist
17. delft
18. zimb
19. skelp
20. prog

21. plash
22. sneck
23. sept
24. bast
25. smutch

26. gursh
27. jauk
28. spoor
29. stirk
30. neum

31. noil
32. rube
33. thurl
34. forb
35. lave

36. scow
37. drupe
38. knur
39. whorl
40. feu

41. crore
42. gault
43. dinge
44. quince
45. kine

46. fadge
47. spline
48. stean
49. reave
50. thraw

51. pawk
52. shirr
53. vare
54. weald
55. mayvin

56. fanwort
57. dacoit
58. cony
59. kibosh
60. leukon

61. smectite
62. thewless
63. higgler
64. emprise
65. deemster

66. premune
67. thrummy
68. grouter
69. forkiest
70. damozel

71. jelutong
72. lomentum
73. unroven
74. paronym
75. scabiosa

76. diaconal
77. iconolatry
78. ephemerid
79. licentiate
80. pastorium

Generic Answer Sheet

1.____
2.____
3.____
4.____
5.____
6.____
7.____
8.____
9.____
10.____
11.____
12.____
13.____
14.____
15.____
16.____
17.____
18.____
19.____
20.____
21.____
22.____
23.____
24.____
25.____
26.____
27.____
28.____
29.____
30.____
31.____
32.____
33.____
34.____
35.____
36.____
37.____
38.____
39.____
40.____
41.____
42.____
43.____
44.____
45.____
46.____
47.____
48.____
49.____
50.____
51.____
52.____
53.____
54.____
55.____
56.____
57.____
58.____
59.____
60.____
61.____
62.____
63.____
64.____
65.____
66.____
67.____
68.____
69.____
70.____
71.____
72.____
73.____
74.____
75.____
76.____
77.____
78.____
79.____
80.____
81.____
82.____
83.____
84.____
85.____
86.____
87.____
88.____
89.____
90.____
91.____
92.____
93.____
94.____
95.____
96.____
97.____
98.____
99.____
100.____
101.____
102.____
103.____
104.____
105.____
106.____
107.____
108.____
109.____
110.____
111.____
112.____
113.____
114.____
115.____
116.____
117.____
118.____
119.____
120.____
121.____
122.____
123.____
124.____
125.____
126.____
127.____
128.____
129.____
130.____
131.____
132.____
133.____
134.____
135.____
136.____
137.____
138.____
139.____
140.____
141.____
142.____
143.____
144.____
145.____
146.____
147.____
148.____
149.____
150.____
151.____
152.____
153.____
154.____
155.____
156.____
157.____
158.____
159.____
160.____

Three Phoneme Words, With Pictures

The pages that follow contain "three phoneme" words and pictures. These are useful for several sorts of exercises for beginning readers.

The five words on the first nine of these pages have different beginning sounds, different ending sounds, and different middle sounds. Thus you can show the learner any one of these pages and do the "Which Word" exercise with beginning, middle, or ending sounds, knowing that there will be only one correct answer. For example: "On the first page there are bag, cob, hen, gum, and six . Which word starts with kuh? Which word starts with guh? Which word ends with nn? Which word ends with ks? Which has an ĕ in the middle? Which has an ĭ in the middle?"

You can also do the blending exercise with these pictures. "I'm thinking of one of these five words: bag, cob, hen, gum, and six. See if you can guess which one: kuh ŏ buh."

You can ask the learner to segment the words on the page. It's easier for the learner to do this when he has heard you say the separate phonemes several times. "You've heard me say the words in three parts, with one sound being the sound of each letter. For example, you've heard me say 'guh ŭ mm' for *gum*. Who can do the same thing with *hen*?"

You can ask letter-sound correspondence questions, asking the learner which sound a certain letter makes in a certain word. For example: "In the word *bag*, what sound does the b make?" "In the word *gum*, what sound does the u make?"

After the learner has done lots of these exercises with the words and pictures, you can cover up the pictures and let the learner look at the three (or four) letters in the word, say the three phonemes that those letters make, and then blend them to say the word. Your uncovering the picture after the learner sounds and blends the word can be a good reinforcer.

Alternatively, you can not bother with covering up the pictures, and simply ask the learner to look at the letters and sound and blend the words, one after another; the learner is assisted in this task by the picture beside the word. Thus the learner's job is to look at the first page and say, "buh ă guh bag. kuh ŏ buh cob. huh ĕ nn hen. guh ŭ mm gum. ss ĭ ks six."

Doing lots of these exercises with just these words gets the learner very much prepared for success on sounding and blending the Words in Word Families.

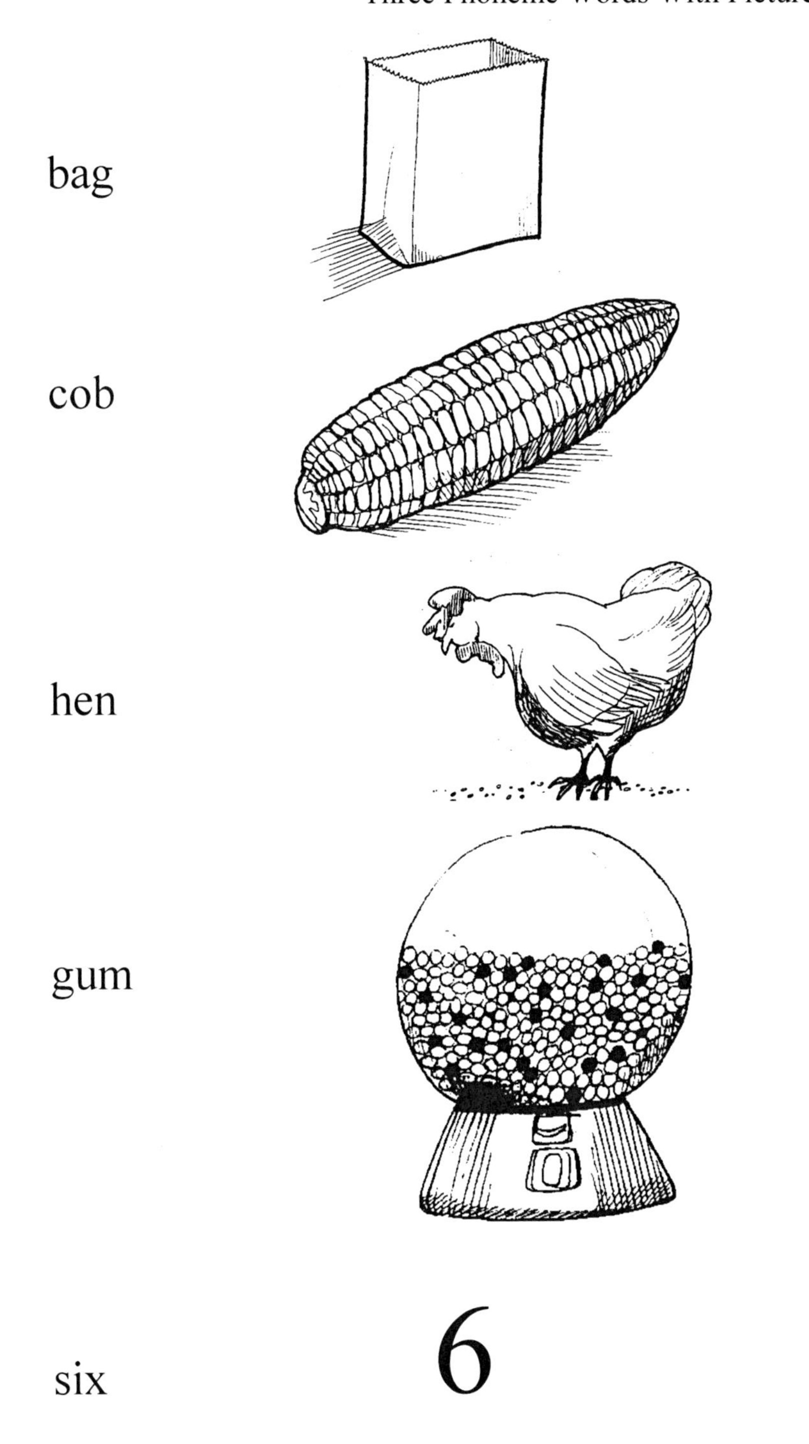
bag
cob
hen
gum
six
6

bat
sun
ten
pig
mop

net

box

cup

man

hill

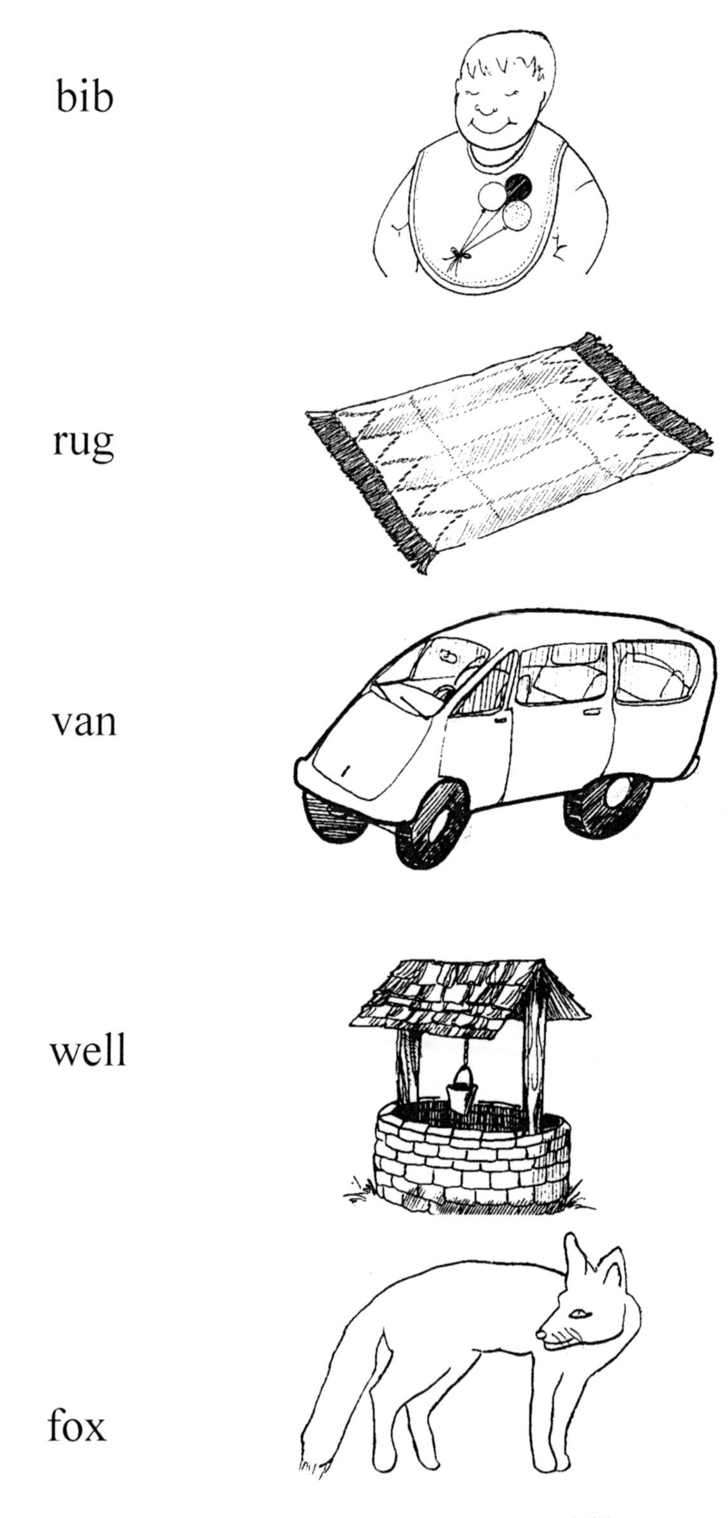
bib
rug
van
well
fox

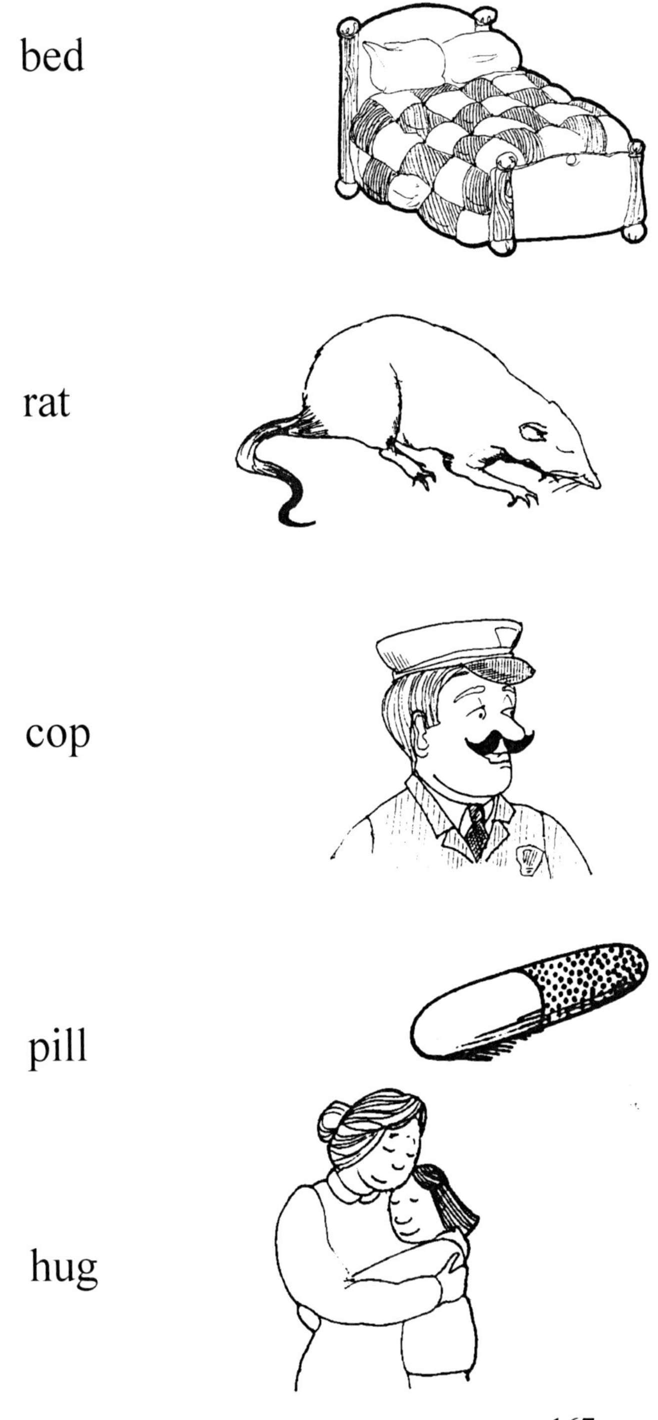

bed

rat

cop

pill

hug

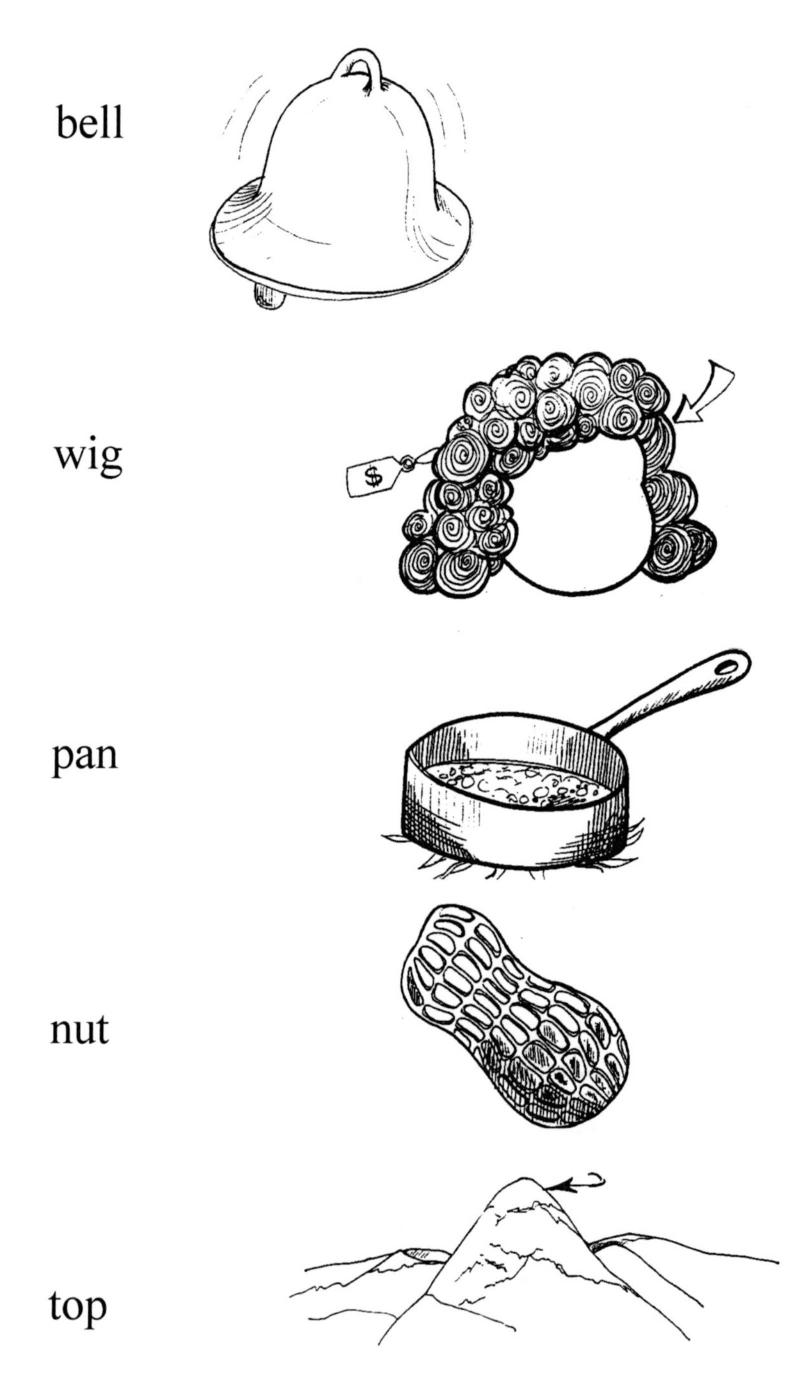
bell
wig
$
pan
nut
top

mud
pen
kiss
log
hat

bug
web
lid
doll
fan

dog

bud

mess

pin

cap

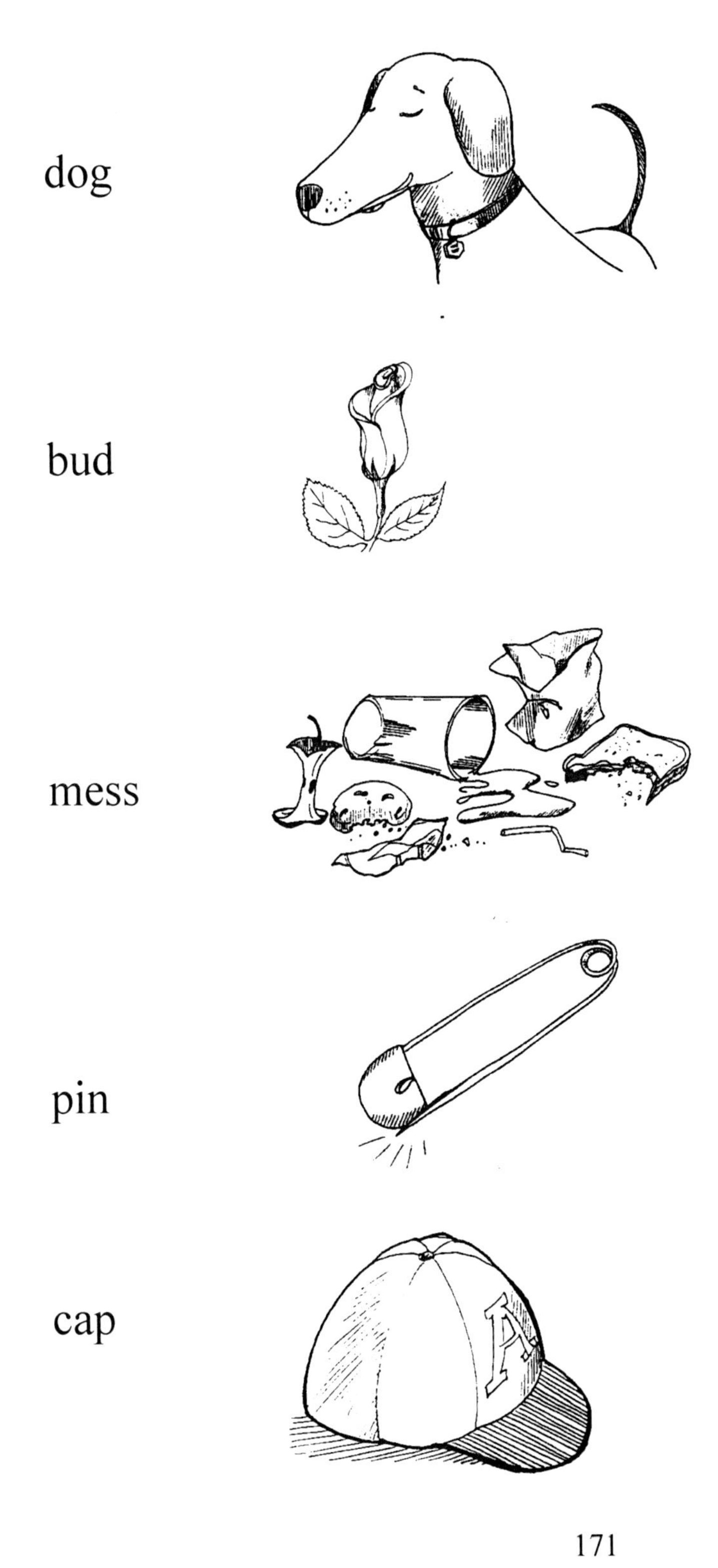

cub
jam
nun
mug
lab

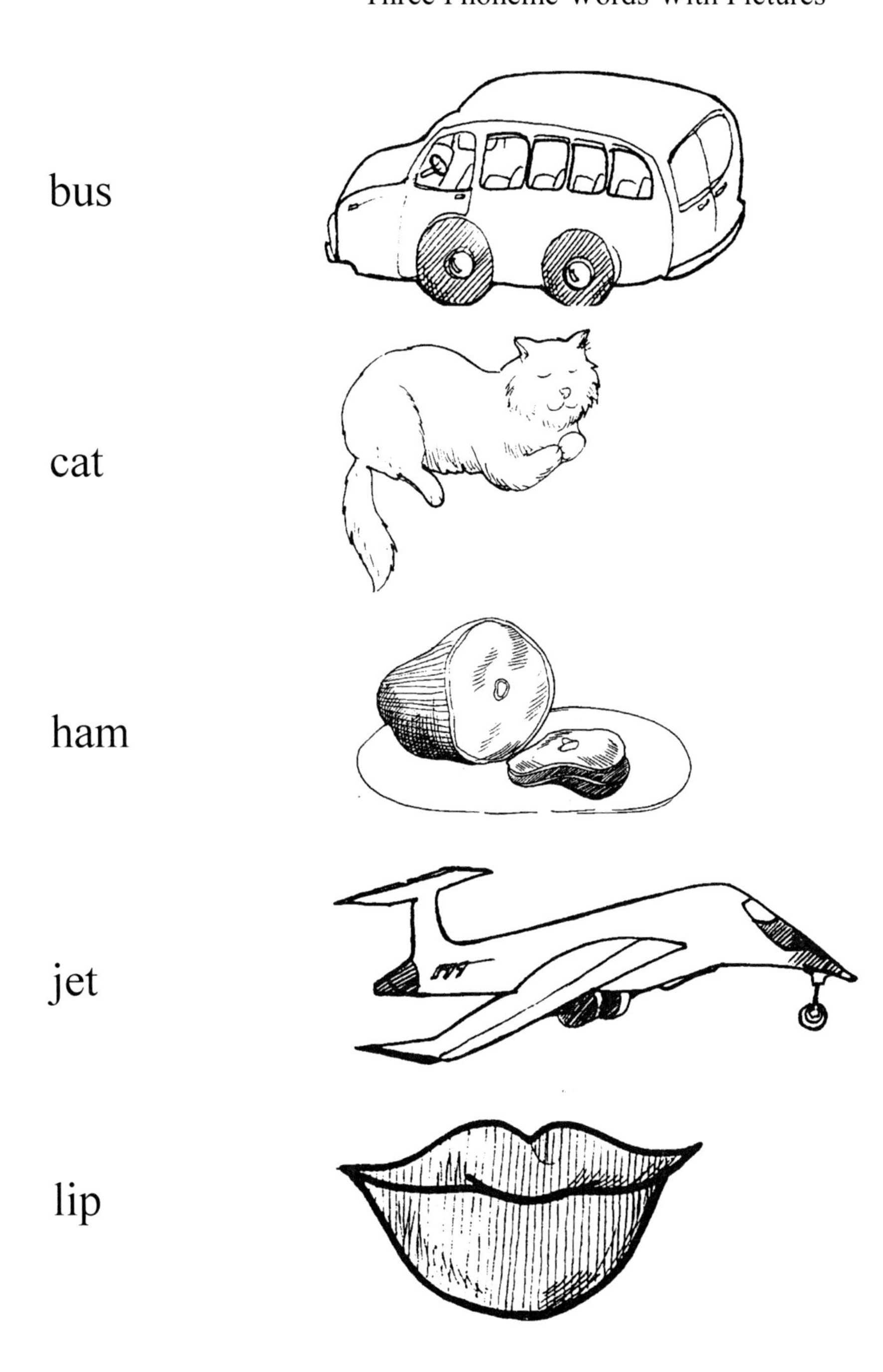
bus
cat
ham
jet
lip

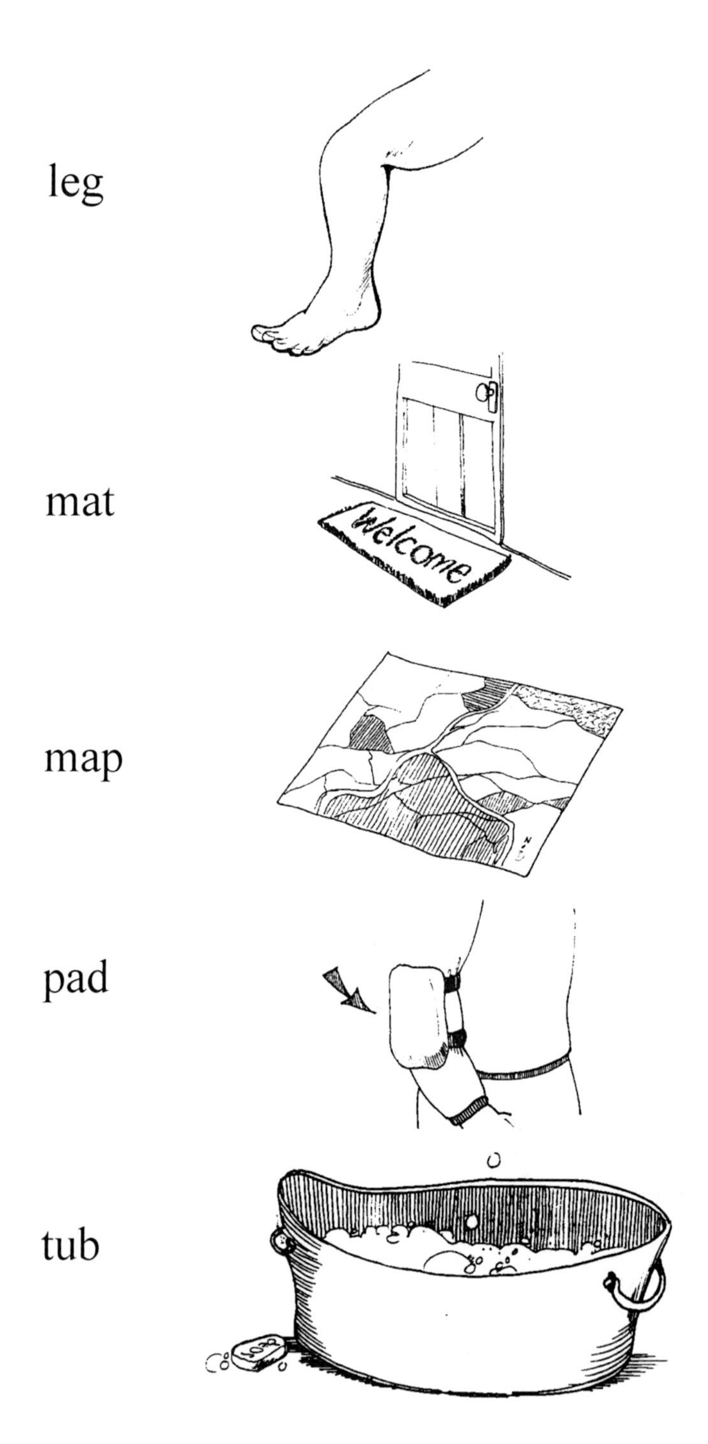
leg
mat
Welcome
map
pad
tub

tag
SALE
can
cab
dad
peg

The Alphabet Page

The alphabet page, which is printed on the page following this, contains one picture for each letter of the alphabet. Each word begins with the letter sound that is usually taught first for that letter. (The exception to this is the word x-ray; for this word you ignore the short e sound that really starts the word and focus on the ks sound immediately after.) The words pictured on the alphabet page are also those sung about in the song "Ă as in Apple," on the CD *What the Letters Say*. You have my permission to photocopy this page and to enlarge it into a big poster to tape onto the wall. You can do various activities with the alphabet page.

1. You can let students point to the pictures while any of the letter sound songs are sung or listened to.

2. You can use the pictures for the blending exercise. "I see, on the alphabet page, a *lll ē fff*. Who can guess what I'm thinking of?"

3. You can use the pictures for the which-word exercise. "I'm thinking of either *snake* or *turtle*. The one I'm thinking of starts with tuh. Can you guess which one?"

4. You can use the pictures for the which-sound exercise with two choices. "Which sound does the word *jar* start with: is it juh or mmm?"

5. You can do the which-sound exercise without two choices. "Which sound does the word moon start with?

6. You can use telling and then asking to teach letter identification, if the student doesn't already know it. "This letter is a, and this is b. What's this one? Good!"

7. The telephone tutor can use the alphabet page to teach letter identification without being able to point. "The letter above the apple is a, and the letter over the bus is b. What's the letter over the bus? Good!"

8. You can teach letter-sound correspondence. What sound does this letter make? (Hint: it's the first sound in the word pictured underneath it.)

9. You can let the students refer to it when testing themselves on letter-sound correspondence, so that the student can have a more nearly "errorless" pathway to expertise. "Look at this list of letters, and say the sound that each one makes. If you forget, feel free to look at the alphabet page."

10. You can use it to teach the concepts of *row* and *left* and *right*. "Can you find the picture that just to the right of the snake?" "Do you see elephant in the top row?"

Alphabet Page

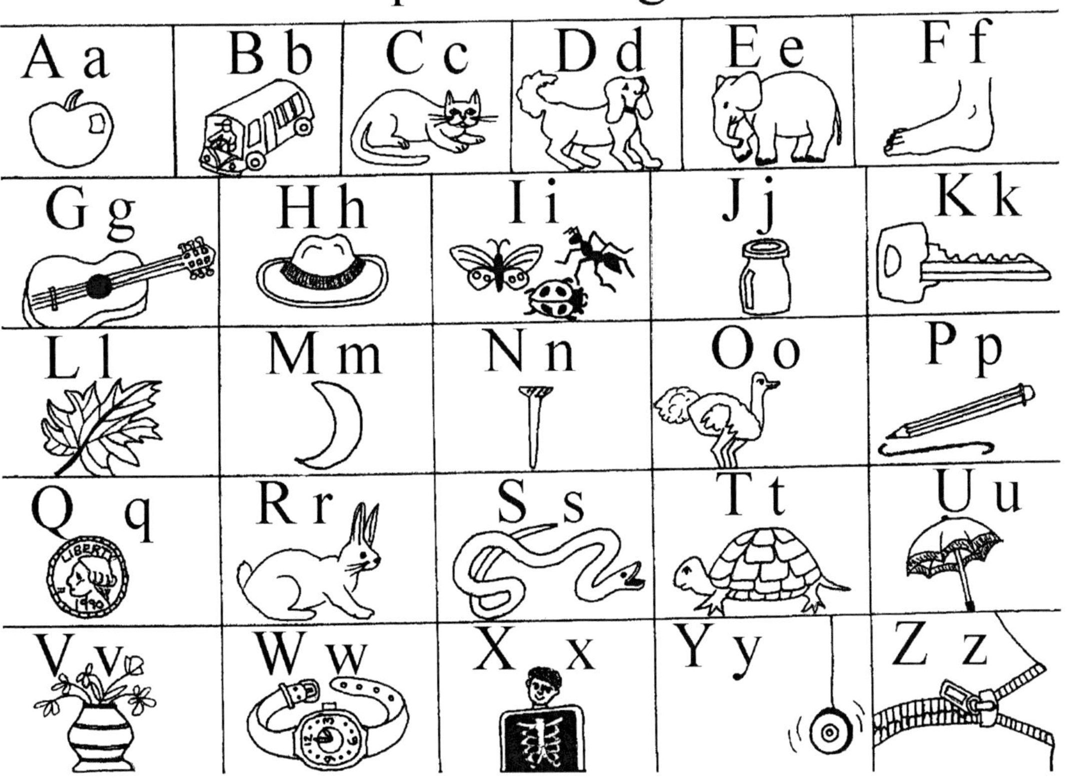

Phonemic Awareness: Sentences for the Blending Exercise

For learners with goals of increasing phonemic awareness, the following exercise will give much practice in blending the separate sounds of words to make the word. For many learners, the sentences give just the right level of clue. The tutor reads the sentence, but for the last word in the sentence, the tutor says the phonemes separately. For example, for sentence 1, the tutor would say "The dog likes to get a puh-aah-tuh." If these are hard for the learner the tutor can run the sounds together. As these get easier, the tutor can separate the sounds more. When they are easier still, the tutor can give the sounds without the sentence clue.

Three Phoneme Words

1. The dog likes to get a pat.
2. It was hot so we used a fan.
3. A space between two things is a gap.
4. They played jazz.
5. Jelly and jam.
6. A steel rod.
7. The balloon didn't pop.
8. A chapped lip.
9. A bear cub.
10. We had fun.
11. We couldn't see because of fog.
12. A science kit.
13. He gave his wife a kiss.
14. The dog likes to beg.
15. Ring a bell.
16. Pay your tax.
17. Bigger than a car, it's a van.
18. He gave his tail a wag.
19. They flew in a jet.
20. More or less.
21. This place is a mess.
22. Caught in a net.
23. Drink from the cup.
24. The knife is dull.
25. A patch of woods is called a dell.
26. The light is dim.
27. At the top of the letter i is a dot.
28. A sea gull.
29. Chewing gum.
30. Cats sometimes hiss.
31. The outer part of a peanut is the hull.
32. Clean the floor with a mop.
33. A goat and a pig.
34. The shirt got a rip.
35. Thou shalt not kill.
36. Jack and Jill.
37. The baby wore a bib.
38. The whale is big.
39. Has the dog been fed?
40. She stumbled and fell.
41. What grade did you get?
42. A rooster and a hen.
43. A corn cob.
44. The police officer was called a cop.
45. He slept on a cot.
46. An almond is a nut.
47. Peas grow in a pod.

48. Whether or not.
49. She held the baby on her lap.
50. He got mad.
51. The song was a rap.
52. She felt sad.
53. If I eat a lot I may get fat.
54. Hit the ball with the bat.
55. If she can't do it, nobody can.
56. Her dad is a good man.
57. Fry it in a pan.
58. Do you like to play tag?
59. An old horse is called a nag.
60. A joke or prank is called a gag.
61. A sweet potato or a yam?
62. A knee pad.
63. A boy is called a lad.
64. Can you tell where we are from the map?
65. Forbidding or saying no is called a ban.
66. First she walked, then she ran.
67. The old witch was called a hag.
68. A poke is called a jab.
69. The scientist worked in a lab.
70. To catch something is to nab.
71. Just a little bit is a little dab.
72. The deer is called a buck.
73. A part of my body I can't see is my back.
74. She gave the ice cream a lick.
75. An argument is called a tiff.
76. Not the bottom but the top.
77. He gave the ball a toss.
78. The spider made a web.
79. A rolling stone gathers no moss.
80. Wipe your feet on the door mat.
81. A girl is called a lass.
82. I have something to sell.
83. It's in our chests, it's a rib.
84. They ate and drank at the pub.
85. I want to take a nap.
86. To keep quiet is to keep mum.
87. Keep your ears warm with the ear muff.
88. Don't look right at the sun.
89. If you won't, I will.
90. Do you have a safety pin?
91. Do you want to make a bet?
92. A school bus.
93. You can sing it or you can hum.
94. Add the numbers and get the sum.
95. A bath tub.
96. A back rub.
97. A Roman Catholic nun.
98. No or yes.
99. The tent is held up by a peg.
100. Not just one guy but several men.
101. The fox went back to his den.
102. A group of things is called a set.
103. A weeping sound is a sob.
104. A type of fish is a cod.
105. My supervisor is called my boss.
106. Short for sister is sis.
107. I'd rather stand than sit.
108. Shot by a gun.
109. The peach is covered with fuzz.
110. He went away mad, in a big huff.
111. She gave her son a hug.
112. A lie is called a fib.
113. Half of twenty is ten.
114. She took the dog to a vet.
115. The water came from a well.
116. I heard a bee buzz.
117. A flower bud.
118. The end of the sleeve is the cuff.
119. He gave the ball a kick.
120. Is that a goose or a duck?
121. I'm feeling a little sick.

122. They pinned it with a tack.
123. Carried books in a back pack.
124. To you I wish good luck.
125. On the window I heard a tap.
126. Our ears produce wax.
127. It's time to go to bed.
128. What other than beer is in a keg?
129. He said he didn't but I know he did.
130. They let us eat our fill.
131. The dog is called a mutt.
132. I just can't tell.
133. Her favorite color was red.
134. Don't make a big fuss.
135. He lived in a little hut.
136. I got dirty from walking in mud.
137. Keep the corn in the bin.
138. How can we pay the hospital bill?
139. He didn't like it one bit.
140. A type of fruit is a fig.
141. The shoes don't fit.
142. He couldn't walk because he hurt his leg.
143. If you sit by the pool you're going to get wet.
144. Don't scream and yell.
145. They ran out of gas.
146. This too shall pass.
147. It's not healthy to try to get a tan.
148. To keep the sun off me, I wear a hat.
149. It's the best lesson I ever had.
150. Did you lose or win?
151. Let me give you a tip.
152. The person is easily led.
153. The computer memory was called ram.
154. The vegetarian never ate ham.
155. A lot of talk is called gab.
156. They rode in a taxi cab.
157. Maple syrup is made from sap.
158. I want to see what you got.
159. The pig is also called a hog.
160. On one foot I can hop.
161. The child played with a doll.
162. Put it into the box.
163. He needed money and wanted a job.
164. In the woods I saw a big log.
165. The jar has a lid.
166. In the Wizard of Oz a man was made of tin.
167. Half of twelve is six.
168. To pull on a rope is to tug.
169. They sat on the rug.
170. How fast can you run?
171. Conjunctions are words like and, or, and but.
172. The fish has a fin.
173. Behind their house is a deck.
174. The boat is at the dock.
175. Is it slow or quick?
176. They used to write with a quill.
177. A little joke is called a quip.
178. Should we keep going or quit?
179. He gave the stuck machine a whack.
180. Who knows where or when?
181. She's a math whiz.
182. What is your first wish?
183. They're sleeping, so hush.
184. Go fast but don't rush.
185. The oyster lives in a shell.
186. Money is called cash.
187. A big cut is a gash.
188. To get clean you take a bath.
189. There were three of them.
190. I didn't know that.

191. What is this?
192. The tools are in the shed.
193. Red marks on the skin are called a rash.
194. A large boat is a ship.
195. The front part of your lower leg is your shin.
196. They went to the store to shop.
197. At the doctor's office she got a shot.
198. Is the door open or shut?
199. A fellow is called a chap.
200. To have a talk is to chat.
201. He wrote a check.
202. A young hen is a chick.
203. Below my mouth is my chin.
204. A potato chip.
205. A friend is called a chum.
206. To get a little smell of something is to take a whiff.
207. We take one of these roads, but I don't know which.
208. A sudden impulse is called a whim.
209. The opposite of without is with.
210. A bad guy is called a thug.
211. Through the woods there ran a path.
212. He went on a diet to get thin.
213. The dictionary is very thick.
214. It looks like a butterfly, but it's a moth.
215. To make something stop is to quell.
216. The duck says quack.
217. Did you pass the quiz?
218. He walked with a cane.
219. They used the oven to bake.
220. The bear lived in a cave.
221. It looked real, but it was fake.
222. Hide and seek.
223. Plant the seed.
224. How do you feel?
225. If you succeed you don't fail.
226. Ice falling from the sky is hail.
227. The deaf person couldn't hear.
228. The mountain top is called a peak.
229. Please have a seat.
230. She rode a bike.
231. The river was long and wide.
232. I pronounce you husband and wife.
233. They put the trash in a big pile.
234. Three times three is nine.
235. A ten cent coin is a dime.
236. Turn on the light.
237. They dug a hole.
238. I want to go home.
239. Would you like to hear a joke?
240. The long story was a bore.
241. What is his weight and height?
242. The operation restored the blind person's sight.
243. The ocean's movement is called a tide.
244. Grapes grow on a vine.
245. Get tough and don't whine.
246. What type of food do you like?
247. We want to keep you safe.
248. They worked with a rake.
249. The window glass is called a pane.
250. What is your name?
251. The opposite of love is hate.
252. Be honest and don't cheat.
253. The man said to his wife, "Yes, dear."
254. They put water on themselves because of the heat.
255. To cry is to weep.

256. What do you need?
257. Can I take just one peek?
258. A bobwhite bird is also called a quail.
259. When do we get paid?
260. The man had to go to jail.
261. A group of players is called a team.
262. He liked to learn and liked to teach.
263. There are 365 days in a year.
264. On the water I see a boat.
265. The black stuff is coal.
266. That flower is a rose.
267. To make people happy is a good goal.
268. A pile of sand is called a dune.
269. The month after May is June.
270. Talking disrespectfully is being rude.
271. I don't know what clothes he wore.
272. The cure for hunger is food.
273. They got into the water to get cool.
274. In the night sky is the moon.
275. I'm in a good mood.
276. He has a loose tooth.
277. I like to read that book.
278. The opposite of bad is good.
279. The horse has a hoof.
280. Let's go take a look.
281. The dog began to bark.
282. They got out of the ocean when they saw a shark.
283. The math problems weren't hard.
284. Our food was grown on a farm.
285. They popped some corn.
286. A knife and fork.
287. South and north.
288. Tall or short.
289. Stuck by a thorn.
290. The light from a torch.
291. Blow on the horn.
292. The sheep travel in a herd.
293. Pull steadily but don't jerk.
294. The birds sound is a chirp.
295. The chirp is made by a bird.
296. He's digging in the dirt.
297. It didn't do any harm.
298. The horse pulled the cart.
299. Three feet make a yard.
300. The bird found a place to perch.
301. A nickel is a type of coin.
302. Dirt is also called soil.
303. Aluminum foil.
304. A sofa is a couch.
305. The referee called a foul.
306. The music is too loud.
307. The doctor looked in her patient's mouth.
308. The kangaroo has a pouch.
309. Don't yell or shout.
310. North and south.
311. The farmer drove to town.
312. A wedding gown.
313. He cut the lawn.
314. They got up at dawn.
315. The sleepy person gave a yawn.
316. The lady wore a shawl.
317. My friend's first name is Paul.
318. They met me in the hall.
319. The basketball player is tall.
320. Pick up the phone and give me a call.
321. Is it up or down?
322. The wolf began to howl.
323. I hope you don't get hurt.
324. After the second comes the third.

Four phoneme words

325. Two hot dog buns.
326. In the paper, make two little cuts.
327. The rabbit hops.
328. I have to pay so many bills.
329. They play in a band.
330. He tightened his belt.
331. The piece of metal got bent.
332. I like that one best.
333. Don't go too close to the edge of the bluff.
334. A light bulb.
335. It wasn't heavy but it had a lot of bulk.
336. Don't let your head get a bump.
337. In the summer they went to camp.
338. Is it really wet, or just a little damp.
339. I like to write at my desk.
340. They took the trash to the dump.
341. The time just before night is called dusk.
342. They used a broom to clean up the dust.
343. It may seem like fiction, but it's a fact.
344. They ran fast.
345. I couldn't tell how she felt.
346. He clenched his fist.
347. They collected money for the charitable fund.
348. I'd like to give you a gift.
349. He got the lemonade and took a big gulp.
350. The tired swimmer called for help.
351. The camel had one hump.
352. The animal rights person refused to fish or hunt.
353. How high can that guy jump?
354. If something is fair, it is just.
355. I want to know what you gave away and what you kept.
356. There is light coming from the lamp.
357. Good luck on your test.
358. On the beach is lots of sand.
359. The airplane can land.
360. Are you first or last?
361. Is it right or left?
362. Where's the computer disk?
363. I'll pay back the money you lent.
364. East and west.
365. Do you need a lift?
366. Walk with a limp.
367. Let's make a list.
368. The patient asked the doctor to check out a lump.
369. Let's do the job with cheefulness and zest.
370. On halloween she wore a mask.
371. The snow began to melt.
372. They slept overnight in a tent.
373. The socks are too torn for me to mend.
374. Cows give milk.
375. I don't know where he went.
376. The candy has the flavor of mint.
377. The future, the present, and the past.
378. It's a hard word to spell.
379. It's too dangerous to take that risk.
380. A bird's nest.
381. There are fish in the pond.
382. A nice present for you to send.
383. What you do to flour is to sift.
384. When the dog is hot, he will pant.

385. At the waterfall there is lots of mist.
386. Take a giant step.
387. When he didn't get his way, he began to sulk.
388. It's a very difficult task.
389. The room was cluttered with lots of stuff.
390. He's tired; he needs to rest.
391. She didn't think her brother was a pest.
392. The steel didn't rust.
393. The day felt colder because of a strong wind.
394. The door closed with a loud bang.
395. He gave thc rope a yank.
396. The dump had lots of junk.
397. A skating rink.
398. Let's play a song.
399. To dip something in water is to dunk.
400. To close and open your eyelid is to wink.
401. The bell has been rung.
402. A street gang.
403. He couldn't wait to be king.
404. You breathe air into your lung.
405. The diver held his air on his back in a tank.
406. They celebrated the baby girl with balloons that were pink.
407. The person passed a scout rank.
408. Each part of a chain is a link.
409. To say how great you are is to brag.
410. The opposite of white is black.
411. Let's walk around the block.
412. A type of smile is a grin.
413. The baby slept in a crib.
414. The bus came to a stop.
415. A long attention span.
416. The book had a good plot.
417. The croaking sound came from a frog.
418. Don't fall into a trap.
419. She wore a dress.
420. A spoiled brat.
421. The branch broke with a loud snap.
422. Seeing his daughters made him glad.
423. The liberty bell has a crack.
424. The paddle hit the water with a loud slap.
425. Hop and skip.
426. Teach her to swim.
427. They roasted the vegetables on a grill.
428. He can play a drum.
429. The doctor searched for the best drug.
430. They took a long trip.
431. Bore a hole with a drill.
432. To stick with a knife is to stab.
433. The rose had thorns on its stem.
434. The plains are flat.
435. The diver did a flip.
436. To push on something is to press.
437. She fixed her hair by using a brush.
438. I'm glad the airplane didn't crash.
439. I saw the lightning flash.
440. A big long hole is called a shaft.
441. The books are on the shelf.
442. She gave her shoulders a shrug.
443. Please take out the trash.
444. He was so impulsive that we called him brash.
445. A piano bench.

446. A whole lot, a big bunch.
447. I don't know, but I have a hunch.
448. A piece of something is a chunk.
449. Between your neck and your belly is your chest.
450. They said it over and over in a chant.
451. Let's eat lunch.
452. Hawaiian punch.
453. The thirst is easy to quench.
454. A dude ranch.
455. A little crack in something is a chink.
456. He ate a grape.
457. The oranges came in a crate.
458. The hero was brave.
459. The cobra is a snake.
460. A little shovel is a spade.
461. The bread has become stale.
462. They went to the rink to skate.
463. A snow flake.
464. The thing hanging near the window is a drape.
465. They traveled on a train.
466. The writing was very faint.
467. Someone who is weak and skinny is called frail.
468. Wheat is a type of grain.
469. He is so good, he is like a saint.
470. As slow as a snail.
471. The water came from the hose in a fine spray.
472. Wanting too much is called greed.
473. To make a car go the right direction is to steer.
474. She gave a good speech.
475. He took the broom and started to sweep.
476. The leaves are green.
477. I had a pleasant dream.
478. A lot of food is a feast.
479. When you say something, you speak.
480. The minister began to preach.
481. When water gets hot enough it turns to steam.
482. The stuff used to make the bread rise is yeast.
483. To steal is a crime.
484. A woman getting married is a bride.
485. To complain is to gripe.
486. She won the prize.
487. When you're proud, you have pride.
488. People look friendlier when they smile.
489. The best one I could find.
490. Treat them nicely; be kind.
491. The winters here are mild.
492. The part of a canteloupe you don't eat is the rind.
493. The horse couldn't be ridden because he was too wild.
494. The man and woman loved their child.
495. My shirt got wet, but it now has dried.
496. The vegetables were stir fried.
497. It's not much, it's very slight.
498. What was that car that you drove?
499. It was so cold that we almost froze.
500. He couldn't see, so all he could do was to grope.
501. They had fun playing even though they didn't keep score.
502. They skiied down the slope.
503. Cigarette smoke.

504. The thief stole.
505. Rock is stone.
506. Cook it in the stove.
507. I like that one most.
508. I'm allergic to mold.
509. They locked the door by moving a bolt.
510. The best story I ever told.
511. A young male horse is a colt.
512. The king is on the throne.
513. The door is open.
514. I caught a cold.
515. He liked to brag and boast.
516. A noise that signals pain is called a groan.
517. A sore throat.
518. Turn the bread into toast.
519. When the flowers don't get water they start to droop.
520. A rough and unkind person is a brute.
521. A dried plum is called a prune.
522. Not rough but smooth.
523. An ice cream scoop.
524. Thread is kept on a spool.
525. Darkness and bad moods are called gloom.
526. To scatter something out is to strew.
527. She kept her neck warm with a scarf.
528. Intelligent equals smart.
529. Bread and potatoes contain starch.
530. It's time to start.
531. Basketball is a sport.
532. A lightning storm.
533. To burn is to scorch.
534. The horse started to snort.
535. The court reporter read back the oath the person had sworn.
536. The strict teacher was stern.
537. Opposite of over is under.
538. A person who does paperwork is a clerk.
539. Opposite of before is after.
540. Opposite of always is never.
541. The woman wore a colorful skirt.
542. To fidget is to squirm.
543. Not drinking causes thirst.
544. What you do with a baton is to twirl.
545. Not second, but first.
546. When something breaks open, it has burst.
547. To roast something near something hot is to broil.
548. To lift something using ropes or chains is to hoist.
549. The knee is a type of joint.
550. A little bit wet is called moist.
551. You have a good point.
552. I don't want the food to spoil.
553. In the sky is a pretty cloud.
554. The tiger waited in a crouch.
555. She showed me what she had found.
556. The irritated person is a grouch.
557. The dog is a hound.
558. When I do good things I feel proud.
559. A circle is round.
560. The nose of some animals is called their snout.
561. No one made even a little sound.
562. The teapot has a spout.
563. A type of fish is the trout.
564. We made the bread from flour.

565. The opposite of a smile is a frown.
566. Flour and sugar are both powder.
567. The king wore a crown.
568. Her skin was dark brown.
569. A funny clown.
570. Sipping through a straw.
571. Look what I have drawn.
572. It's not your fault.
573. Pale and thin is gaunt.
574. They took the boat and started to launch.
575. A light-hearted trip is a jaunt.
576. A teasing thing someone says is a taunt.
577. A fat belly is sometimes called a paunch.
578. Cheating someone out of money is fraud.
579. No hair means bald.
580. Write on the blackboard with chalk.
581. To stop is to halt.
582. Opposite of big is small.
583. A storm is a squall.
584. To try to get more time is to stall.
585. To speak is to talk.
586. In the hall, don't run, but walk.
587. Mr. Disney's first name was Walt.

Spatial Awareness Exercises

The pages that follow are the stimuli for 8 types of exercises. These are especially useful for the child who has trouble telling the difference between b and d, or telling the difference between p and q. They also are especially helpful for the child who reads or writes words or other letters backwards. They are useful for learners who have difficulties with right-left distinctions. But they are probably helpful for most beginning readers. The notion is that these are exercises in "spatial awareness," a skill that is to vision what "phonemic awareness" is to hearing.

The exercises are as follows.

1. Same or different with pictures.
2. Same or different with b-d and p-q.
3. Which letter is at the left or right (of a three letter word)?
4. Which side of the word is this letter on?
5. Which picture is not like the others?
6. Which letter is not like the others? with b-d and p-q
7. Is the ball at the left or right of the stick (with b-d, p-q).
8. Name the letter or say the sound (with b-d, p-q).

Same or Different With Arrows

Here the learner looks at pairs of arrows, and says whether they are pointing in the same direction, or in different directions. This is the "entry level" spatial awareness exercise; most learners will not find it difficult. The only tricky part comes with arrows like this:

which are pointing in different directions, even though they could be pointing at the same little object right between the arrows. You can explain to the learner that if you keep following the arrow on the left, you'll wind up in a different place than if you keep following the one one the right, and thus we say they're going in different directions. You can also show the learner pairs of arrows like

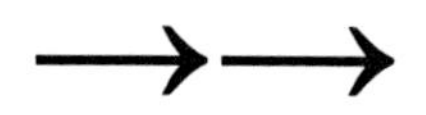

and like

and explain that we're going to call these pairs the same, but we call the pair with one going right and the other going left, different.

Left and Right with Arrows

In this exercise, the learner looks at one arrow and simply says whether it is pointing to the right or the left. Since the number of the item in this exercise is always to the left of the arrow, a learner can remember which is right and which is left by the phrase "right away": the arrows pointing to the right point away from the numbers, whereas the arrows pointing to the left point toward the numbers. If you do this exercise to the criterion of fluency, that is when the learner can do it quickly and automatically, the rest of spatial awareness will be much easier.

Same or Different With Pictures

In this exercise the learner looks at pairs of pictures, and says whether they are exactly the same, or whether they are different. The pairs of pictures in a section to come are made for this exercise. You will notice that some of the pictures are identical. Some have been "flipped" horizontally, so that one picture is the mirror image of the other. (The mirror image relationship is the same as that between b and d, and between p and q.) For some of these pictures, the differences are clear; for others the differences are more subtle. All of these pictures give the learner practice in distinguishing a picture from its mirror image.

With this and all other spatial awareness exercises, the goal is not just to do them. The goal is to become able to do them very quickly. Almost instant answers are eventually desired. If the learner has to take a while to decide which is which, he or she will be too slowed down in the process of reading.

Same or Different with b-d or p-q

This exercise is just like the same or different with pictures exercise, only in this exercise the learner is presented with pairs of letters, for example b and d. The learner's job is to say whether the two letters in the pair are the same or different.

Which Letter Is Farthest Left or Right (With Three Letter Words)

In this exercise, you use the three letter words provided to ask questions like this: "What's the name (or the sound) of the letter that's farthest left (or right) in that word?" So for example, if the word is *get*, you would ask, "What's the name of the letter that's farthest right?" The answer would be t. If you ask, "What's the sound of the letter that's farthest right," the answer would be tuh. If you're working on letter sounds, you can use this exercise to drill on letter sounds while at the same time working on left-right distinctions.

Which Side of the Word is This Letter On? (With Three Letter Words)

In this exercise, you still use the three letter words presented in this section. Now rather than giving a side and asking for the letter name or sound, you give a letter name or sound and ask which side it's on. So for example, if the word is *get*, you would say, "In that word, find the letter g. Is that on the left, or on the right?" Or, you can ask, "In that word, there's a letter that says guh. Is that on the left, or the right?"

Which Picture Is Not Like the Others?

This exercise is done with the sets of three pictures in this section. The three pictures in each set are identical except that one of them is flipped around its axis -- usually flipped horizontally. (The first couple of pictures are flipped to create an upside-down drawing.) The task of the learner is to say which of the three pictures is not like the other two. Is it the drawing on the left, on the right, or in the middle?

This exercise gives a workout to the part of the brain that tells left from right. Left-right orientation is involved both in finding the odd picture out and in deciding what to call it.

Which Letter Is Not Like the Others?

This exercise is done with sets of three letters, b's, d's, p's, or q's. This is done in exactly the same way as Which Picture Is Not Like the Others, only now rather than using drawings, we have sets of three letters. The learner tells which of the three is not like the others, answering left, right, or middle as before.

Is the Ball At the Left or Right of the Stick?

This exercise is done with single letters, b, d, p, or q. You explain to the learner that the letters b and d and p and q are made of a ball and a stick. For b and p, the ball is on the right side of the stick. For d and q, the ball is at the left side of the stick. In this exercise, the learner looks at these letters and simply says whether the ball is at the right or left of the stick.When the stimulus is b, the learner just says "right," because in b the ball is to the right of the stick. Remind the learner that we are talking of where the ball is, not where the stick is; do this by asking, "Which side is the ball on?"

Name the Letter or Say the Sound (with b, d, p, q)

This exercise is done with the same set of b's, d's, p's, and q's included in this section. The learner looks at each one and says what the letter is. The nonsense mnemonic "bright pright" can help some learners remember that for b and p, the ball is on the right. You get this by putting b and right together to get bright, and by put p and right together to get pright, (even though pright isn't a real word). An alternative way to do this exercise is to ask the learner to say, not the name of the letter, but the sound of the letter. So in this exercise the learner is going down the list and saying buh, duh, puh, or quuh.

When the learner can do these exercises very fast, I think you will find that he or she is much better equipped to do the right-left discriminations that are crucial to reading.

Spatial Awareness 1: Same or different directions?

1. ↑↑
2. ↑↓
3. →→
4. ↓↓
5. ←→
6. ←←
7. ↓→
8. →→
9. ←←
10. →←
11. ←→
12. ↑↓
13. ←→
14. ↓←
15. ←←
16. →←
17. →→
18. ←←
19. →←
20. →→
21. ↓↓
22. ←→
23. ↓→
24. ←←
25. →→
26. →←
27. ←→
28. ↓←
29. ↑↑
30. ←←

Is the Arrow Pointing Right or Left?
(Remember "right away" from the numbers.)

1. →
2. →
3. →
4. ←
5. ←
6. →
7. ←
8. ←
9. ←
10. →
11. →
12. ←
13. →
14. ←
15. ←
16. ←
17. →
18. →
19. ←
20. ←
21. →
22. →
23. ←
24. →
25. ←
26. →
27. →
28. ←
29. ←
30. →

Same or Different With Pictures

Figure 1

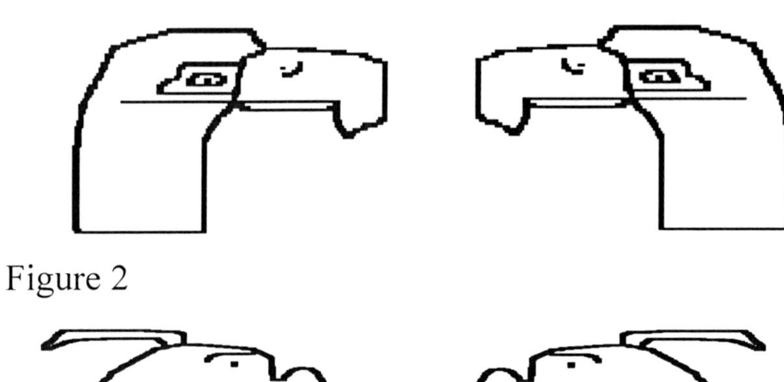

Figure 2

Figure 3

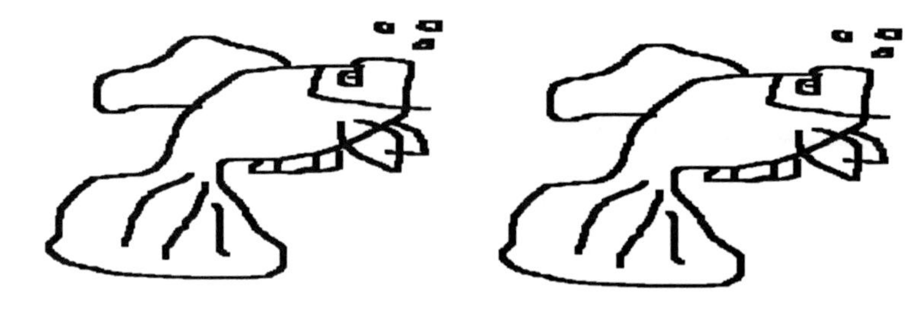

Figure 4

Figure 5

Figure 6

Figure 7

Figure 8

Figure 9

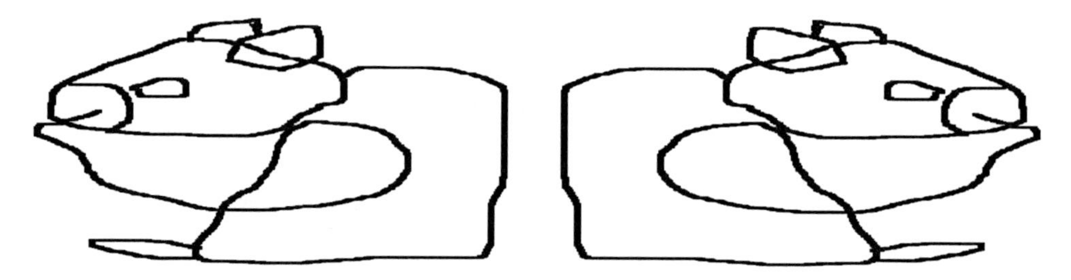

Figure 10

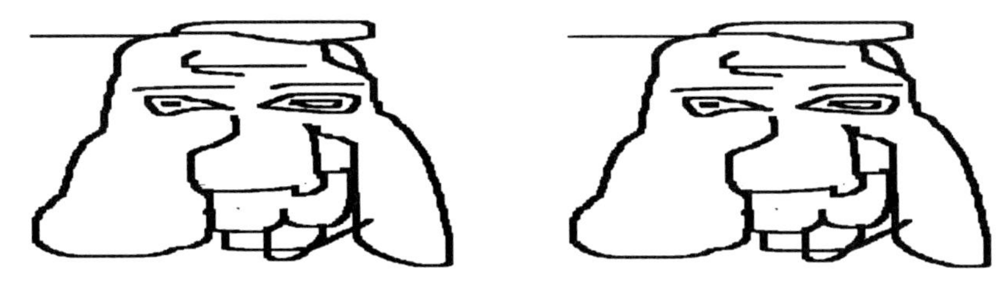

Figure 11

Figure 12

Figure 13

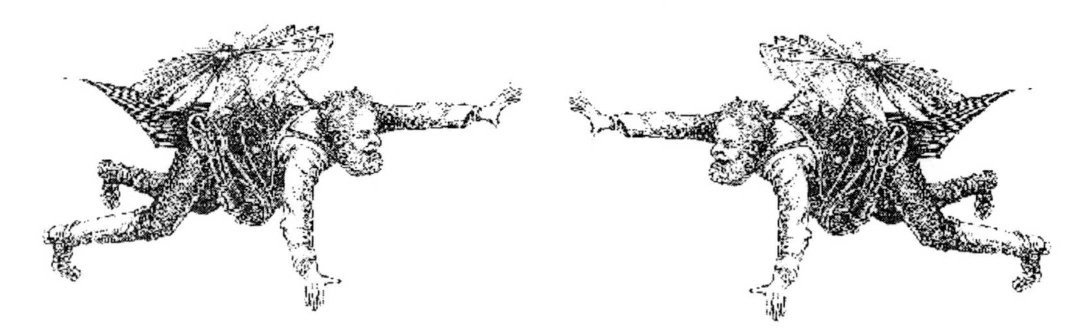

Figure 14

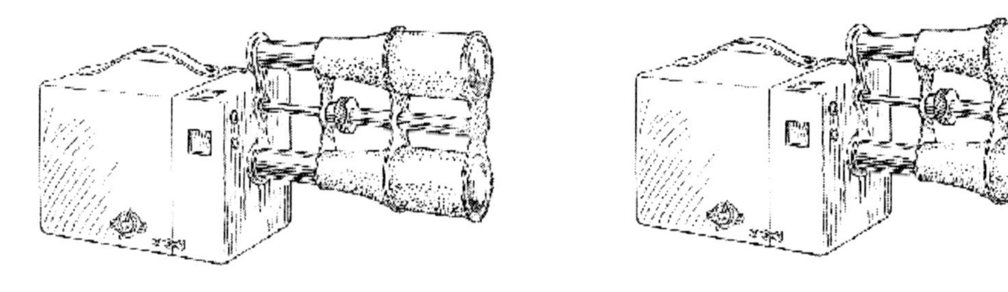

Figure 15

Figure 16

Figure 17

Figure 18

Figure 19

Figure 20

Figure 21

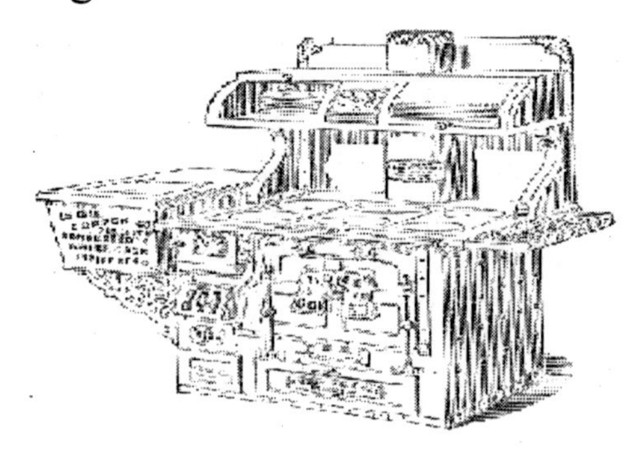
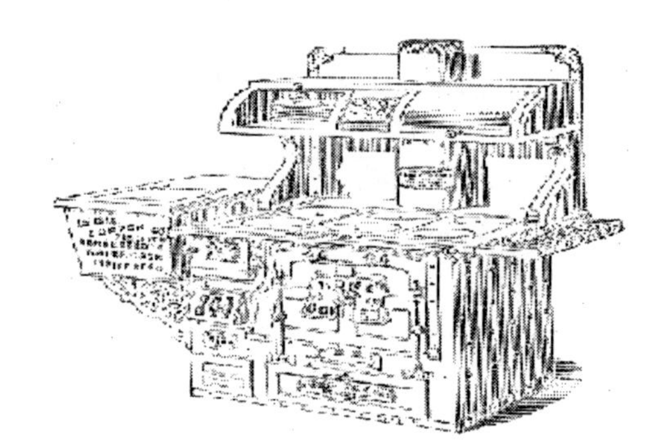

Figure 22

Figure 23

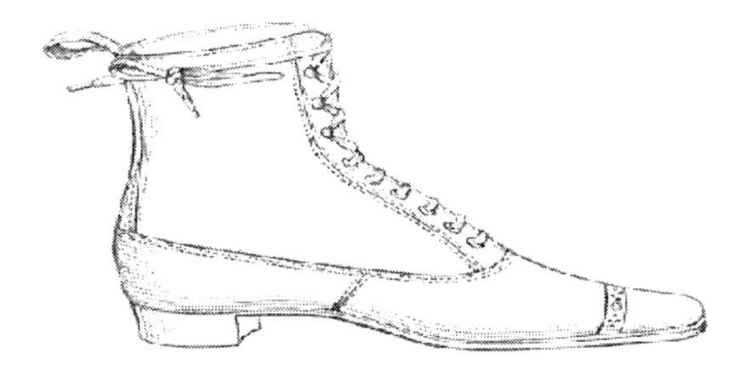
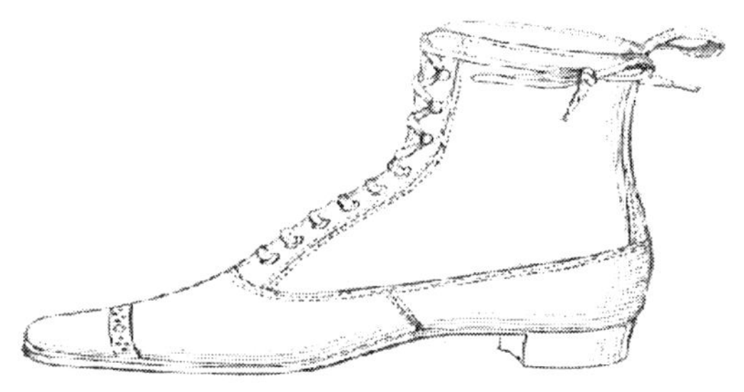

Figure 24

Figure 25

Figure 26

Figure 27

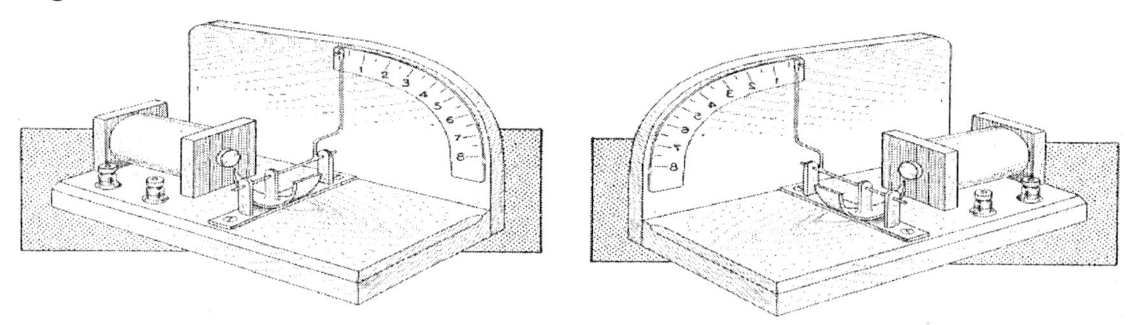

Figure 28

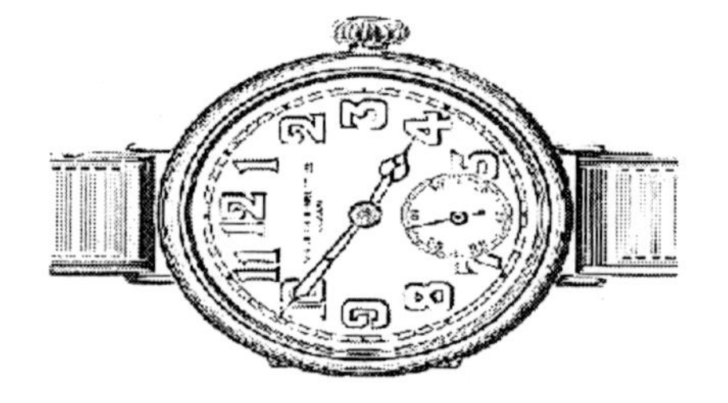

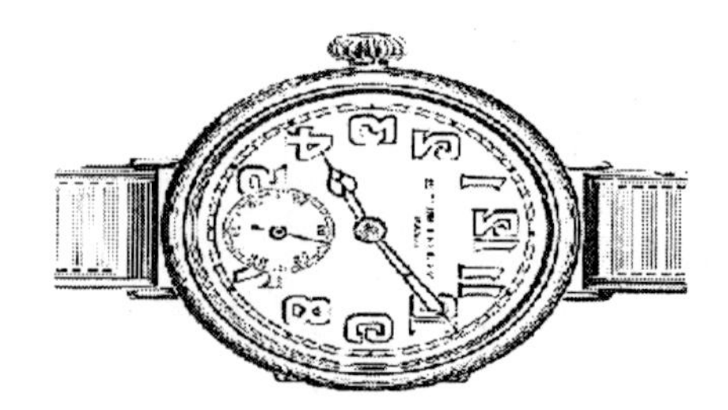

Figure 29

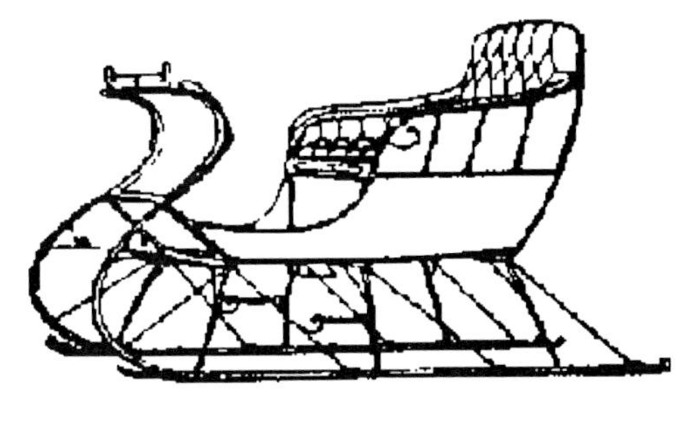

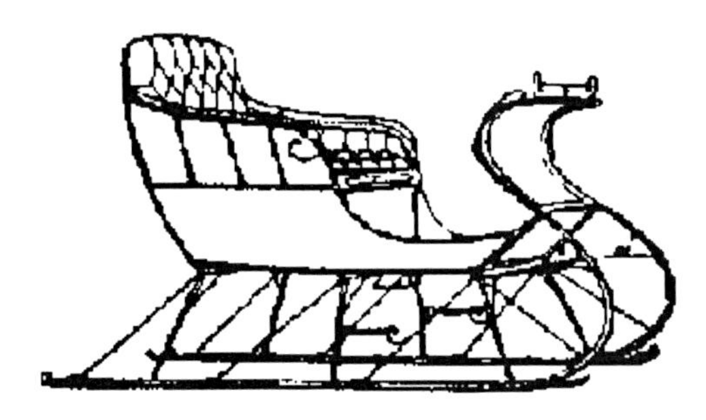

Figure 30

Figure 31

Figure 32

Figure 33

Figure 34

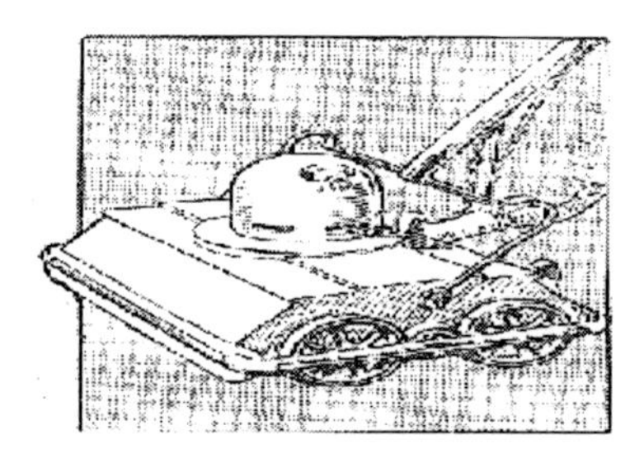

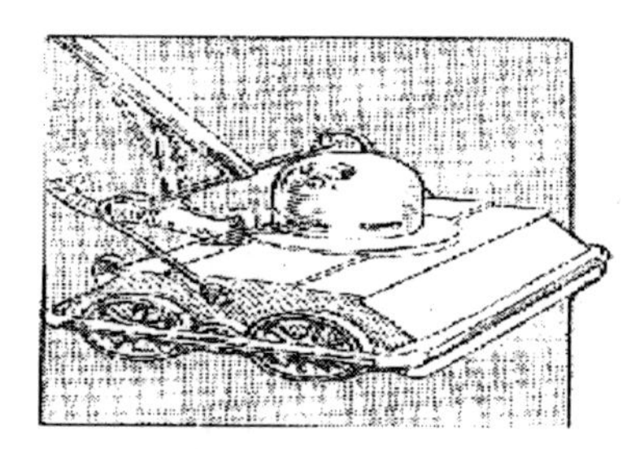

Figure 35

Figure 36

Figure 37

Figure 38

Same or Different with b-d and p-q

1. b b
2. d d
3. b d
4. d b
5. b d
6. d d
7. b b
8. b b
9. d d
10. b d
11. b b
12. d d
13. b d
14. d b
15. b b
16. d d
17. d b
18. b d
19. d d
20. b b
21. p p
22. p q
23. q p
24. q q
25. p q
26. q p
27. p p
28. q q
29. p p
30. q p

31. q q
32. p q
33. q p
34. p p
35. p p
36. p q
37. q q
38. q p
39. p p
40. p q

Which Letter Is Farthest Left (Or Right)? and Which Side of the Word is the Letter On?

1. get
2. win
3. nag
4. kit
5. fox
6. sun
7. wig
8. fan
9. man
10. rug
11. vat
12. hen
13. mat
14. jam
15. leg
16. run
17. tag
18. win
19. yak
20. jazz

Which Picture Is Not Like the Others?

Answering with "left," "right," or "middle" is harder than answering by pointing.

Figure 39

Figure 40

Figure 41

Figure 42

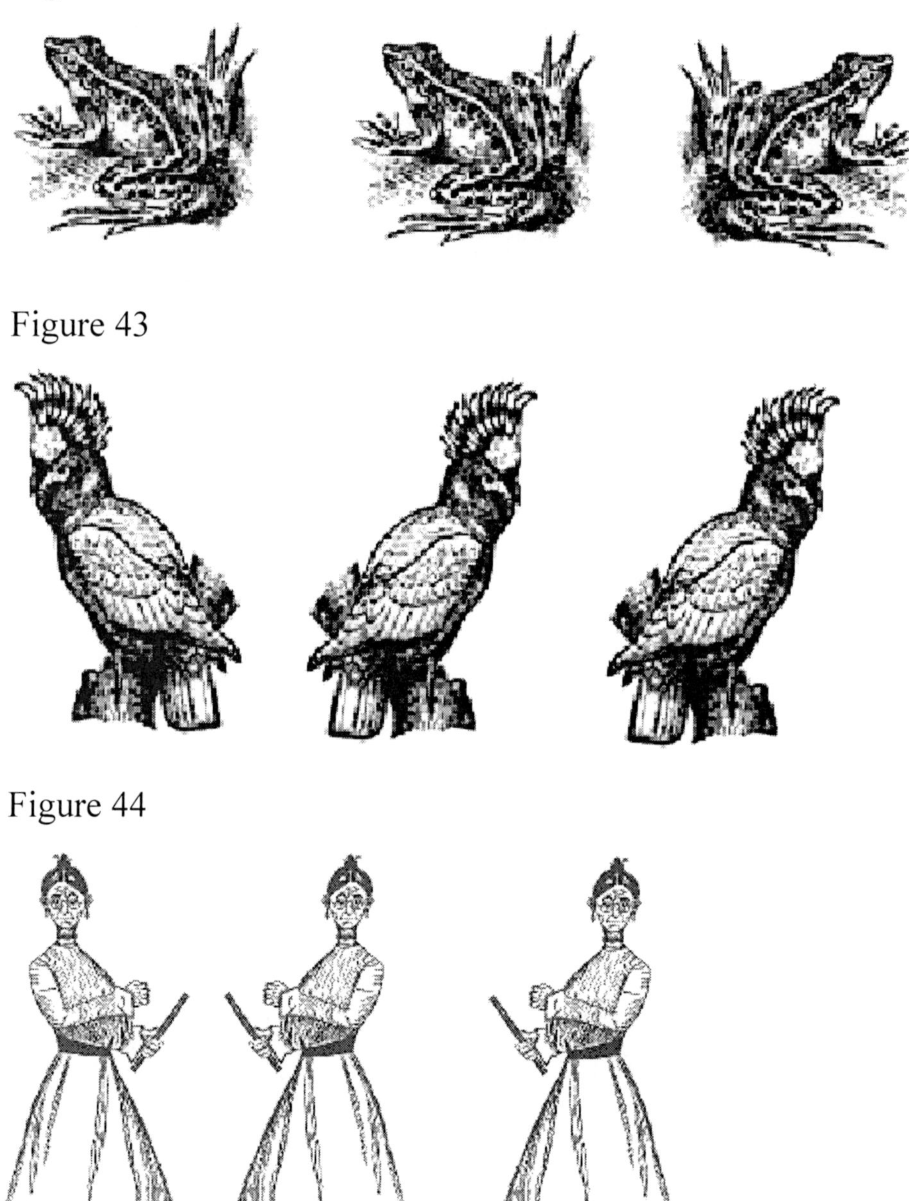

Figure 43

Figure 44

Figure 45

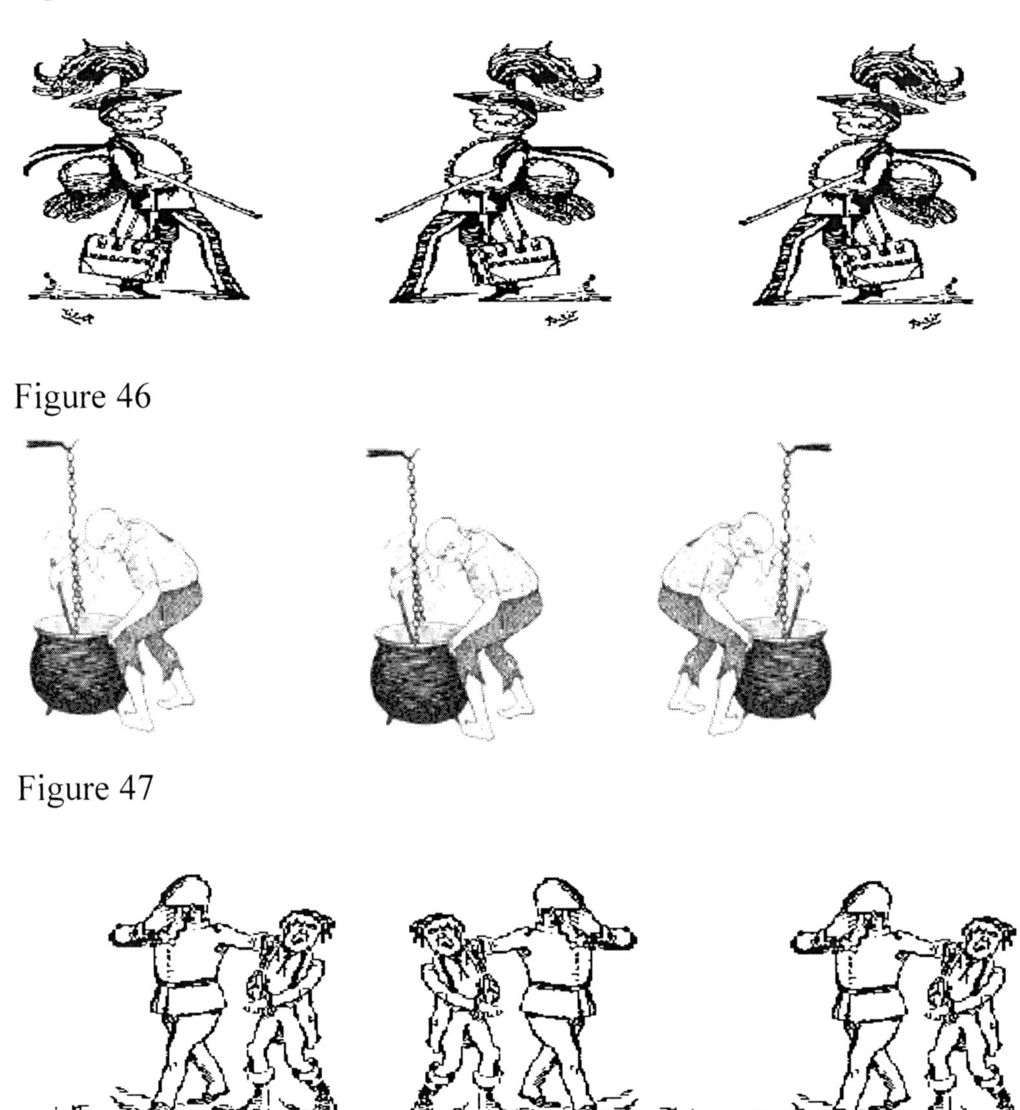

Figure 46

Figure 47

Figure 48

Figure 49

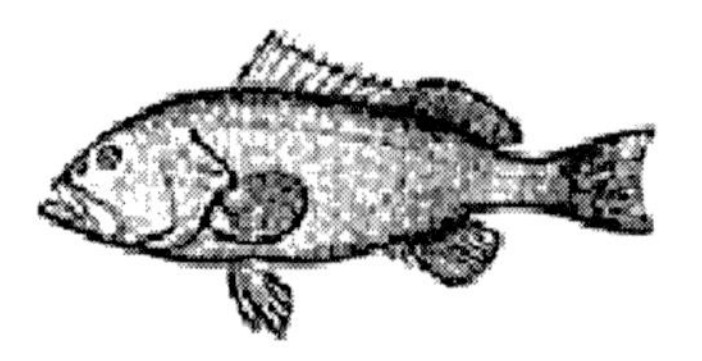
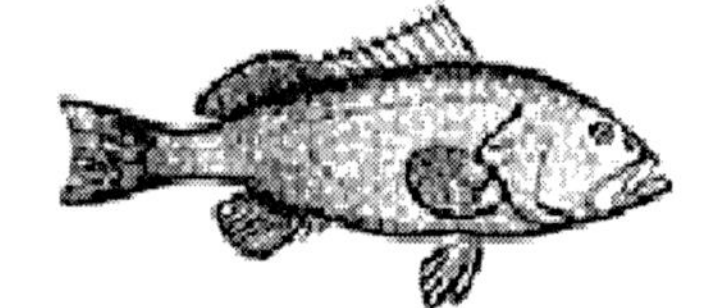
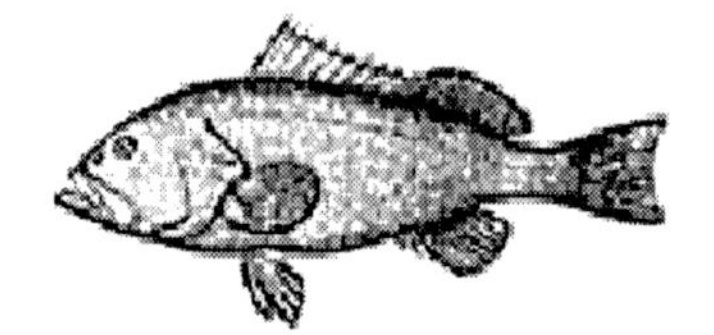

Figure 50

Figure 51

Figure 52

Figure 53

Figure 54

Figure 55

Figure 56

Figure 57

Figure 58

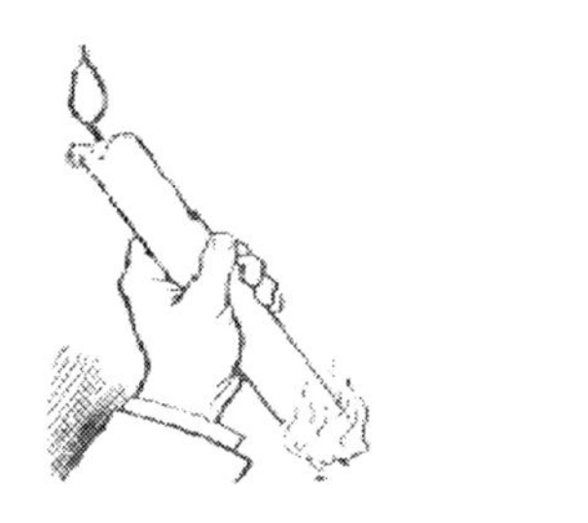
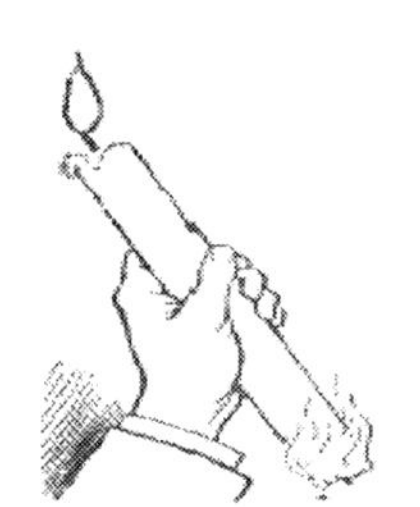
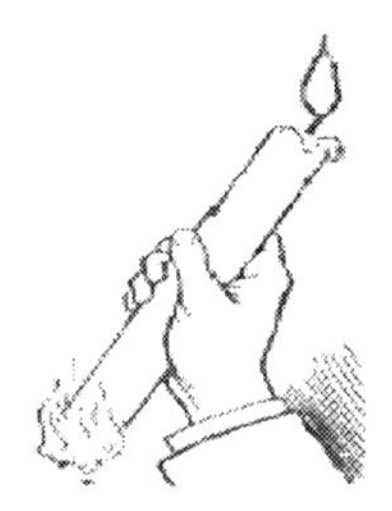

Figure 59

Figure 60

Figure 61

Figure 62

Figure 63

Figure 64

Figure 65

Figure 66

Figure 67

Figure 68

Figure 69

Figure 70

Figure 71

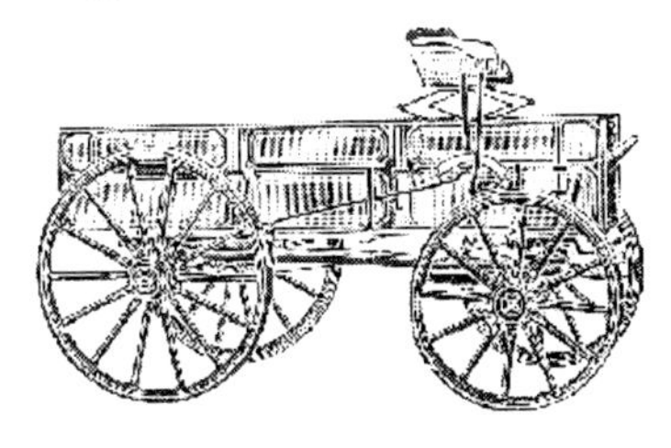
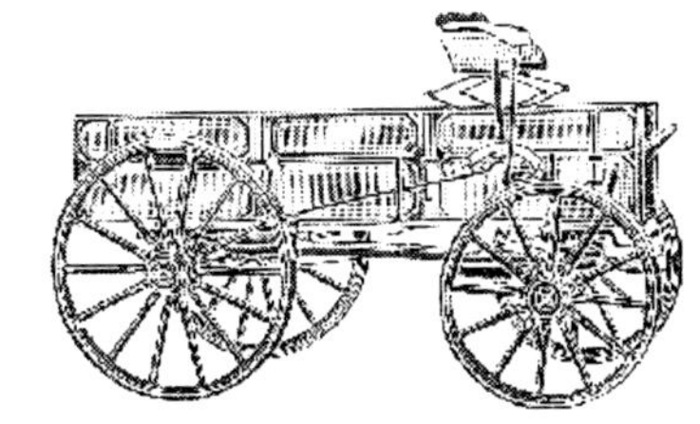
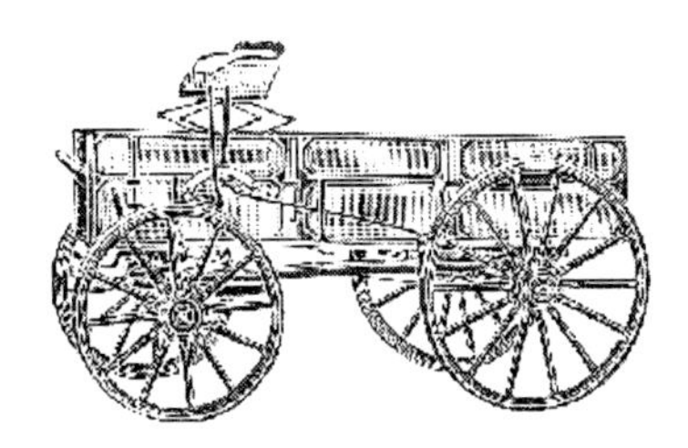

Figure 72

Figure 73

Figure 74

Figure 75

Figure 76

Figure 77

Figure 78

Figure 79

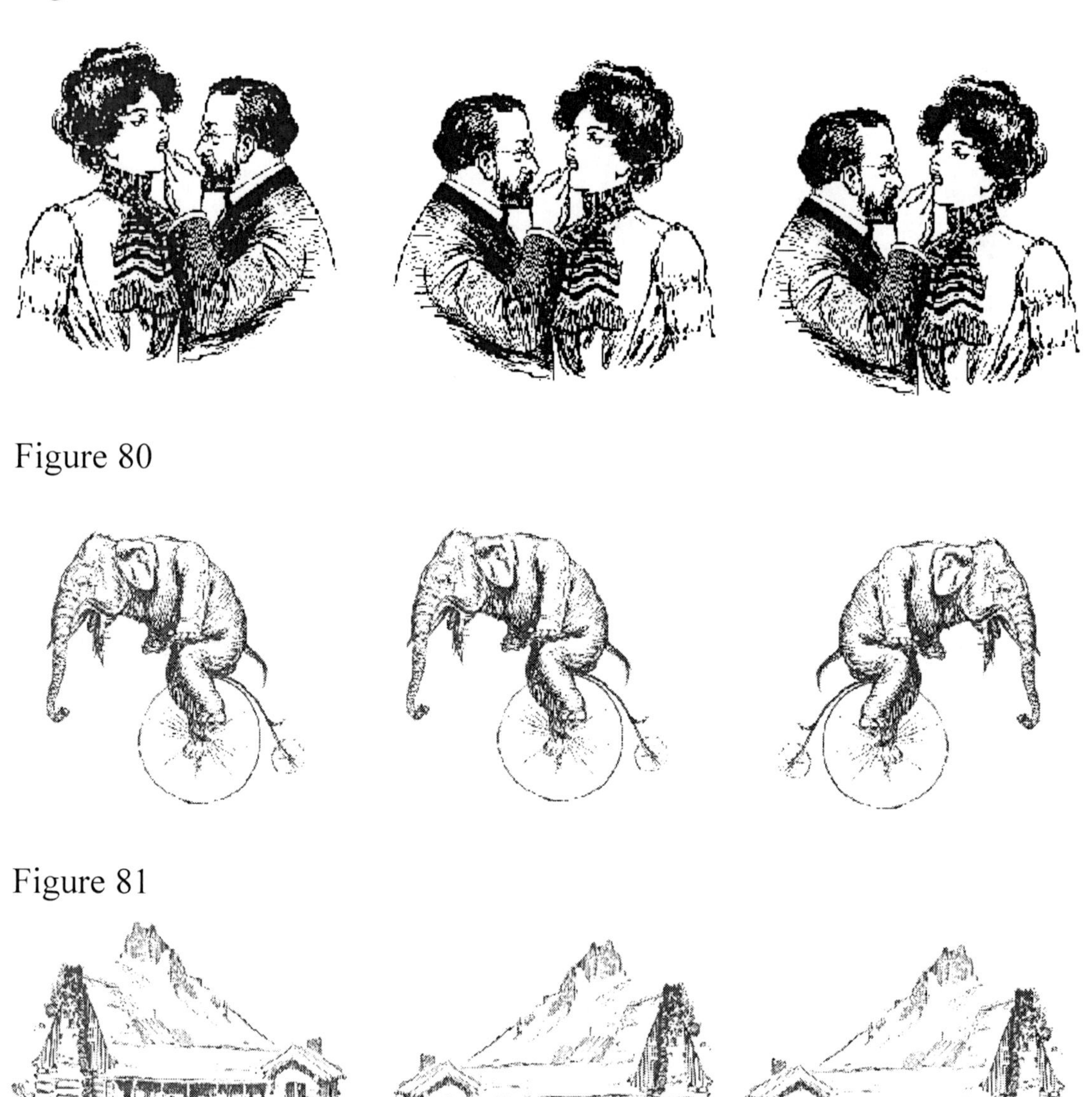

Figure 80

Figure 81

Figure 82

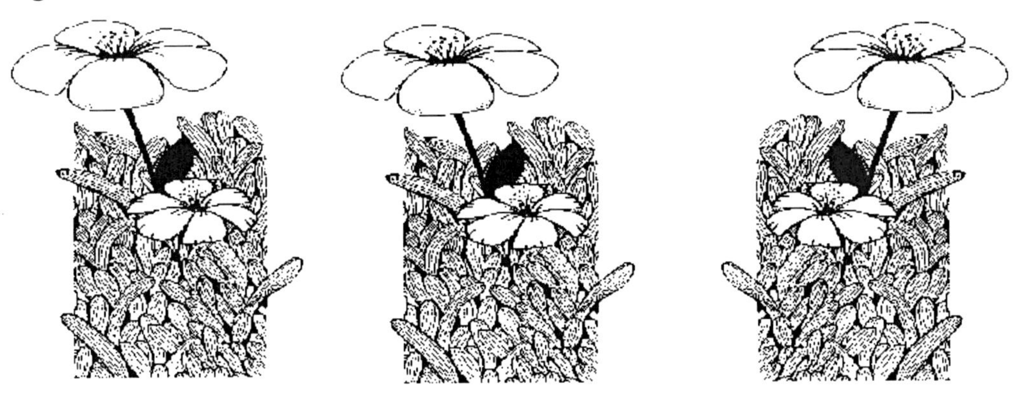

Figure 83

Figure 84

Figure 85

Figure 86

Figure 87

Figure 88

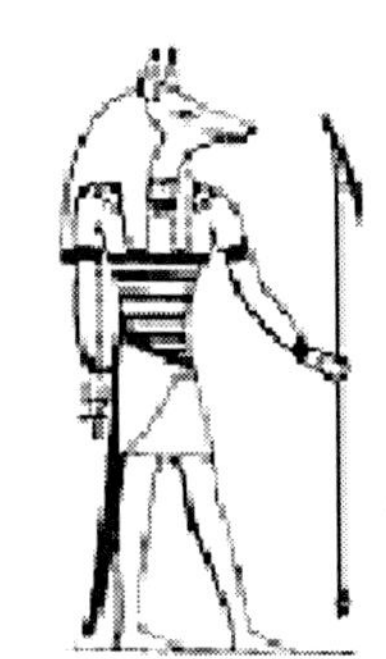
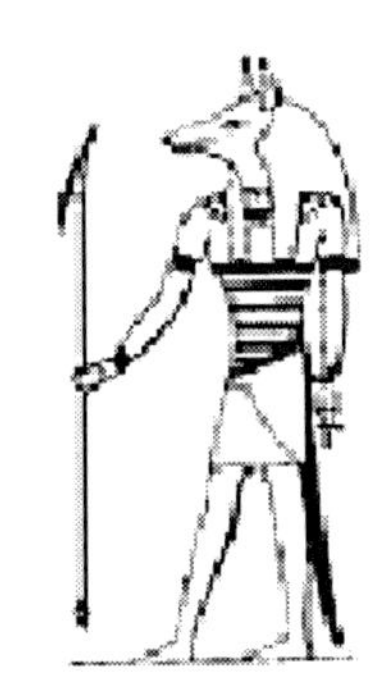

Which Letter Is Not Like the Others?

1. b b d
2. b d d
3. d d b
4. d b d
5. d b b
6. b d b
7. b d d
8. b b d
9. d b d
10. d b d
11. d b b
12. b d b
13. d b d
14. d b d
15. d d b
16. b d d
17. b b d
18. b d b
19. d b b
20. d b d
21. b b d
22. b d b
23. b d d
24. d d b
25. b d d
26. d b d
27. b d b
28. b b d
29. d b b
30. d b d
31. d d b
32. b d d
33. b b d
34. b d b
35. d b b
36. d d b
37. b d b
38. b b d
39. d d b
40. d b d
41. b d b
42. d b b
43. b d d
44. b b d
45. d d b
46. b d b
47. d d b
48. b d d

49. d b d
50. b d b
51. p p q
52. q p p
53. p q p
54. q q p
55. p q q
56. q q p
57. p p q
58. q p p
59. p q q
60. q p q
61. p q q
62. p q p
63. q p p
64. p p q
65. q p p
66. p q p
67. p q q
68. p p q
69. q q p
70. q p q
71. q q p
72. p q q
73. p q p
74. q p q
75. q p p
76. p p q
77. p q p
78. q p p
79. p p q
80. q q p
81. p q q
82. q p q
83. q p p
84. p q q
85. p p q
86. q p p
87. q q p
88. q p q
89. q p p
90. q q p
91. p p q
92. p q q
93. q q p
94. q p q
95. p q p
96. p q p
97. q p q
98. p p q
99. q q p
100. q p p

Is the Ball At the Left or Right of The Stick? and: Name the Letter or Say the Sound

1. b
2. d
3. b
4. b
5. d
6. d
7. b
8. d
9. d
10. b
11. b
12. b
13. d
14. d
15. d
16. b
17. b
18. b
19. d
20. b
21. d
22. b
23. d
24. b
25. b
26. d
27. b
28. d
29. b
30. d
31. b
32. d
33. b
34. d
35. b
36. d
37. d
38. d
39. b
40. b
41. d
42. b
43. b
44. b
45. b
46. d
47. d
48. b

49. b
50. d
51. p
52. q
53. q
54. p
55. q
56. q
57. p
58. q
59. p
60. p
61. p
62. q
63. p
64. q
65. q
66. q
67. q
68. p
69. p
70. p
71. q
72. q
73. p
74. p
75. q
76. p
77. p
78. p
79. q
80. p
81. p
82. q
83. p
84. q
85. p
86. p
87. p
88. q
89. p
90. p
91. q
92. q
93. q
94. p
95. p
96. q
97. q
98. q
99. p
100. q

Four-Letter Pages: For Letter-Sound Correspondence Training

The four-letter pages have a letter in the upper left, upper right, lower left, and lower right. If the learner gets the question or gives the answer using these four phrases, rather than by pointing, the learner gets some practice in left-right distinction as well as letter-sound correspondence practice. To make the exercise easier, you can use pointing instead. In telephone tutoring, the verbal phrases must be used.

In the beginning, we teach only one sound per letter. These are the sounds that begin the words on the alphabet page; they're the sounds that are used in the letter sound songs; they are the short vowels, the hard g and c, "kiss" minus the short i sound for x, and "yuh" for y.

There are two types of exercises to be done with these pages. In both, the tutor first explains to the learner the sounds that the four letters make. If the tutor wants to make sure not to overload the student's working memory, the tutor can start with just two or three letters instead of all four. It's good to ask the tutor to repeat the sound after it's given for each letter. For example: "the one in the upper left says luh. Can you please say luh?"

For the first exercise, the tutor says the sound of the letter, and the learner either points to the letter or tells its position. So for example, with the first page, the tutor would say "buh" and the student would say "lower left."

For the second exercise, the tutor says or points to the position of the letter, and the student says its sound. So, for example, using our first page, the tutor says "upper right" and the student answers "huh."

A big rcsponsibility of the tutor is to decide the ratio of practice and review to learning of new sounds. Learners can vary widely in the speed with which they can learn to associate the letters with their sounds. If the tutor bites off small enough chunks for practice, the work of any learner should be close to errorless. As the learner is just beginning, one page per lesson is often plenty; as the learner gets more proficient, doing all the pages from beginning to end should become easy.

The letters on the following pages are Times Roman letters, the most commonly used in printed books. Some learners may need separate practice with different fonts. The letters are also the lower case letters. Some may benefit from similar pages with the upper case letters. For most learners, the first two lists of letters in the "words in word families" lists will be sufficient for learning and practicing naming the sounds of the upper case letters.

In addition to learning the sounds of the letters, it's also good to learn their names. Thus the four-letter pages can also be a way for the learner to practice saying the names of the letters given their positions, or the positions given the names. If one is to choose between learning the names of the letters and the sounds, the sounds are obviously more important for reading. But learning the names is also a part of becoming an educated person, and there's no reason not to get on with it!

l

h

b

e

f j

t g

y z

m u

n

w

d

x

p o

k i

q

a

c

r

s v

u y

Illustrated Stories that Model Psychological Skills: Primer

The pages that follow are the *Illustrated Stories that Model Psychological Skills, Primer*. The student is usually ready to read this when she has worked up to about list 30 in the "Words in Word Families" lists. But you can start reading the stories to the student from the beginning of the program. The student may be able to read or tell you back the stories before she is thoroughly familiar with the sounds that are in all the words. If so, this is to be celebrated. As soon as the student can take pleasure in reading these, that's the time to do it. Using memory traces as an aid to sounding and blending skills at the beginning is not only permissible, but also encouraged. For this reason, it's sometimes useful to read the story to the student immediately before the student reads it to you.

Let the student know ahead of time that these stories are meant to be read several times, not just once.

In the chapter following this one, there is a brief definition of sixteen skills and principles that constitute psychological health. The stories in the *Primer*, like those in *Programmed Readings*, are meant to model at least one of the sixteen groups of psychological skills, as follows: Jeff Helps With the Jet, productivity and courage; Ann Helps with the Cat, kindness; Fran Helps Nan with a Pen, kindness; Bill Cuts the Grass, compliance, productivity, and self-discipline; The Doc Helps Pam, productivity, joyousness; Jan Helps Tom with the Van, kindness; Jill Helps Pick Up, compliance, productivity; Sam Gets Less Fat, self-discipline; Jill Helps the Man Get Unstuck, good decisions, kindness; Russ Helps Tug the Rock, productivity, kindness; Rick Lost Well, fortitude; Jon Can Sing Well, joyousness; Mick Stops Alcohol, self-discipline, joyousness; The Cop Helps the Man Get Back on Track, kindness, productivity.

Thus each of these stories can be a puzzle, just as are the stories in *Programmed Readings*. After you read that Fran helped Nan by lending her a pen, you can ask, did Fran do an example of kindness or self-discipline?

With these stories, what's most important is to be joyous that the learner can read them!

Jeff Helps with the Jet

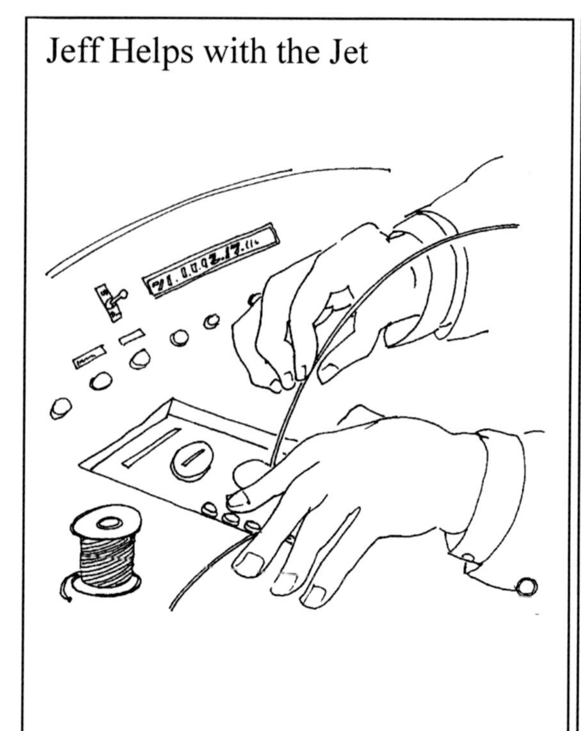

The jet is up.

Jeff is on the jet.

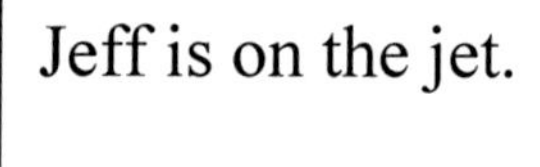

The men must fix the jet.

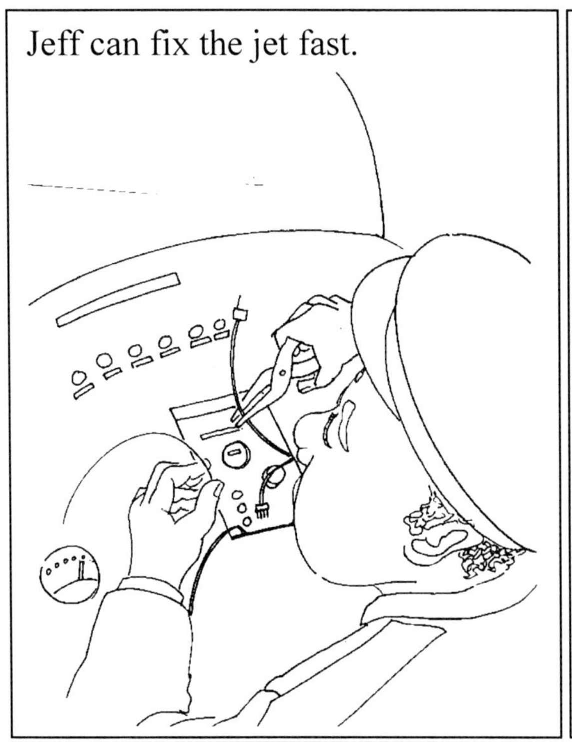
Jeff can fix the jet fast.

The jet can land.

“Thanks, Jeff!”

Ann Helps with the Cat

Matt's cat ran.

Matt yells, "Cat! Cat!"

Matt is sad. Matt can not get the cat.

Ann ran. The cat ran.

Ann pets the cat.

Ann picks the cat up.

Matt is glad. Matt has his cat.

"Thanks, Ann!"

Fran Helps Nan with a Pen

Fran and Nan can print with a pen.

Nan is sad. Nan's pen can not print.

Fran has six pens.

Nan can print with Fran's pen.

Nan is glad. "Thanks, Fran!"

Bill Cuts the Grass
This is Bill's dad.
"Bill is big. Bill can cut grass."
Bill did cut grass.

The sun is hot. Bill is hot.

"The grass is cut! Thanks, Bill!"

Bill drinks and drinks!

The Doc Helps Pam

Pam is not well. Pam is sick.

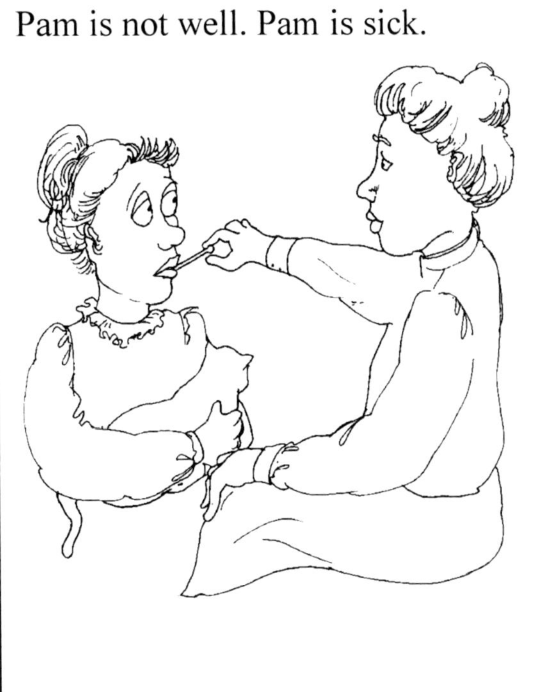

Pam asks the doc, "Is the sickness bad?"

"Yes, but Pam will get well."

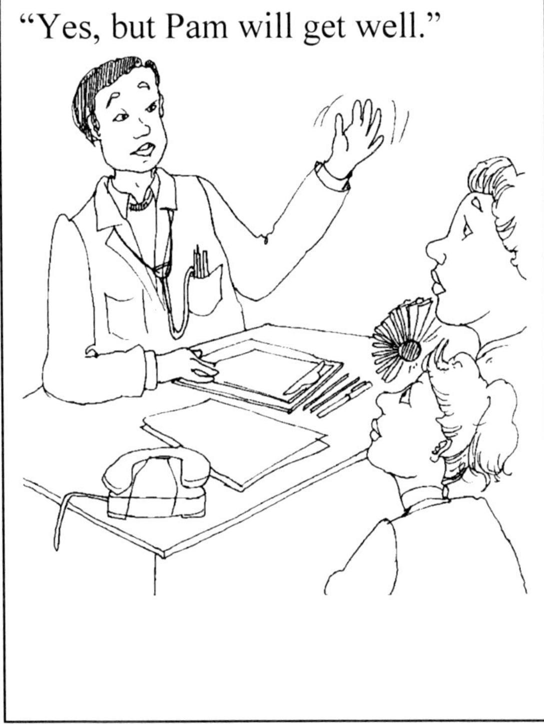

The doc has pills.

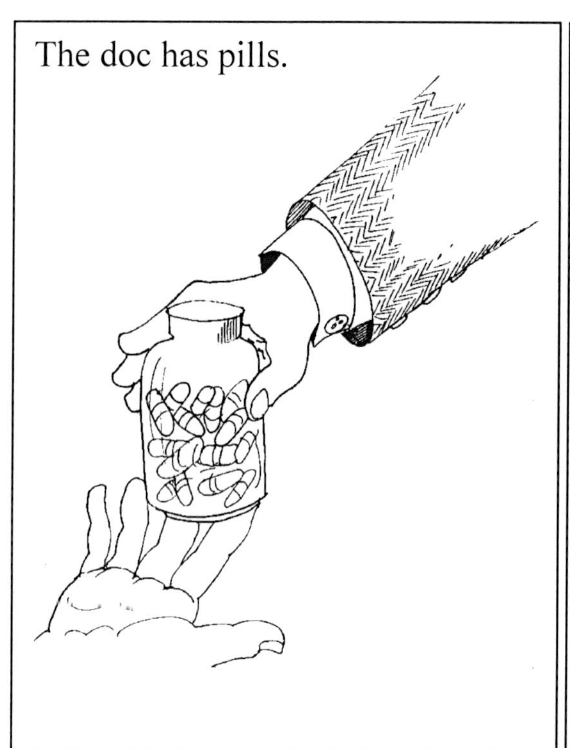

Pam gets a pill.

Pam rests.

Pam is glad. Pam is well!

"Thanks, doc!"

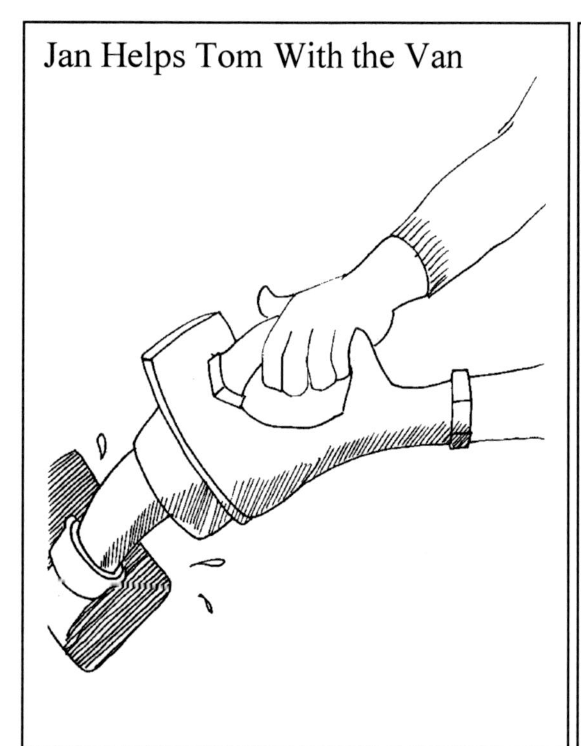
Jan Helps Tom With the Van

Tom is in his van.

Tom is sad. The van will not run!

Jan stops.

Gas is not in the van!

Jan and Tom get gas.

Jan and Tom get the gas in the van's tank.

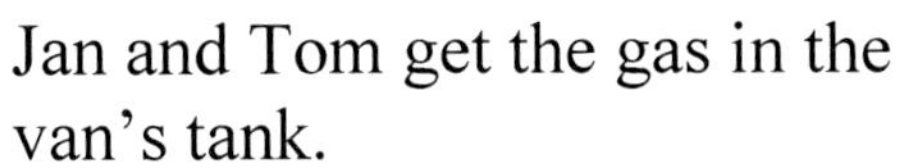

Tom is glad. The van will run!

"Thanks, Jan!"

Jill Helps Pick Up

Mom is sad and mad.

"Bats! Cats! Men! Caps! Socks! Cups!"

"Rest, mom. Jill will pick up."

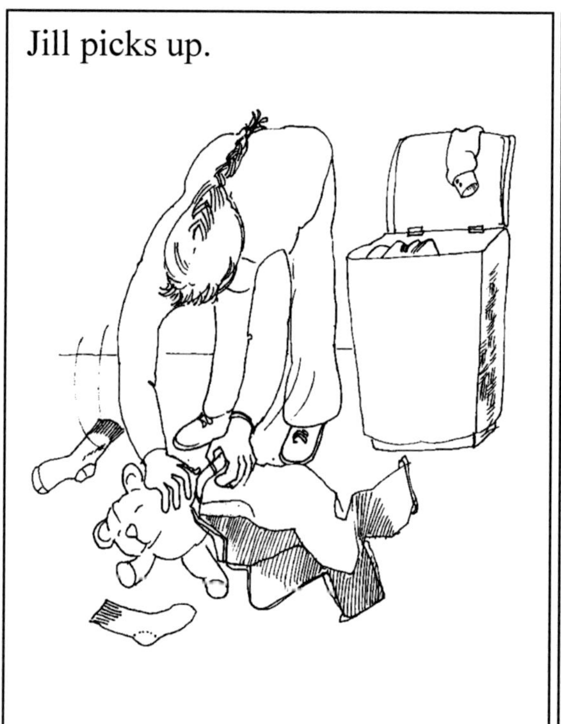
Jill picks up.

"It's up in a snap, Mom!"

Mom is glad. Mom hugs Jill.
"Thanks, Jill!"

Sam Gets Less Fat

Sam had lots of chips. Sam had lots of pop.

Sam had lots of junk.

Sam did not get up and run.

Sam got fat.
"Sam will get less fat!"
Sam ran and ran.
"Chips? Pop?"
"I will not, thanks."

The job is long. Still Sam runs.
Still Sam will not get chips.
JUNE
7

Sam is not fat! Sam is thin!
"Congrats, Sam!"

Jill Helps the Man Get Unstuck

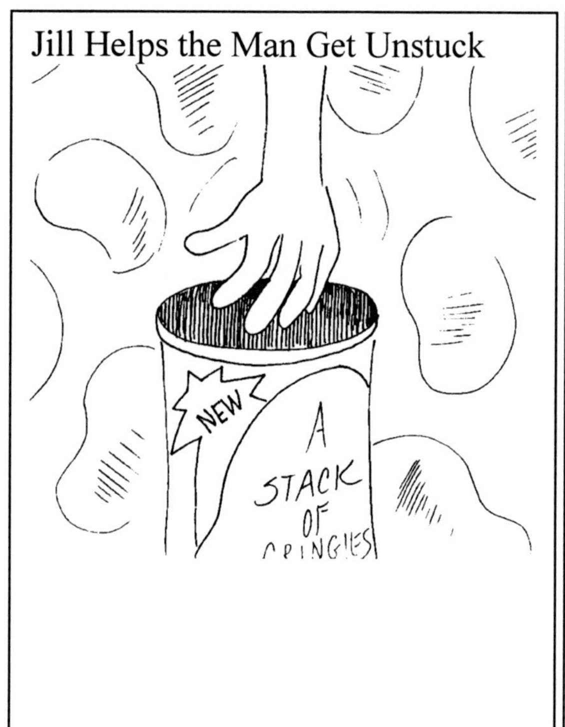

This is a can.

The man put his hand in the can.

The man's hand got stuck.

WL 12,920 TW 307

Russ Helps Tug the Rock

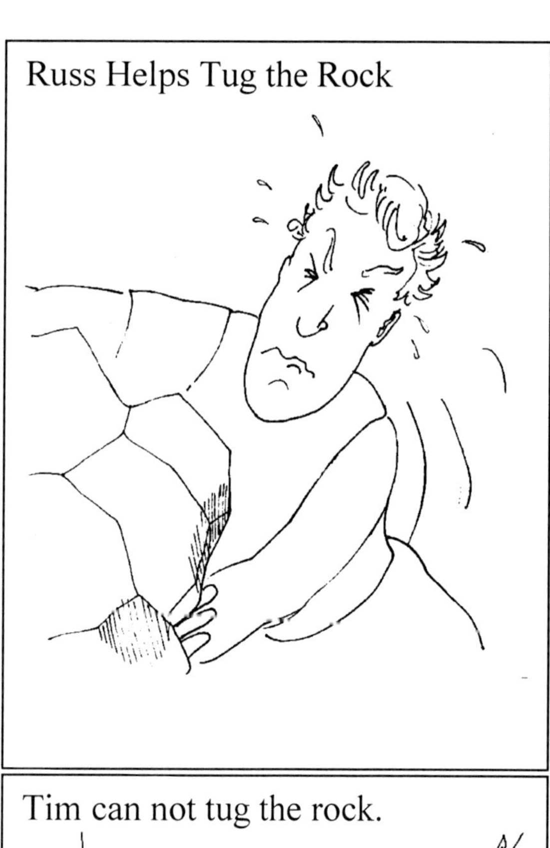

A rock fell.

Tim can not tug the rock.

Tim is sad. Tim can not get the van.

Russ is a big man. Russ can help.

Russ and Tim can tug the rock.

Tim is glad. Tim can get the van.

"Thanks, Russ!"

Rick Lost Well

Rick bets that Rick will win.

Rick thinks and thinks.

Sal thinks, and wins. Sal thinks, "Will Rick get upset?"

Rick is not upset. Rick thinks Sal won well.

"Congrats, Sal!"
"Thanks, Rick!"

Jon Can Sing Well

Jon is with Ed, Ben, Lil, and Erin.

"Jon can sing well. Sing, Jon!"

Ben can strum.

Jon sings six songs.

Ed, Ben, Lil, and Erin sing with Jon.

Singing well is fun. "Thanks, Jon!"

Mick Stops Alcohol
Mick drinks alcohol. Mick drinks lots and lots.
If Mick drinks alcohol, Mick gets mad.
Mick's kid is sad.

Mick went to the doc.

“Mick must not drink alcohol!”

“Just a bit, doc?”

“Not a bit! Not a drop!”

Mick sits and thinks.
ALCOHOL AND HEALTH

"Mick will not drink alcohol!
Mick will stop it!"

"Drink up, Mick!"
"Not for Mick, thanks!"

Mick is not mad. Mick's kid is glad.

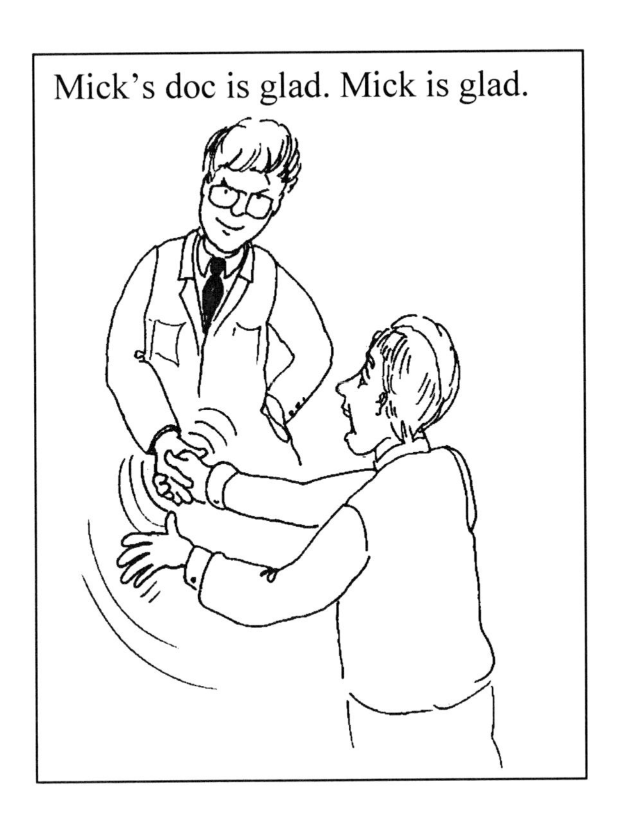

Mick's doc is glad. Mick is glad.

The Cop Helps the Man Get Back on Track

The bus runs. It turns and turns.

The man is lost.

The map is not on the bus! The man is mad.

The cop is in his van. The cop stops.

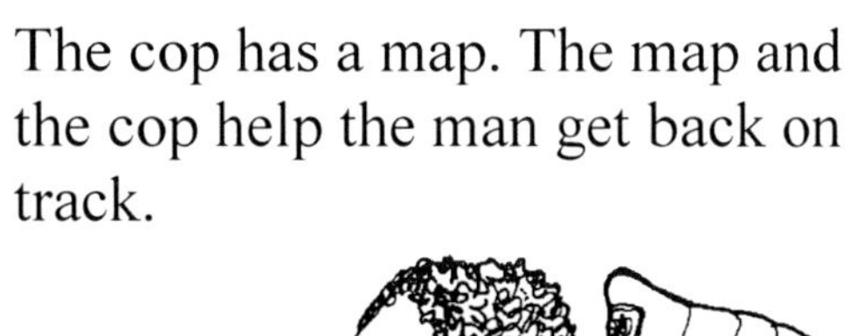
The cop has a map. The map and the cop help the man get back on track.

The man is not lost. "Thanks, cop!"

Sixteen Skills and Principles

I mentioned earlier that the purpose of reading and writing is to save worthwhile ideas so that they can be recalled. The sixteen maxims that follow define the sixteen groups of psychological skills that I have used to organize many ideas on what constitutes psychological health. Even though the reading level is not at the very bottom, beginning readers can learn to read these maxims after hearing them several times. The vignettes that follow, the first twenty from *Programmed Readings for Psychological Skills*, are easier reading.

To make it much easier for learners to get these skills and principles into their minds, you can refer to the song entitled "What Are the Qualities" from the *Spirit of Nonviolence* recording.

The vignettes from *Programmed Readings* give examples of the psychological skill concepts, together with practice in easy reading. *Programmed Readings* contains about a thousand more vignettes, illustrating a variety of psychological skill-related concepts.

Sixteen Skills and Principles

1. Work hard. (productivity)
2. Be cheerful. (joyousness)
3. Be kind. Make people happy. (kindness)
4. Tell the truth. (honesty)
5. When you don't get what you want, handle it. (fortitude)
6. Think carefully about what to do. Talk calmly when you don't agree with someone. (good decisions)
7. Don't hurt or kill. (nonviolence)
8. Don't use hurtful talk. (respectful talk, not being rude)
9. Build good relations with people. (friendship building)
10. Do what's best even when it isn't the most fun. (self-discipline)
11. Stick by people who have been good to you. (loyalty)
12. Don't waste the earth's resources. (conservation)
13. Take care of yourself. (self-care)
14. Obey when it is good and right to obey. (compliance)
15. In your fantasy, practice doing good things. Don't have fun

pretending people are hurt. (positive fantasy rehearsal)

16. Be brave enough to do what's best. (courage)

Examples of Sixteen Skills

1. Jack was with his pal Jed. They were in the woods. Jed saw a bug. Jed said, "I will step on the bug."

Jack said, "No, Jed. Let the bug live. The bug will not hurt us. Let us not hurt or kill when it does no good."

Jed said, "OK, Jack." Jed did not kill the bug.

Jack felt good.

A. productivity,
or
B. nonviolence?

2. Peg had a plan. Peg's pal Ann was to come and be with Peg. But Ann called. Ann said, "I am sick. I can't come."

Peg was sad. But Peg said, "I can take it." Peg did not get too upset. Peg wrote a note to Ann. The note said, "I hope you get well soon, Ann." Then Peg read a book. The book was fun.

Peg was glad she had put up with it when Ann could not come.

A. fortitude,
or
B. conservation?

3. Sam's mom let Sam swim. Sam was glad to swim. Sam wanted to swim a long time.

But Sam's mom said, "We must stop swimming now, Sam. We must go."

Sam was not glad. Sam did not want to go. But Sam said, "Yes, mom." Sam got up to go.

Sam's mom said, "You did well, Sam. You made your mom glad."

A. compliance,
or
B. self-care?

4. A man liked junk food. He liked candy bars. He liked pop. He liked lots of cake.

The man read a book. The book said that junk food was not good for him. The man wanted to stay well. The man decided to eat much less junk. He ate more peas and beans and other veggies. He ate more fruit.

The man felt good about what he did for himself.

A. honesty and nonviolence,
or
B. self-care and self-discipline?

5. Two men waited for a bus. The bus was late. The first man got angry. He said, "Why is the bus late?"

The other man had fun. He said, "Now I have a chance to read. Now I have some time to rest. Now I have a chance to think about my plans." He looked at the sky. He felt good.

When the bus came, that man said to himself, "I'm glad the bus is here. But I had fun waiting for it, too."

A. kindness,
or
B. joyousness?

6. A man was rich. Some rich men get lots of big cars. Some rich men get lots of big things. But this man did not spend his money on things. He paid people to help people read. He paid people to help people grow food. He paid people to clean up the earth. He felt good about how he used his money.

A. self-care and compliance,
or
B. kindness and conservation?

7. Rick had a job to do. He wanted to cut with a saw. He took his dad's saw.

When Rick did the job, he felt glad. But he did not put the saw back.

Rick's dad looked for the saw. He got mad. He said, "Who took my saw?"

Rick felt bad. But he said, "I took it. I will get it for you."

Rick's dad was still mad. He said, "If you take it, put it back!"

Later, Rick's dad said, "Rick, I'm glad you told me the truth. Some kids would not have told the truth. But you did."

Rick felt good to hear this.

A. honesty and courage,
or
B. positive fantasy rehearsal and loyalty?

8. Tom had lots of work to do. He had to do math. He had words to learn to spell. He had lots to read.

A good show came on TV. Tom said, "It would feel good now to watch TV. But the work would not get done. I would feel bad tomorrow."

Tom did the work. He did not watch the show. It was hard. But he did what was best.

A. joyousness,
or
B. self-discipline?

9. Liz loved dogs. Dogs loved Liz. Liz wanted to have a dog. She wanted it all the time.

But her dad said, "We can not get a dog. I know this makes you feel bad." Her dad told Liz why they could not get a dog.

Liz did not cry or scream. Liz did not get angry. Liz said, "I can take it." Liz was nice to her dad.

Liz's dad said, "Thank you for taking it, Liz."

A. fortitude,
or
B. productivity?

10. Tim had a good friend. A big boy was being mean. The big boy said bad things to the friend. The big boy said, "He is dumb. Isn't he, Tim?"

Tim said, "He is not dumb. He is my good friend."

The big boy said, "You are dumb too."

Tim said, "You can think what you want."

Later, Tim's friend said, "Thanks, Tim."

Tim said, "I wanted to stick up for my friend."

A. loyalty,
or
B. joyousness?

11. A man had some money. But a bad man stole the money. The man could not get it back. Now the man did not have much.

The man had two kids. The man said, "I will work hard to feed my kids." The man worked at two jobs. He tried to do his best. He worked a long time each day.

The man worked so much that he made the money back. He said to himself, "Now I know my kids can eat."

A. honesty,
or
B. productivity?

12. Jan drew pictures. Kim drew too. Jan saw what Kim had drawn. Jan had the urge to say, "That drawing is bad." But then she thought, "I don't want to make Kim sad."

So Jan just said, "It's fun to draw. Isn't it, pal?" Jan smiled at Kim.

Kim felt good. Jan was glad that she had not been rude.

A. respectful talk,
or
B. compliance?

13. Ted was with Mack. Mack said, "Let's watch this."

Ted said, "What is it?"

Mack said, "It's a movie on tape. There's much blood. Lots of men are killed."

Ted said, "I don't want to have fun pretending that people are hurt. I'd rather not see that movie."

They did some other thing with each other.

Ted was glad he did not have fun with the killing in the movie.

A. positive fantasy rehearsal,
or
B. productivity?

14. Bob and Pat were at the river. Bob said to Pat, "I dare you to dive off the cliff."

Pat said to himself, "I want to decide with care." Pat thought, "If the water is deep and safe, it would be fun." But then Pat thought, "If a rock is at the wrong place, I could get hurt or killed."

Pat said to Bob, "The risk is too big. I will not dive."

Later, Pat told his dad what he had done. Pat's dad said, "I am glad that you think before you act. I love my son. I do not want my son to be hurt or killed. You chose well."

Pat felt good that he had made a good choice.

A. good decisions,
or
B. compliance?

15. Min was at a party. Min saw a girl who was alone. The girl did not know the rest of the girls at the party.

Min wanted to help the girl have a good time. She said to the girl, "Hi, I'm Min. What's your name?"

The girl said, "My name is Sal. I'm glad to meet you, Min."

Min said, "I had fun with the game we just played. Did you?"

Sal said, "Yes, I like playing guessing games. What other games do you like, Min?"

Min and Sal talked a lot. They got to know each other.

At the end of the party Sal said to Min, "I feel good that I made a new friend." Min felt good too.

A. honesty and compliance,
or
B. friendship-building and kindness?

16. Pam played the piano. Someone said, "Pam, will you play for our group? Do you like to play for lots of people?"

Pam said, "Yes, that will be fun."

The time came for her to play. There were many people. Pam looked at them. She felt scared.

She got the urge to run away. But then she thought, "I will try to be brave. I will play even though I am scared."

Pam's fingers shook. But she played the songs. She kept going until the end. She got less scared.

Pam felt good that she had not run away. She was glad she had been brave.

A. courage,
or
B. friendship-building?

17. Mick wanted to learn to read. One day Mick's mom said, "Mrs. Ling will help you read."

Mrs. Ling asked Mick to work for a long time each day.

At times Mick did not feel like working. But Mrs. Ling said, "We work to make good things happen. If you can work even when you don't feel like it, you've learned a very good thing."

Mick thought about that. He worked, even when he felt like playing.

The more Mick worked, the more work Mick could do.

One day Mrs. Ling said, "You can do six times more work than when we started." Mick was glad to hear this.

One day Mick was able to read very well. Mrs. Ling said, "You did it by learning to work hard and long." Mick felt good.

A. self-discipline and productivity,
or
B. nonviolence and positive fantasy rehearsal?

18. Ann was at school. At talk time, the boys and girls got to talk. They said what they thought.

Ron said a wrong thing. Ann got the urge to say, "Ron, you don't know a thing." But then Ann thought, "Why make Ron feel bad?" So Ann said, "I have a different idea." She told what she thought.

Ron did not mind this. Ann was glad she had not been rude to Ron.

A. respectful talk
or
B. compliance?

19. Biff was very strong. Biff was very fast. Lunk said to Biff, "I'll fight you. You can't win."

Lots of kids said, "Get him, Biff. Show Lunk he's wrong."

Biff said to Lunk, "Why should I hurt you? Why should you hurt me? That would be dumb."

Lunk said, "You are just scared."

Biff said, "You can think what you will."

The kids were sad. Biff said to them, "To watch a fight should not be fun for you."

The kids knew Biff was right.

A. nonviolence,
or
B. productivity?

20. Jan and her dad went out. They walked in the woods. Jan's dad hurt his leg. He could not walk.

Jan said, "I will run for help." She ran a long way.

Jan got tired. She felt like giving up. She felt like stopping to rest. But Jan said to herself, "I don't care what I feel like. I need to get that help."

She kept going fast. Then she found people to help! They went to her dad. They brought her dad to the doctor.

Later, Jan's dad was OK. He said, "Thanks, Jan."

Jan thought, "I'm glad I kept on."

A. self-discipline,
or
B. conservation?

Supplemental Books

The reading grade levels listed for some of these works were obtained by using the Flesch-Kincaid reading level assessment that comes with *Microsoft Word*.

Works by Joseph Strayhorn:

Illustrated Stories That Model Psychological Skills, Primer. Included within this volume. Meant to be among the first exercises in text-reading for the beginning reader. The first couple of stories have reading grade level 0.0, reading ease rating 100%.

Illustrated Stories That Model Psychological Skills. Over a hundred illustrated stories, bound into one volume, meant to give practice for beginning readers and model psychologically skillful patterns.

The Letter Stories. About thirty illustrated stories, bound into one volume, in which the characters are letters who communicate with people by getting together with each other and saying their individual phonetic sounds. Meant to be read aloud to pre-readers and beginning readers, as an introduction to phonemic awareness and letter sound correspondence. A random story was rated at 1.0 reading level.

Programmed Readings for Psychological Skills. Over a thousand vignettes, approximately one hundred words each, written at a beginning level. The vignettes illustrate psychological skill concepts, and picking which concept is illustrated is a comprehension check for the reader. These have been successfully used as a major reading text for beginning readers. Unillustrated. First 50 stories have average reading level grade 1.3.

Basic Concept Illustrations. Meant for the student who needs work in oral language development, with concepts such as left, right, row, top, bottom, and so forth. There are a few illustrations of a concept, and then the listener (the student) is asked to pick among a couple of illustrations for the next example. The vignettes chosen to model these basic concepts also model prosocial behavior.

Illustrated Math Stories. These are similar in format to the *Illustrated Stories that Model Psychological Skills*. The stories are meant to show the young student why certain math concepts are useful – beginning with counting, and going to adding, to calculating distance from rate and time, and eventually to the methods of a controlled experiment.

As with the other stories, each is meant to model prosocial behavior.

Works by Other Authors:

Highlights for Children Magazine. Each issue includes at least some stories or nonfiction earmarked as embodying "moral values." This is a great magazine for children of a wide age range; there are easy and hard stories and articles.

Easy Picture Books

Maslen, Bobby Lynn, and Maslen, John R. *The Bob Books*. These start with the easiest three letter words. Useful for very first books.

Eastman, P.D., et al. *The Big Blue Book of Beginner Books* and *The Big Red Book of Beginner Books*. These each contain six beginner books, including *Go Dog Go*, *Robert the Rose Horse*, and others. In our tutoring program we've used these to great advantage: they're a little harder than the primer illustrated stories in this book, and easier than *Illustrated Stories That Model Psychological Skills*. They've helped many students make the transition.

Hoff, Syd. *Chester, Sammy the Seal, Danny and the Dinosaur, The Horse in Harry's Room*, and other easy readers. These are good for young beginning readers. There's a nice comfortable and secure feeling about Syd Hoff's stories and drawings.

Dr. Seuss. *Green Eggs and Ham, Dr. Seuss's ABC, The Cat in the Hat, Hop on Pop, Horton Hatches the Egg, Horton Hears a Who,* etc. *Hop on Pop* is a very easy reader, good for a first book.

Frith, Michael K., and Eastman, P.D. *I'll Teach My Dog 100 Words*. Nice whimsical book for young beginning readers.

Lobel, Arnold. *Frog and Toad Are Friends*. Easy reading, quirky humor.

Rylant, Cynthia: The *Henry and Mudge* series. Lots of good illustrated stories about a boy and his dog, written for beginning readers.

Rylant, Cynthia: The *Mr. Putter and Tabby* series. Good picture books, easy to read.

Standiford, Natalie, and Cook, Donald. *Bravest Dog Ever*. Step Into Reading, Step 2. The story of Balto, a dog who pulled a dogsled to get medicine to sick people. If you search with the keywords "Step Into Reading" on Amazon.com, you'll find over 200 books published by Random House, graded according to reading level. The easiest level is called "early"; after that come step 1, step 2, etc. Many other publishers also have early readers of graded difficulty.

Bulla, Clyde Robert. *Singing Sam*. Step Into Reading, Step 3. A story about a selfish child and a kind child and a dog. The dog will "sing" for the child who loves him but not for the child who wants to use him. Who will eventually be able to keep the dog?

Harder Picture Books

Value Tale Series By Ann Donegan Johnson or Spencer Johnson. These are great books for children throughout early grade school, or perhaps later. They are biographies of people who illustrate a certain value: Harriet Tubman for the Value of Helping, Benjamin Franklin for the Value of Saving, Ralph Bunche for the Value of Determination, Elizabeth Fry, Jane Addams, Marie Curie, Charles Dickens, and others. These are out of print, but you can find them on the Internet.

Boudart, J., Rowitz, M, Toast, S., 1998. *Treasury of Virtues: Courage, Love, Honesty*. Lincolnwood, Illinois: Publications International, Ltd. 7373 North Cicero Avenue, Lincolnwood, Illinois 60646. Pretty color illustrations on every other page, and text on the facing page. Includes stories such as the Lion and the Mouse, the Honest Woodcutter, The Selfish Giant, King Midas, The North Wind, The Velveteen Rabbit. A little of the problem being resolved through the death of the adversary, in Jack and the Beanstalk. Appropriate for early grade school children. Reading grade level about 2.4.

Havill, Juanita: *Jamaica's Find*. A picture book in which a young girl finds something she likes a lot on a playground, uses self-discipline to turn it in, and as a result finds something even better: a friend, the owner of the object. For young readers. Protagonist is African American. Reading grade level about 2.2.

Martin, Bill, and Archambault, John. *Knots on a Counting Rope*. A very moving story about a blind Native American boy and his relationship to his grandfather. Reading level about 2.1.

Wisniewski, David. *The Warrior and the Wise Man*. A story about two brothers who quest to become the next king, one in a warlike way and one in a gentle way. A beautifully illustrated picture book. Reading grade level 6.1.

Golenbock, Peter. *Teammates*. When Jackie Robinson became the first African-American player in major league baseball, he experienced a good deal of harrassment and rejection, some even from his own teammates. His teammate Pee Wee Reese supported him, in this moving true story.

Paterson, Katherine. *The Tale of the Mandarin Ducks*. A moving and beautifully illustrated story, celebrating nonviolence. This is an all-time great, in my opinion. Reading level about 5.1.

Mahy, Margaret. *The Seven Chinese Brothers*. An entertaining tale in which each of the 7 brothers has some sort of unusual power, and all look alike. They trade places with each other to help each other withstand onslaughts. Reading grade level about 4.1.

Steptoe, John. *Mufaro's Beautiful Daughters*. A tale set in Africa, about two beautiful daughters, one kind and the other selfish. Reading grade level about 3.2.

Ada, Alma Flor. *The Gold Coin*. A thief pursues, encounters, and is transformed by a woman who goes around doing good. This is a very moving one. Grade level 4.5.

Seeger, Pete, Jacobs, Paul Dubois, Hays, Michael: *Abiyoyo Returns*. Very prosocial book in which a giant is tamed, not killed; main protagonists are African American.

Bennett, W.J., & Hague, M. (1995). The Children's Book of Virtues, Illustrated version. New York, Simon & Schuster. Beautiful Illustrations. In St. George and the Dragon, problem solved by death of adversary. In the King and His Hawk, a story that can be very upsetting to tender-hearted children. Other than these stories this book is appropriate for younger children and grade school children.

For a list of many more picture books that exemplify ethical values and good writing, check the following web site: www.heartwoodethics.org.

Chapter Books

White, E.B. *Charlotte's Web, The Trumpet of the Swan, and Stuart Little*. These are well-written, enjoyable, nonviolent classics. *Charlotte's Web* is in the latter part of third grade reading level.

Warner, Gertrude Chandler. *The Boxcar Children*. This is a good one for this program because it's chapter book that doesn't feel too juvenile, but the reading level is easy. A large series of "mystery" books involving these characters followed, many of which are also good. Four siblings are the main characters; they are very supportive and kind to one another. The other ingredient that makes these books useful is nonviolence. Often the mystery revolves around some sort of signs that some unknown person is around, creating a scary enough story to be interesting, but the unknown person turns out not to be malevolent. When there are actual bad guys in this series, they are total bunglers, not the type that give nightmares. Reading grade level for the first book in the series is about 1.6.

Burnett, Frances Hodgson. *The Secret Garden.* In addition to the original version, there is an abridged and illustrated version retold by Resnick, Jane Parker, and Illustrated by Dale Crawford. Philadelphia: Courage Books, 1990. This beautifully illustrated book is appropriate for older preschoolers and young grade school children. The unabridged version is good for older grade schoolers up. It's the story, among other things, of an overindulged child becoming unspoiled. The unabridged version has an embarrassing brief conversation where the characters make some racist remarks. Also the unabridged version has a lot of nonstandard spelling that is used to depict the accents of the characters. So my recommendation for this project is the illustrated and abridged version.

Dodge, Mary. *Hans Brinker.* For readers in this project, the recommendation is the greatly abridged and illustrated version in the Great Illustrated Classics series. Lots of prosocial behavior by the characters, nonviolent. The abridged version makes the plot unfold at a very rapid pace. Reading grade level for abridged version about 6.9.

More Challenging Books

O'Brien, Robert: *Mrs. Frisby and the Rats of NIMH.* Conly, Jane: *Racso and the Rats of NIMH.* These are gripping novels. The first won the Newbery Award. The sequel was written after the death of the author by his daughter, who is also a prominent writer of children's books. There are many examples of kindness, helpfulness, courage, ethical decision-making, delay of gratification, and other psychological skills. *Racso and the Rats of NIMH*, in addition to having an enthralling plot, is a character development story in which the title character moves from being narcissistic and focussed on building up his own image, to becoming a more generous and loyal and mature character.

Greer, Colin, & Kohl, Herbert, Editors, 1995. *A Call to Character: A Family Treasury of stories, poems, plays, proverbs, and fables to guide the development of values for you and your children.* New York: Harper Collins. No pictures. Selections from much good writing, including E.B. White, Shakespeare, Walt Whitman, Hans Christian Andersen, Albert Einstein, James Herriot, and many others. When the child has achieved the ability to enjoy hearing pictureless stories with fairly complex vocabulary, this is a great one. Selections chosen to embody values such as courage, integrity, creativity, playfulness, loyalty, generosity, empathy, honesty, adaptability, idealism, compassion, responsibility, balance, fairness, love.

Bennett, William J. (1993). The Book of Virtues: A Treasury of Great Moral Stories. New York, Simon and Schuster. Enough to keep you reading for a long time. No pictures. Level of difficulty varies.

Bennett, William J. (1995). The Moral Compass: Stories for a Life's Journey. New York, Simon and Schuster.

Words In Word Families

List 1: Upper case letters, in order.

1. A
2. B
3. C
4. D
5. E
6. F
7. G
8. H
9. I
10. J
11. K
12. L
13. M
14. N
15. O
16. P
17. Q
18. R
19. S
20. T
21. U
22. V
23. W
24. X
25. Y
26. Z

List 2: Upper case letters, out of order.

1. T
2. J
3. D
4. O
5. Z
6. G
7. U
8. H
9. I
10. Y
11. C
12. E
13. L
14. N
15. Q
16. A
17. R
18. X
19. M
20. F
21. P
22. K
23. W
24. S
25. V
26. B

List 3: Lower case letters, in order.

1. a
2. b
3. c
4. d
5. e
6. f
7. g
8. h
9. i
10. j
11. k
12. l
13. m
14. n
15. o
16. p

17. q
18. r
19. s
20. t
21. u
22. v
23. w
24. x
25. y
26. z

List 4: Lower case letters, out of order.

1. b
2. l
3. h
4. e
5. t
6. f
7. g
8. j
9. m
10. y
11. z
12. u
13. d
14. n
15. w
16. x
17. o
18. p
19. k
20. q
21. i
22. a
23. c
24. r
25. s
26. v

List 5: In this list, the a t at the end of the word says at.

1. pat
2. hat
3. fat
4. cat
5. mat
6. rat
7. bat
8. Nat
9. sat
10. vat

List 6: In this list, the a n says an.

1. an
2. ban
3. can
4. Dan
5. fan
6. man
7. Nan
8. pan
9. ran
10. tan
11. van

List 7: In this list, the a p says ap.

1. cap
2. gap
3. lap
4. map
5. nap
6. pap
7. rap
8. sap
9. tap
10. zap

List 8: In this list, the a g says ag.

1. bag
2. gag
3. hag
4. lag
5. nag
6. rag
7. sag
8. tag
9. wag

List 9: In this list, the a d at the end of the word says ad.

1. add
2. bad
3. dad
4. mad
5. sad
6. had
7. fad
8. lad
9. pad
10. rad

List 10: In this list, the a m at the end of the word says am.

1. am
2. jam
3. Pam
4. yam
5. ram
6. Sam
7. ham

List 11: In this list, the a b says ab.

1. cab
2. dab
3. fab
4. gab
5. jab
6. lab
7. nab
8. tab

List 12: In this list, the a says ă as in apple.

1. an
2. ax
3. bag
4. bat
5. dad
6. Dan
7. fan
8. fat
9. gas
10. had
11. hag
12. ham
13. jam
14. jazz
15. lap
16. mad
17. map
18. mass
19. Nat
20. pad
21. Pam
22. pan
23. pass
24. pat
25. rap
26. sad
27. tag
28. tan

29. tap
30. tax
31. van
32. wag
33. wax

List 13: In this list the e says ĕ as in elephant.

1. bed
2. beg
3. bell
4. Ben
5. den
6. fed
7. fell
8. get
9. hen
10. jet
11. keg
12. leg
13. less
14. led
15. let
16. men
17. mess
18. net
19. peg
20. pen
21. pet
22. red
23. set
24. tell
25. ten
26. vet
27. well
28. wet
29. yell
30. yes

List 14: In this list the i says ĭ as in insects.

1. bib
2. big
3. bill
4. bin
5. bit
6. did
7. dig
8. fib
9. fig
10. fill
11. fit
12. fix
13. hill
14. him
15. hit
16. if
17. it
18. Jill
19. kid
20. kill
21. Kim
22. kiss
23. kit
24. lid
25. lip
26. lit
27. mill
28. miss
29. mix
30. nip
31. pig
32. rip
33. sin
34. sip
35. sis
36. sit
37. six
38. Tim
39. till
40. tin
41. tip
42. win

29 13,470
+ 29

43. wig
44. zip

List 15: In this list the o says ŏ as in ostrich.

1. Bob
2. boss
3. box
4. cob
5. cod
6. cop
7. cot
8. doll
9. Don
10. fog
11. God
12. got
13. hog
14. hop
15. hot
16. job
17. log
18. lot
19. mop
20. nod
21. not
22. on
23. off
24. ox
25. pod
26. pop
27. rod
28. sob
29. Tom

List 16: In this list the u says ŭ as in umbrella.

1. bud
2. but
3. buzz
4. cub
5. cuff
6. cup
7. dull
8. fun
9. fuss
10. fuzz
11. gun
12. Gus
13. huff
14. hug
15. hum
16. hut
17. mud
18. mug
19. mutt
20. nun
21. nut
22. puff
23. rub
24. rug
25. run
26. sum
27. tub
28. tug
29. up

List 17: Here is a set of words for practice on all five short vowels.

1. bet
2. bus
3. dell
4. dim
5. dot
6. gull
7. gum
8. hiss
9. hull
10. hum
11. Jim

12. Ken
13. lass
14. mat
15. max
16. moss
17. muff
18. mum
19. nap
20. odd
21. pin
22. pub
23. rib
24. rim
25. sell
26. sun
27. tiff
28. top
29. toss
30. web
31. will

List 18: Here are some words ending in s.

1. beds
2. bets
3. bills
4. bugs
5. buns
6. cats
7. cops
8. cuffs
9. cups
10. cuts
11. digs
12. dogs
13. fins
14. guns
15. hats
16. hens
17. hills
18. hops
19. hums
20. lips
21. mats
22. pets
23. pigs
24. pills
25. rips
26. sells
27. sips
28. tops
29. tubs
30. wells
31. wigs

List 19: In this list the ck says kuh as in cat and key.

1. back
2. buck
3. deck
4. dock
5. duck
6. hack
7. kick
8. lack
9. lick
10. lock
11. luck
12. mock
13. Nick
14. pack
15. pick
16. rack
17. rock
18. sack
19. sick
20. sock
21. tack
22. tick
23. tuck

List 20: In this list you get practice in blending two consonants.

1. act
2. and
3. ask
4. band
5. belt
6. bend
7. bent
8. best
9. bluff
10. bond
11. bulb
12. bulk
13. bump
14. camp
15. damp
16. desk
17. disk
18. dump
19. dusk
20. dust
21. elf
22. end
23. fact
24. fast
25. felt
26. fist
27. fond
28. fund
29. gift
30. gulp
31. help
32. hump
33. hunt
34. its
35. jump
36. just
37. kept
38. lamp
39. land
40. last
41. left

List 21: More practice in blending consonant sounds.

1. lent
2. lift
3. limp
4. list
5. lump
6. mask
7. melt
8. mend
9. milk
10. mint
11. mist
12. must
13. nest
14. pant
15. past
16. pest
17. pond
18. pump
19. rest
20. risk
21. rust
22. sand
23. self
24. send
25. sift
26. silk
27. spell
28. spend
29. stamp
30. step
31. stuck
32. stuff
33. sulk
34. task

35. tent
36. test
37. vest
38. went
39. west
40. wind
41. zest

List 22: In this list you practice with the blends ng and nk.

1. bang
2. bank
3. dunk
4. gang
5. hang
6. ink
7. junk
8. king
9. link
10. long
11. lung
12. mink
13. pink
14. plank
15. rank
16. rink
17. rung
18. sank
19. sing
20. song
21. tank
22. wing
23. wink
24. yank

List 23: More practice with blending consonants.

1. black
2. blend
3. blink
4. block
5. clamp
6. clap
7. click
8. clip
9. clump
10. flag
11. flat
12. flint
13. flip
14. flock
15. flop
16. glad
17. glint
18. held
19. lamp
20. lump
21. next
22. plot
23. plum
24. plump
25. scamp
26. skip
27. slack
28. slap
29. slick
30. slink
31. slip
32. slot
33. snap
34. snip
35. span
36. spill
37. spit
38. splint
39. stab
40. stem
41. stick
42. stop
43. stub
44. swell

45. swept
46. swim
47. twin

List 24: Practice in blending with the letter r.

1. brag
2. brand
3. brat
4. brim
5. bring
6. brink
7. brisk
8. crab
9. crack
10. craft
11. cramp
12. crank
13. crest
14. crib
15. crock
16. crust
17. drab
18. drank
19. dress
20. drill
21. drink
22. drip
23. drug
24. drum
25. Fran
26. frank
27. Fred
28. frills
29. frock
30. frog
31. from
32. grand
33. grill
34. grin
35. grip
36. grunt
37. prank
38. press
39. print
40. prompt
41. scrub
42. spring
43. strap
44. string
45. strip
46. strong
47. tramp
48. trap
49. trick
50. trip
51. trot
52. truck
53. trust

List 25: In these words there's a th as in this.

1. than
2. that
3. them
4. then
5. this

List 26: In this list, there's a th as in thick.

1. bath
2. broth
3. cloth
4. moth
5. path
6. smith
7. thank
8. thick
9. thin
10. think
11. thrift

12. thrill
13. throb
14. throng
15. thug
16. thump
17. with

List 27: In this list qu says kwuh as in quarter.

1. quack
2. quell
3. quest
4. quick
5. quill
6. quilt
7. quip
8. quit
9. quiz

List 28: In this list wh says hwuh as in when.

1. whack
2. when
3. whet
4. which
5. whiff
6. whim
7. whip
8. whit
9. whiz

List 29: In this list sh says sh as in ship.

1. ash
2. bash
3. brash
4. brush
5. cash
6. crash
7. flash
8. gash
9. hush
10. lash
11. mush
12. rash
13. rush
14. sash
15. shaft
16. shall
17. shed
18. shell
19. shelf
20. shift
21. shin
22. ship
23. shock
24. shop
25. shot
26. shrimp
27. shrug
28. shut
29. slash
30. splash
31. thrash
32. thrush
33. trash
34. wish

List 30: In this list ch says ch as in chin.

1. batch
2. bench
3. branch
4. bunch
5. catch
6. chap
7. chant
8. chat
9. check

10. chest
11. chick
12. chill
13. chin
14. chink
15. chip
16. chop
17. chum
18. chunk
19. clinch
20. clutch
21. crunch
22. crutch
23. ditch
24. fetch
25. hitch
26. hunch
27. itch
28. latch
29. lunch
30. match
31. much
32. notch
33. patch
34. pinch
35. punch
36. quench
37. ranch
38. sketch
39. snatch
40. stitch
41. stretch
42. such
43. switch
44. trench
45. witch

List 31: Review.

1. bed
2. bench
3. box
4. brand
5. brat
6. broth
7. chap
8. chop
9. clip
10. cloth
11. cob
12. cod
13. crunch
14. dad
15. deck
16. drill
17. dusk
18. fix
19. flock
20. grunt
21. hands
22. hitch
23. junk
24. lunch
25. mats
26. melt
27. mix
28. moth
29. next
30. pin
31. plum
32. press
33. quack
34. quell
35. quill
36. quip
37. quit
38. sack
39. shrimp
40. splash
41. such
42. tax
43. than
44. that
45. them
46. then
47. this
48. thrash

49. van
50. whack
51. when
52. whiff
53. with
54. yes

List 32: In this list, e
says long e as in me.

1. be
2. he
3. me
4. she
5. the
6. we

List 33: In this list, o says oo in who.

1. do
2. to
3. into
4. who

List 34: In this list, o says o as in so.

1. ago
2. go
3. hello
4. no
5. pro
6. so

List 35: in this list, y makes the long i sound as in sky.

1. by
2. cry
3. dry
4. fly
5. fry
6. ply
7. pry
8. shy
9. sky
10. sly
11. spy
12. try
13. why

List 36: This list has words to memorize. The letters often make sounds different from what they usually make.

1. a
2. been
3. begin
4. are
5. was
6. were
7. come
8. some
9. done
10. have
11. here
12. there
13. where
14. their
15. I
16. any
17. many
18. of
19. once
20. one
21. said

22. they
23. two
24. woman
25. you
26. your
27. yours
28. could
29. should
30. would
31. what
32. does
33. pcople

List 37: Long a sounds, with silent e at the end.

1. ape
2. ate
3. bake
4. blame
5. blaze
6. brave
7. came
8. cane
9. cape
10. case
11. cave
12. crate
13. date
14. Dave
15. daze
16. drape
17. fade
18. fake
19. fame
20. fate
21. flake
22. game
23. gape
24. gate
25. gave
26. grapes
27. grate
28. grave
29. hate
30. haze
31. Jane
32. Kate
33. lake
34. lame
35. lane
36. late
37. made
38. make
39. male
40. maze

List 38: More long a words with silent e at the end.

1. name
2. pane
3. paste
4. pave
5. plane
6. plate
7. quake
8. rake
9. rate
10. safe
11. sale
12. same
13. shake
14. shame
15. shape
16. shave
17. skate
18. slate
19. slave
20. snake
21. spade
22. stale
23. tame
24. take
25. tape

26. taste
27. trade
28. wake
29. waste
30. wave
31. whale

List 39: Here ai makes the long a sound.

1. aid
2. aim
3. bait
4. braid
5. brain
6. chain
7. claim
8. drain
9. fail
10. faint
11. faith
12. frail
13. gain
14. grain
15. hail
16. jail
17. maid
18. mail
19. main
20. paid
21. pail
22. pain
23. paint
24. plain
25. quail
26. quaint
27. raid
28. rail
29. rain
30. sail
31. saint
32. snail
33. stain
34. strain
35. tail
36. trail
37. train
38. vain
39. wail
40. wait

List 40: ay makes the long a sound.

1. away
2. always
3. bay
4. bray
5. clay
6. day
7. gay
8. gray
9. hay
10. jay
11. lay
12. may
13. maybe
14. pay
15. play
16. pray
17. ray
18. say
19. slay
20. spray
21. stay
22. stray
23. sway
24. today
25. tray
26. way

List 41: Long e, with silent e at the end.

1. Crete

2. eke
3. eve
4. here
5. Pete
6. Swede
7. Zeke

List 42: ee makes the long e sound.

1. bee
2. breed
3. cheek
4. creep
5. deep
6. deer
7. feed
8. feel
9. feet
10. flee
11. free
12. greed
13. green
14. heel
15. keel
16. keep
17. meet
18. need
19. peek
20. peel
21. peep
22. queen
23. queer
24. screen
25. see
26. seed
27. seek
28. seem
29. seen
30. sheep
31. sheer
32. sheet
33. sleep
34. speech
35. steel
36. steer
37. street
38. sweep
39. sweet
40. teem
41. teeth
42. three
43. tree
44. weed
45. week
46. weep
47. wheel

List 43: In this list ea makes the long e sound as in beach.

1. beach
2. bead
3. beak
4. beam
5. bean
6. beast
7. cheap
8. cheat
9. clean
10. clear
11. cream
12. dear
13. dream
14. ear
15. east
16. eat
17. fear
18. feast
19. flea
20. gear
21. heap
22. hear
23. heat
24. leaf

25. lean
26. leap
27. meat
28. near
29. neat
30. peach
31. peak
32. preach
33. reach
34. reap
35. scream
36. seal
37. seam
38. seat
39. speak
40. spear
41. squeak
42. steal
43. steam
44. stream
45. tea
46. teach
47. team
48. veal
49. weak
50. wheat
51. year
52. yeast
53. zeal

List 44: Long i with silent e at the end.

1. beside
2. bike
3. bite
4. bride
5. chime
6. crime
7. dike
8. dime
9. dine
10. dive
11. file
12. fine
13. fire
14. five
15. glide
16. gripe
17. hide
18. hike
19. hire
20. hive
21. kite
22. life
23. like
24. lime
25. line
26. live
27. Mike
28. mile
29. mine
30. nine
31. pile
32. pine
33. pride
34. prize
35. quite
36. ride
37. ripe
38. shine
39. side
40. site
41. size
42. smile
43. spine
44. spite
45. strike
46. stripe
47. tide
48. tile
49. time
50. tire
51. vine
52. while
53. whine

54. white
55. wide
56. wife
57. wine
58. wire

List 45: i makes long i sound by itself in these words.

1. bind
2. blind
3. child
4. find
5. grind
6. hi
7. kind
8. mild
9. mind
10. rind
11. wild

List 46: ie makes the long i sound in these.

1. cries
2. die
3. died
4. dried
5. flies
6. fried
7. lie
8. pie
9. tried

List 47: igh makes the long i sound for these words.

1. bright
2. fight
3. flight
4. fright
5. height
6. knight
7. light
8. lightning
9. might
10. mighty
11. night
12. plight
13. sigh
14. sight
15. slight
16. thigh
17. tight
18. tonight

List 48: Silent e at the end, and long o.

1. before
2. bone
3. bore
4. chore
5. cone
6. cope
7. core
8. dole
9. dome
10. doze
11. drove
12. froze
13. globe
14. grope
15. hole
16. home
17. hope
18. joke
19. lobe
20. mope
21. more
22. note

23. poke
24. pole
25. robe
26. Rome
27. rope
28. rose
29. scope
30. score
31. shore
32. slope
33. smoke
34. snore
35. sole
36. sore
37. spoke
38. stole
39. stone
40. store
41. stove
42. throne
43. tone
44. vote
45. woke
46. wore
47. wove

List 49: o says long o by itself in these words.

1. bold
2. bolt
3. both
4. cold
5. colt
6. don't
7. fold
8. go
9. hold
10. jolt
11. mold
12. most
13. old
14. open
15. over
16. poll
17. roll
18. scold
19. scroll
20. stroll
21. told
22. toll

List 50: ow makes the long o sound in these words.

1. below
2. blow
3. blown
4. crow
5. flow
6. follow
7. glow
8. grow
9. grown
10. growth
11. low
12. mow
13. own
14. row
15. show
16. shown
17. slow
18. throw
19. window
20. yellow

List 51: oa makes long o in these.

1. boast
2. boat
3. coach
4. coal
5. coast

6. float
7. foal
8. foam
9. goal
10. goat
11. groan
12. load
13. loaf
14. loan
15. moan
16. moat
17. oak
18. oath
19. oats
20. road
21. roam
22. roar
23. roast
24. soak
25. soap
26. throat
27. toad
28. toast

List 52: oe makes the long o.

1. doe
2. foe
3. hoe
4. Joe
5. Poe
6. roe
7. toe
8. woe

List 53: With silent e at the end, u makes long u as in rude.

1. brute
2. crude
3. duke
4. dune
5. flute
6. June
7. Luke
8. lute
9. prune
10. rude
11. rule
12. tube
13. tune

List 54: With silent e at the end, u often makes long u as in the word you.

1. cube
2. cure
3. cute
4. fume
5. hue
6. mule
7. pure
8. tube
9. use

List 55: In this list oo says oo as in cool.

1. bloom
2. boot
3. booth
4. brood
5. broom
6. coo
7. cool
8. doom
9. drool
10. droop
11. food
12. fool

13. gloom
14. groom
15. hoop
16. loop
17. moo
18. mood
19. moon
20. pool
21. roof
22. room
23. root
24. scoop
25. shoot
26. smooth
27. soon
28. spool
29. spoon
30. stool
31. stoop
32. too
33. tool
34. tooth
35. troop
36. woo
37. zoo

List 56: In this list ew says oo as in new.

1. blew
2. brew
3. chew
4. crew
5. dew
6. drew
7. flew
8. grew
9. Jew
10. new
11. news
12. stew
13. strew
14. strewn

List 57: In this list ue says oo as in blue.

1. blue
2. clue
3. due
4. glue
5. Sue
6. true

List 58: In this list oo says oo as in foot.

1. book
2. cook
3. foot
4. good
5. hood
6. hoof
7. hook
8. look
9. shook
10. soot
11. stood
12. took
13. wood
14. wool

List 59: In this list the ar says ar as in yard.

1. arch
2. arm
3. art
4. bar
5. bark
6. car

7. card
8. Carl
9. cart
10. chart
11. dark
12. darn
13. dart
14. far
15. farm
16. hard
17. harm
18. jar
19. lard
20. lark
21. march
22. mark
23. marsh
24. park
25. part
26. scar
27. scarf
28. shark
29. sharp
30. smart
31. star
32. starch
33. start
34. tar
35. yard
36. yarn

List 60: In this list or sounds like the word or.

1. cord
2. cork
3. corn
4. for
5. fork
6. form
7. horn
8. lord
9. north
10. or
11. porch
12. pork
13. port
14. scorch
15. scorn
16. short
17. snort
18. sort
19. sport
20. storm
21. sworn
22. thorn
23. torch
24. torn
25. worn

List 61: er as in her.

1. after
2. Bert
3. clerk
4. ever
5. her
6. herd
7. hers
8. jerk
9. never
10. number
11. perch
12. stern
13. under

List 62: ir makes the same sound er usually makes.

1. bird
2. birch
3. birth
4. chirp
5. dirt

6. fir
7. firm
8. first
9. girl
10. shirt
11. sir
12. skirt
13. squirm
14. stir
15. third
16. thirst
17. twirl
18. whirl

List 63: ur also makes the er sound.

1. burn
2. burr
3. burst
4. church
5. curb
6. furl
7. hurl
8. hurt
9. purr
10. spur
11. surf
12. turn

List 64: oy says oy as in boy.

1. boy
2. coy
3. joy
4. ploy
5. Roy
6. soy
7. toy

List 65: oi says oy as in oil.

1. broil
2. coin
3. foil
4. hoist
5. joint
6. loin
7. moist
8. oil
9. point
10. soil
11. spoil

List 66: Here ou says ou as in ouch.

1. about
2. around
3. bound
4. cloud
5. couch
6. crouch
7. flour
8. foul
9. found
10. grouch
11. ground
12. hound
13. house
14. loud
15. mouth
16. ouch
17. our
18. out
19. pouch
20. pound
21. pout
22. proud
23. round
24. scout
25. shout

26. snout
27. sound
28. sour
29. south
30. spout
31. trout

List 67: Here ow says ow as in ouch.

1. bow
2. brow
3. brown
4. clown
5. cow
6. crown
7. down
8. drown
9. fowl
10. frown
11. gown
12. growl
13. how
14. howl
15. now
16. owl
17. powder
18. town
19. vow
20. vowel
21. wow

List 68: aw says aw as in saw.

1. bawl
2. claw
3. crawl
4. dawn
5. draw
6. drawn
7. flaw
8. jaw
9. law
10. lawn
11. paw
12. raw
13. saw
14. shawl
15. sprawl
16. straw
17. thaw
18. yawn

List 69: au says aw as in saw.

1. daunt
2. fault
3. fraud
4. gaunt
5. haul
6. haunch
7. haunt
8. launch
9. flaunt
10. jaunt
11. Paul
12. paunch
13. taunt

List 70: The a before l says aw as in saw.

1. all
2. always
3. bald
4. balk
5. ball
6. call
7. chalk
8. fall
9. gall
10. hall
11. halt

12. malt
13. mall
14. pall
15. salt
16. small
17. squall
18. stalk
19. stall
20. talk
21. tall
22. walk
23. wall
24. Walt

List 71: This list reviews letter combinations. Say the sound or sounds. There's a word beside it to give you a clue.

1. ai	rain
2. ar	star
3. au	haul
4. aw	straw
5. ay	day
6. ch	chain
7. ea	each
8. ee	see
9. er	her
10. ew	new
11. igh	night
12. ir	sir
13. oa	boat
14. oe	Joe
15. oi	oil
16. oo	moon
17. or	for
18. ou	out
19. oy	boy
20. qu	quit
21. sh	shut
22. ue	blue
23. ur	curl
24. wh	when

List 72: Review.

1. a
2. all
3. are
4. ball
5. bar
6. be
7. bead
8. bike
9. boast
10. book
11. boy
12. braid
13. by
14. car
15. cart
16. chart
17. chase
18. child
19. coin
20. come
21. cope
22. cook
23. crew
24. cue
25. doe
26. draw
27. dune
28. ear
29. eve
30. flute
31. fly
32. fold
33. fried
34. frown
35. gape
36. glue
37. go
38. good

39. have
40. he
41. hear
42. here
43. hold
44. hood
45. hook
46. hound
47. I
48. into
49. joint
50. Junc
51. lark
52. law
53. lay
54. leaf
55. lies
56. life
57. load
58. look
59. loud
60. mail

List 73: More review.

1. main
2. many
3. mate
4. me
5. moist
6. mouth
7. my
8. need
9. no
10. note
11. of
12. once
13. one
14. or
15. part
16. pew
17. pipe
18. pool
19. port
20. pouch
21. pound
22. purr
23. queer
24. quite
25. room
26. Roy
27. said
28. saw
29. scoop
30. seen
31. she
32. shirt
33. shook
34. shoot
35. short
36. shout
37. sir
38. sky
39. sly
40. smart
41. smooth
42. snort
43. so
44. soak
45. soil
46. soot
47. sport
48. stain
49. stay
50. stew
51. stir
52. take
53. tall
54. the
55. they
56. third
57. to
58. tooth
59. toys
60. train
61. tray

62. tried
63. tune
64. twirl
65. two
66. veal
67. vote
68. was
69. we
70. why
71. woman
72. wool
73. worn
74. yawn
75. you

List 74: In these words, are says air as in the word care.

1. aware
2. blare
3. care
4. fare
5. flare
6. glare
7. hare
8. mare
9. rare
10. scare
11. share
12. snare
13. spare
14. square
15. stare

List 75: In these words air sounds like the word air.

1. air
2. chair
3. fair
4. flair
5. hair
6. lair
7. pair
8. stair

List 76: In these words, ear says air as in bear.

1. bear
2. pear
3. tear
4. wear

List 77: wa usually says wah as in water.

1. swamp
2. swan
3. wall
4. wan
5. want
6. wash
7. watch
8. water

List 78: This list has words where letters make sounds they don't often make.

1. again
2. build
3. busy
4. buy
5. door
6. eye
7. floor
8. friend
9. fruit

10. guess
11. gone
12. juice
13. minute
14. school
15. science
16. shoe
17. straight
18. sure
19. sugar
20. though
21. through
22. war
23. warm
24. work
25. word
26. world
27. worse

List 79: Here are some common contractions.

1. aren't
2. can't
3. couldn't
4. didn't
5. don't
6. hasn't
7. he'll
8. he's
9. I'd
10. I'll
11. I'm
12. I've
13. isn't
14. it's
15. let's
16. mustn't
17. she'll
18. she's
19. shouldn't
20. there's
21. there'll
22. they'll
23. they're
24. they've
25. wasn't
26. we'll
27. we're
28. we've
29. weren't
30. what's
31. where's
32. who'd
33. who'll
34. who's
35. won't
36. wouldn't
37. you'd
38. you'll
39. you're
40. you've

List 80: In these words, ed at the end of the word says duh as in called.

1. boiled
2. buzzed
3. called
4. canned
5. charmed
6. crawled
7. filled
8. followed
9. growled
10. helped
11. nagged
12. pinned
13. played
14. robbed
15. rolled
16. sailed

17. slammed
18. sneezed
19. squeezed
20. trailed
21. wheeled

List 81: In this list the ed at the end of the word says tuh as in jerked.

1. asked
2. baked
3. balked
4. cracked
5. crashed
6. dropped
7. fished
8. fixed
9. helped
10. hissed
11. hitched
12. huffed
13. hushed
14. jerked
15. jumped
16. kissed
17. leaped
18. matched
19. mixed
20. parked
21. patched
22. pinched
23. preached
24. puffed
25. scratched
26. skipped
27. smoked
28. snapped
29. sniffed
30. splashed
31. stacked
32. stitched
33. stopped
34. tipped
35. trapped
36. tripped
37. whipped
38. wiped
39. wished

List 82: In this list s says zz as in nose.

1. as
2. because
3. cause
4. cheese
5. choose
6. close
7. closed
8. daisy
9. easy
10. excuse
11. fuse
12. hose
13. is
14. noise
15. nose
16. pause
17. please
18. raise
19. rise
20. rouse
21. tease
22. those
23. use
24. wise

List 83: In this list there is a silent b.

1. comb
2. crumb
3. debt
4. dumb

5. limb
6. plumber
7. thumb

List 84: In this list there is a silent g.

1. gnat
2. gnaw
3. gnome
4. gnu

List 85: In this list there is a silent k.

1. knack
2. knave
3. knee
4. kneel
5. knelt
6. knife
7. knob
8. knock
9. know
10. known

List 86: In this list the w is silent.

1. answer
2. whole
3. wrap
4. wreath
5. wreck
6. wrestle
7. wretch
8. wretched
9. wrist
10. write
11. written
12. wrong
13. wrote

List 87: In this list ought and aught say ought as in bought.

1. bought
2. brought
3. fought
4. ought
5. sought
6. thought
7. caught
8. daughter
9. naught
10. naughty
11. taught

List 88: In this list there is a silent l.

1. balm
2. calm
3. palm
4. calf
5. half
6. folk
7. yolk

List 89: In this list eigh says long a as in eight.

1. eight
2. eighty
3. freight
4. neighbor
5. sleigh
6. weigh
7. weight

List 90: In this list gh says ff as in enough.

1. cough
2. enough
3. laugh
4. rough
5. tough

List 91: In this list ea says short e as in head.

1. bread
2. breakfast
3. breath
4. dead
5. deaf
6. death
7. dread
8. feather
9. heads
10. health
11. heaven
12. heavy
13. instead
14. leather
15. meant
16. ready
17. spread
18. steady
19. sweat
20. sweater
21. thread
22. threat
23. treads
24. wealth

List 92: In some words ea says long a as in steak.

1. break
2. great
3. steak

List 93: In some words ear says ur as in learn.

1. earth
2. heard
3. learn
4. pearl
5. search

List 94: Sometimes the c makes an s sound as in city.

1. ace
2. brace
3. Bruce
4. cell
5. cent
6. chance
7. choice
8. cinch
9. city
10. dance
11. face
12. forced
13. glanced
14. lace
15. mice
16. ounce
17. pace
18. peace
19. place
20. pounce
21. prince
22. race
23. raced
24. rice

25. since
26. slice
27. spaced
28. spruce
29. truce
30. twice
31. voice

List 95: In this list the g says juh as in huge.

1. age
2. bridge
3. budge
4. bulge
5. cage
6. change
7. charge
8. dodge
9. edge
10. forge
11. fringe
12. fudge
13. gem
14. gene
15. George
16. germ
17. gym
18. hedge
19. huge
20. ledge
21. lodge
22. nudge
23. orange
24. page
25. pledge
26. rage
27. sledge
28. sludge
29. smudge
30. stage
31. strange
32. urge
33. wage

List 96: u can say the same sound as the oo in good, or the u in put.

1. bull
2. bush
3. Butch
4. full
5. pull
6. push
7. put

List 97: o can make a short u sound in some words, such as son.

1. above
2. front
3. glove
4. honey
5. love
6. money
7. monks
8. monkey
9. month
10. son
11. sonny
12. ton

List 98: In this list ie or i says ee as in babies.

1. brief
2. chief
3. field
4. fiend

5. fierce
6. niece
7. pierce
8. priest
9. shield
10. shriek
11. shrieked
12. siege
13. thieves
14. yield

List 99: In this list th says th as in gather.

1. bathe
2. breathe
3. loathe
4. seethe
5. soothe
6. these
7. those

Words to Sound and Blend by Syllables, Part 1

The learner who can sound and blend by phonemes the words in the preceding set of lists, and who can read off the lists rapidly without sounding and blending, has gained great skill in reading. However, sometimes this skill is not enough to progress to the next level, that of being able to decode polysyllabic words. A breakthrough in our tutoring technique has been the discovery that concentrated practice in sounding and blending by syllables can raise the learner from about third or fourth grade level on tests of decoding to about the sixth grade level. (After this, vocabulary learning is the determinant of reading level rather than decoding skill per se.)

Sounding and blending by syllables means that you say, separately, each syllable of the word, then put them together to say the word normally. For example: pol ly syl lab ic polysyllabic. It's often useful for the learner to see the word broken into syllables when sounding the syllables separately.

The various tutoring activities, and the hierarchy used in sounding and blending by syllable are exactly analogous to those done in sounding and blending by phoneme. They are:

Activity 0: Tutor says the word, learner repeats it.
Activity 1: Tutor says the individual syllables, learner puts them together to say the word.
Activity 2: Tutor says the individual syllables, then the word after it (i.e. sounds and blends by syllables). The learner then repeats the sounding and blending after the tutor.
Activity 3: The learner sounds and blends the words by syllables.
Activity 4: The learner reads off the words, aiming for fast and fluent and comfortable reading.

For the purpose of this exercise, it is not essential that the syllables are broken where the dictionary would say they should be broken. I've broken the words into syllables in an approximation of the process a good reader uses.

Sounding and blending by syllables puts the finishing touches on the learner's becoming an expert in reading decoding. After this, the learner improves by doing lots of reading, both silently and aloud, of progressively more complex text, and studying vocabulary.

List 100: In this list there are compound words.

1. base ball	baseball
2. bath tub	bathtub
3. belt way	beltway
4. birth day	birthday
5. book case	bookcase
6. class room	classroom
7. foot ball	football
8. grand mom	grandmom
9. her self	herself
10. him self	himself
11. home work	homework
12. in side	inside
13. log jam	logjam
14. mail box	mailbox
15. note book	notebook
16. out side	outside
17. play ground	playground
18. rail road	railroad
19. snow man	snowman
20. Sun day	Sunday
21. sun set	sunset
22. tug boat	tugboat
23. un der stand	understand
24. wash rag	washrag
25. watch dog	watchdog
26. with out	without

List 101: er at the end of the word says ur as in slipper. When there are two consonants before er, the vowel is usually short.

1. bet ter	better
2. big ger	bigger
3. black er	blacker
4. clat ter	clatter
5. din ner	dinner
6. dip per	dipper
7. dress er	dresser
8. drum mer	drummer
9. flick er	flicker
10. ham mer	hammer
11. jug gler	juggler
12. jump er	jumper
13. lad der	ladder
14. let ter	letter
15. or der	order
16. pedd ler	peddler
17. pep per	pepper
18. plat ter	platter
19. print er	printer
20. rub ber	rubber
21. shop per	shopper
22. skip per	skipper

23. slip per	slipper
24. snick er	snicker
25. stop per	stopper
26. sum mer	summer
27. trig ger	trigger
28. tum bler	tumbler
29. up per	upper
30. win ner	winner

List 102: When there is one consonant before er, the vowel is usually long.

1. ca per	caper
2. ca ter	cater
3. cra ter	crater
4. la ser	laser
5. la ter	later
6. pa per	paper
7. Pe ter	Peter
8. ra cer	racer
9. ra ter	rater
10. su per	super
11. vo ter	voter
12. wai ter	waiter
13. wea ver	weaver

List 103: If there are two consonants before ing, the vowel is usually short.

1. bed ding	bedding
2. bet ting	betting
3. brim ming	brimming
4. bud ding	budding
5. buz zing	buzzing
6. can ning	canning
7. dig ging	digging
8. dip ping	dipping
9. drum ming	drumming
10. fib bing	fibbing
11. fit ting	fitting
12. grab bing	grabbing
13. hop ping	hopping
14. hug ging	hugging
15. let ting	letting
16. lick ing	licking
17. nag ging	nagging
18. pad ding	padding
19. pur ring	purring
20. quit ting	quitting
21. rub bing	rubbing
22. run ning	running
23. sag ging	sagging
24. set ting	setting
25. ship ping	shipping

26. shop ping shopping
27. skim ming skimming
28. skip ping skipping
29. sled ding sledding
30. slip ping slipping
31. sob bing sobbing
32. spel ling spelling
33. spin ning spinning
34. spit ting spitting
35. stir ring stirring
36. stun ning stunning
37. tip ping tipping
38. top ping topping
39. trim ming trimming
40. tug ging tugging
41. whip ping whipping

List 104: If there is only one consonant before ing, the vowel is usually long.

1. bla ming blaming
2. cha fing chafing
3. co ping coping
4. fa ding fading
5. gli ding gliding
6. gra ting grating
7. ho ping hoping
8. li ning lining
9. mo ping moping
10. na ming naming
11. pi ping piping
12. ra ting rating
13. ra ving raving
14. sa ving saving
15. sli ding sliding
16. slo ping sloping
17. ta ming taming
18. wi ping wiping

List 105: In this list y says ee as in happy.

1. ba by baby
2. ber ry berry
3. Bet sy Betsy
4. Bob by Bobby
5. bun ny bunny
6. can dy candy
7. car ry carry
8. chil ly chilly
9. co zy cozy
10. dad dy daddy
11. dai ly daily
12. diz zy dizzy
13. ev er y every
14. fair y fairy
15. fam i ly family

16. fif ty fifty
17. fog gy foggy
18. for ty forty
19. fun ny funny
20. fus sy fussy
21. glad ly gladly
22. gra vy gravy
23. han dy handy
24. hap pi ly happily
25. hap py happy
26. hard ly hardly
27. hur ry hurry
28. i vy ivy
29. jur y jury
30. kit ty kitty
31. la dy lady
32. la zy lazy
33. like ly likely
34. Mar y Mary
35. mud dy muddy
36. na vy navy
37. near ly nearly
38. nut ty nutty
39. on ly only
40. par ty party
41. Peg gy Peggy
42. pen ny penny
43. pret ty pretty
44. po ny pony
45. real ly really
46. sad ly sadly
47. sha dy shady
48. six ty sixty
49. sleep i ly sleepily
50. snap py snappy
51. sor ry sorry
52. stor y story
53. stud y study
54. thirst y thirsty
55. thir ty thirty
56. twen ty twenty
57. ug ly ugly
58. wit ty witty
59. ver y very

List 106: In this list ie or i says ee as in babies.

1. ba bies babies
2. be lief belief
3. be lieve believe
4. ber ries berries
5. bod ies bodies
6. brown ie brownie
7. can dies candies
8. car ries carries
9. Char lie Charlie
10. chil li er chillier

11. dir ti est dirtiest
12. fair ies fairies
13. fun ni er funnier
14. fun ni est funniest
15. hap pi er happier
16. hap pi est happiest
17. hur ries hurries
18. la dies ladies
19. par ties parties
20. po nies ponies
21. room i er roomier
22. scur ried scurried
23. sil li est silliest
24. stor ies stories
25. sun ni est sunniest
26. ug li er uglier

List 107: In these words, ed says ed as in seated.

1. act ed acted
2. add ed added
3. bless ed blessed
4. count ed counted
5. fit ted fitted
6. mat ted matted
7. need ed needed
8. pad ded padded
9. pat ted patted
10. point ed pointed
11. rest ed rested
12. rug ged rugged
13. seat ed seated
14. shout ed shouted
15. spot ted spotted
16. wick ed wicked

List 108: In this list th says th as in gather.

1. bath ing bathing
2. both er bother
3. broth er brother
4. fath er father
5. gath er gather
6. lath er lather
7. moth er mother
8. oth er other
9. rath er rather
10. seeth ing seething
11. sooth ing soothing
12. teeth ing teething
13. wheth er whether
14. with er wither

List 109: In this list le says ul as in table.

1. a ble able
2. an gle angle
3. an kle ankle
4. ap ple apple
5. bot tle bottle
6. brit tle brittle
7. can dle candle
8. cat tle cattle
9. crack le crackle
10. crip ple cripple
11. cud dle cuddle
12. dan gle dangle
13. driz zle drizzle
14. ex am ple example
15. fid dle fiddle
16. fiz zle fizzle
17. fum ble fumble
18. grum ble grumble
19. guz zle guzzle
20. han dle handle
21. hob ble hobble
22. hum ble humble
23. jin gle jingle
24. jug gler juggler
25. jun gle jungle
26. ket tle kettle
27. la dle ladle
28. man gle mangle
29. med dle meddle
30. mud dle muddle
31. nee dle needle
32. prat tle prattle
33. puz zle puzzle
34. rid dle riddle
35. sad dle saddle
36. set tle settle
37. sick le sickle
38. sim ple simple
39. sin gle single
40. siz zle sizzle
41. snug gle snuggle
42. sprink le sprinkle
43. ta ble table
44. tack le tackle
45. tan gle tangle
46. ti tle title
47. tur tle turtle
48. un cle uncle

List 110: In this list the c says ss as in city.

1. ad vice advice
2. boun cing bouncing
3. cen ter center
4. ci der cider
5. cig ar cigar

6. cin der   cinder
7. cir cle   circle
8. cit i zen   citizen
9. cit y   city
10. con cert   concert
11. dan ces   dances
12. de cide   decide
13. fa ces   faces
14. fan cy   fancy
15. fenc ing   fencing
16. Fran cis   Francis
17. gro cer ies   groceries
18. i cing   icing
19. la cy   lacy
20. mer cy   mercy
21. min cing   mincing
22. no tice   notice
23. off i cer   officer
24. oun ces   ounces
25. pen cil   pencil
26. sli cing   slicing

List 111: In this list the g says juh as in huge.

1. budg ing   budging
2. cab bage   cabbage
3. charg ing   charging
4. dam age   damage
5. dan ger   danger
6. dig it   digit
7. en gine   engine
8. en gin eer   engineer
9. fid get y   fidgety
10. frin ges   fringes
11. gar bage   garbage
12. gen er al   general
13. gen tle   gentle
14. gin ger   ginger
15. lar ger   larger
16. ma gic   magic
17. man a ger   manage
18. or ange   orange
19. pack age   package
20. pas sage   passage
21. pi geon   pigeon
22. stin gy   stingy
23. ur gent   urgent

List 112: In this list there is a silent t.

1. cast le   castle
2. christ en   christen
3. hast en   hasten
4. jost le   jostle
5. list en   listen
6. nest le   nestle

7. oft en	often
8. rust le	rustle
9. thist le	thistle
10. wrest le	wrestle

List 113: In this list, ph says ff as in phone.

1. al pha bet	alphabet
2. el e phant	elephant
3. graph ics	graphics
4. hyph en	hyphen
5. neph ew	nephew
6. or phan	orphan
7. pam phlet	pamphlet
8. phar ma cy	pharmacy
9. Phil ip	Philip
10. pho net ic	phonetic
11. pho to	photo
12. phras ing	phrasing
13. pro phet	prophet
14. tri umph	triumph
15. tro phy	trophy

List 114: u can say the same sound as the oo in good, or the u in put.

1. aw ful	awful
2. aw ful ly	awfully
3. bash ful	bashful
4. bul let	bullet
5. butch er	butcher
6. care ful	careful
7. cush ion	cushion
8. grate ful	grateful
9. help ful ly	helpfully
10. pud ding	pudding
11. re spect ful	respectful
12. thank ful	thankful
13. truth ful	truthful
14. waste ful	wasteful

List 115: o can make a short u sound in some words, such as son.

1. a bove	above
2. com fort	comfort
3. com pan ies	companies
4. com pare	compare
5. hon ey	honey
6. Mon day	Monday
7. mon ey	money
8. mon key	monkey
9. son ny	sonny
10. won der	wonder

List 116: ou sometimes says short u as in touch.

1. coun try	country
2. cou ple	couple
3. cou sin	cousin
4. cu ri ous	curious
5. dan ger ous	dangerous
6. dou ble	double
7. e nor mous	enormous
8. fa mous	famous
9. gen er ous	generous
10. gor geous	gorgeous
11. jeal ous	jealous
12. joy ous	joyous
13. mar vel ous	marvelous
14. ner vous	nervous
15. se ri ous	serious
16. touch y	touchy
17. trou ble	trouble

List 117: tion and sion say shun as in nation.

1. ac tion	action
2. ad di tion	addition
3. at ten tion	attention
4. de ci sion	decision
5. ed u ca tion	education
6. ex cep tion	exception
7. ex pres sion	expression
8. fic tion	fiction
9. frac tion	fraction
10. man sion	mansion
11. men tion	mention
12. na tion	nation
13. oc ca sion	occasion
14. pen sion	pension
15. per mis sion	permission
16. ques tion	question
17. sta tion	station
18. tel e vi sion	television
19. va ca tion	vacation
20. vi sion	vision

List 118: tious and cious and xious say shus as in vicious, and cial says shul as in social.

1. anx ious	anxious
2. cau tious	cautious
3. de li cious	delicious
4. pre cious	precious
5. sus pi cious	suspicious
6. vi cious	vicious
7. so cial	social
8. spe cial	special

List 119: tur or ture can say chur as in picture.

1. fu ture	future
2. lec ture	lecture
3. mix ture	mixture
4. na tur al	natural
5. na ture	nature
6. pic ture	picture
7. tor ture	torture

List 120: sure can say zhur as in measure.

1. lei sure	leisure
2. mea sure	measure
3. plea sure	pleasure
4. trea sure	treasure

List 121: ive says iv as in active.

1. act ive	active
2. at ten tive	attentive
3. cap tive	captive
4. de tec tive	detective
5. ex pen sive	expensive
6. na tive	native
7. neg a tive	negative
8. pas sive	passive
9. pos i tive	positive
10. pro duc tive	productive

List 122: or at the end of the word says or, or er.

1. act or	actor
2. con duc tor	conductor
3. doc tor	doctor
4. el ev a tor	elevator
5. fa vor	favor
6. fla vor	flavor
7. in struc tor	instructor
8. jan i tor	janitor
9. mo tor	motor
10. ra zor	razor
11. sai lor	sailor
12. trai tor	traitor
13. vis i tor	visitor

List 123: Here are words that include some and come.

1. be come	become
2. com ing	coming
3. hand some	handsome
4. in come	income
5. some bod y	somebody

6. some how somehow
7. some one someone
8. some thing something
9. some times sometimes
10. tire some tiresome
11. wel come welcome

List 124: Words that include ance and ence.

1. ap pear ance appearance
2. com pli ance compliance
3. con fi dence confidence
4. im por tance importance
5. in flu ence influence
6. per form ance performance
7. pref er ence preference
8. prov i dence providence
9. res i dence residence
10. sen tence sentence

List 125: Words ending with ment.

1. ce ment cement
2. ex cite ment excitement
3. fer ment ferment
4. gov ern ment government
5. mo ment moment
6. move ment movement
7. re quire ment requirement

List 126: More good words to know.

1. ad mit admit
2. al li ga tor alligator
3. al low allow
4. a larm alarm
5. a maze amaze
6. a mount amount
7. an i mal animal
8. au tumn autumn
9. a wake awake
10. be came became
11. be gan began
12. be have behave
13. be ing being
14. bot tom bottom
15. chick en chicken
16. col lect collect
17. cred it credit
18. cour age courage
19. cow ard coward
20. dur ing during
21. en er gy energy
22. en joy enjoy
23. ex pect expect

24. ex plain	explain
25. fan ta sy	fantasy
26. fin ish	finish
27. for ev er	forever
28. friend ship	friendship
29. for ti tude	fortitude
30. gar den	garden
31. in dex	index
32. les son	lesson
33. loy al	loyal
34. mit ten	mitten
35. mod el	model
36. no thing	nothing
37. o bey	obey
38. per fect	perfect
39. plas tic	plastic
40. plea sant	pleasant
41. plur al	plural
42. pos si ble	possible
43. pre tend	pretend
44. pub lic	public
45. pump kin	pumpkin
46. re joice	rejoice
47. re turn	return
48. six teen	sixteen
49. tel e phone	telephone
50. thou sand	thousand
51. to mor row	tomorrow
52. tow ard	toward
53. tow er	tower
54. u ni ted	united
55. un til	until
56. vi o lence	violence
57. vis it	visit
58. wor ry	worry
59. yes ter day	yesterday

Words to Sound and Blend by Syllables, Part 2

By this stage, the learner has had a good bit of experience with sounding and blending by syllables. Some learners will not need any more such drill. But for some, getting some more practice in sounding and blending by syllables is the magic ingredient to make their reading really fluent.

By this stage, many learners can take on 100 new words to sound and blend by syllables each day, plus review words from previous days, in a session under 30 minutes. Thus although there are many words in the lists to follow, the time expenditure represented is not burdensome. If it is burdensome and tedious, the tutor and learner probably need to work toward more fluency in earlier tasks.

List 127

1. a bil i ty — ability
2. a bu sive — abusive
3. a ca de my — academy
4. a da mant — adamant
5. an gri er — angrier
6. an gri ly — angrily
7. a pol o gy — apology
8. a rou sal — arousal
9. ar ti cle — article
10. bat ter y — battery
11. ben e fit — benefit
12. cap i tol — capitol
13. cur i ous — curious
14. de ny ing — denying
15. de vel op — develop
16. ear li er — earlier
17. ed u cate — educate
18. e lec ted — elected
19. e mo tion — emotion
20. em path y — empathy
21. eth i cal — ethical
22. e ven ing — evening
23. ex act ly — exactly
24. ex am ine — examine
25. ex am ple — example
26. ex cit ed — excited
27. ex er ted — exerted
28. fan ta sy — fantasy
29. fed er al — federal
30. gen er al — general
31. il le gal — illegal
32. im ag er y — imagery
33. im i tate — imitate
34. im mor al — immoral
35. log i cal — logical
36. loy al ty — loyalty
37. mar i tal — marital
38. nu cle ar — nuclear
39. ob vi ous — obvious
40. op er ate — operate
41. o pin ion — opinion
42. o ver all — overall
43. par a dox — paradox
44. pen al ty — penalty
45. pri va cy — privacy
46. re cy cle — recycle
47. reg u lar — regular
48. re la ted — related
49. ri gid ly — rigidly
50. sar casm — sarcasm
51. so ci e ty — society
52. ther a py — therapy
53. to tal ly — totally
54. ur gen cy — urgency
55. u su al ly — usually
56. var i ous — various
57. vic tor y — victory
58. vi o lent — violent
59. vi si ble — visible
60. vi vid ly — vividly
61. war ri or — warrior
62. ab nor mal — abnormal
63. a ca dem ic — academic
64. ac ci dent — accident
65. ac cu rate — accurate
66. ac tiv i ty — activity

67. ac tu al ly	actually
68. ad dic ted	addicted
69. ad di tion	addition
70. ad mir ers	admirers
71. ad vis ing	advising
72. af fec ted	affected
73. a gi ta ted	agitated
74. al ler gic	allergic
75. al low ing	allowing
76. ap pen dix	appendix
77. ap pro val	approval
78. ar gu ment	argument
79. ar rang es	arranges
80. ar rest ed	arrested
81. ar riv ing	arriving
82. ar ti cles	articles
83. as sem ble	assemble
84. ath let ic	athletic
85. at ti tude	attitude
86. au di ence	audience
87. a void ing	avoiding
88. a wak ened	awakened
89. aw ful ize	awfulize
90. bar ri ers	barriers
91. be com ing	becoming
92. be hav ing	behaving
93. be hav ior	behavior
94. ben e fits	benefits
95. broc co li	broccoli
96. ca pa ci ty	capacity
97. ca te gor y	category
98. chem i cal	chemical
99. cin na mon	cinnamon
100. ci ti zens	citizens

List 128

1. ci vil i ty	civility
2. cle ver ly	cleverly
3. clin i cal	clinical
4. col on ies	colonies
5. con si der	consider
6. con tin ue	continue
7. cour te sy	courtesy
8. cow ard ly	cowardly
9. co work er	coworker
10. cre a tion	creation
11. cre a tive	creative
12. crim i nal	criminal
13. crit i cal	critical
14. de ba ting	debating
15. de ci sion	decision
16. def i cits	deficits
17. def in ite	definite
18. del i cate	delicate
19. de tec tor	detector
20. de vel ops	develops
21. de vo ting	devoting
22. di rec ted	directed
23. di rect ly	directly
24. di rec tor	director
25. dis a bled	disabled
26. dis a gree	disagree
27. dis as ter	disaster
28. dis cov er	discover
29. dis eas es	diseases
30. dis or der	disorder
31. di vid ing	dividing

32. dra mat ic dramatic
33. ed u cat ed educated
34. e lec tric electric
35. el i gi ble eligible
36. e mo tions emotions
37. en er gize energize
38. en forc es enforces
39. en tire ly entirely
40. en ti tled entitled
41. ep i sodes episodes
42. e ven ings evenings
43. ev er y day everyday
44. ev er y one everyone
45. ev i dence evidence
46. ex am ined examined
47. ex am ines examines
48. ex am ples examples
49. ex cit ing exciting
50. ex cus ing excusing
51. ex e cut ed executed
52. ex er cise exercise
53. ex pert ly expertly
54. ex po sure exposure
55. ex ter nal external
56. ex tort ed extorted
57. fa mil i ar familiar
58. fes ti val festival
59. for ci bly forcibly
60. gen er ate generate
61. gen er ous generous
62. gov er nor governor
63. hap pi est happiest
64. hol i days holidays
65. hom i cide homicide
66. hor ri ble horrible
67. hos pi tal hospital
68. hu man i ty humanity
69. hu mil i ty humility
70. hu mor ous humorous
71. i den ti fy identify
72. ig nor ant ignorant
73. ig nor ing ignoring
74. i ma gin al imaginal
75. i ma gined imagined
76. im ply ing implying
77. im po lite impolite
78. in ci dent incident
79. in di cate indicate
80. in ex pert inexpert
81. in ju ries injuries
82. in jur ing injuring
83. in san i ty insanity
84. in sul ted insulted
85. in ter act interact
86. in ter est interest
87. in ter nal internal
88. in ter net internet
89. in vest ed invested
90. jea lous y jealousy
91. jo king ly jokingly
92. joy ous ly joyously
93. ju di cial judicial
94. la bor ers laborers
95. lec tur er lecturer
96. le vel ing leveling
97. li ter a cy literacy
98. low er ing lowering
99. mag a zine magazine

100. ma te ri al material

List 129

1. me di a tor mediator
2. med i cine medicine
3. mem o rize memorize
4. men tal ly mentally
5. mil i tar y military
6. mne mon ic mnemonic
7. mod el ing modeling
8. mor al i ty morality
9. mo ti vate motivate
10. mus cu lar muscular
11. nar row ly narrowly
12. neg a tive negative
13. oc ca sion occasion
14. of fen ded offended
15. of fer ing offering
16. of fi cers officers
17. o lym pics olympics
18. o pin ions opinions
19. op po nent opponent
20. op po site opposite
21. or gan ize organize
22. or i ent ed oriented
23. par a noi a paranoia
24. par a noid paranoid
25. pen ta gon pentagon
26. per son al personal
27. phys i cal physical
28. po lite ly politely
29. po si tion position
30. pos i tive positive
31. pow er ful powerful
32. pres tige prestige
33. pre vi ous previous
34. pri or i ty priority
35. prob ab ly probably
36. pro duc es produces
37. prop er ty property
38. proph e cy prophecy
39. pu ni tive punitive
40. pur pos es purposes
41. pur su ing pursuing
42. ran dom ly randomly
43. ra tion al rational
44. re act ing reacting
45. re ac tion reaction
46. re al ized realized
47. re al iz es realizes
48. re cent ly recently
49. re cord ed recorded
50. re cord er recorder
51. re cov ers recovers
52. re cy cled recycled
53. re fu sals refusals
54. re fu sing refusing
55. re gar ded regarded
56. re ject ed rejected
57. re la ting relating
58. re la tion relation
59. rel a tive relative
60. re lax ing relaxing
61. rel e vant relevant
62. re li a ble reliable
63. re li gion religion
64. re mem ber remember

65. re mind ed reminded
66. re mind er reminder
67. re peate ed repeated
68. re port ed reported
69. re sist ed resisted
70. re sult ed resulted
71. re ward ed rewarded
72. rid i cule ridicule
73. ri gid i ty rigidity
74. ro man tic romantic
75. sad is tic sadistic
76. san i tar y sanitary
77. se cret ly secretly
78. se cur i ty security
79. se lect ed selected
80. sep ar ate separate
81. se vere ly severely
82. so lu tion solution
83. spe cif ic specific
84. stim u lus stimulus
85. strat e gy strategy
86. stud y ing studying
87. sur gi cal surgical
88. sur vi val survival
89. sym pa thy sympathy
90. ten den cy tendency
91. ter ri ble terrible
92. ter ri bly terribly
93. tol er ate tolerate
94. to mor row tomorrow
95. to tal i ty totality
96. trav el er traveler
97. tu tor ing tutoring
98. u ni verse universe
99. un just ly unjustly
100. un kind ly unkindly

List 130

1. un want ed unwanted
2. va ca tion vacation
3. ver bal ly verbally
4. vi o lence violence
5. work a ble workable
6. a bil i ties abilities
7. ac a dem ics academics
8. ac a dem ies academies
9. ac cept ing accepting
10. ac cor ding according
11. a chiev ing achieving
12. ac tiv ists activists
13. ad mir a ble admirable
14. a dult hood adulthood
15. ad van tage advantage
16. ad ver sar y adversary
17. af fec tion affection
18. af ter noon afternoon
19. af ter ward afterward
20. a gree ment agreement
21. al ter nate alternate
22. am big u ous ambiguous
23. am bi tious ambitious
24. a muse ment amusement
25. an ces tors ancestors
26. an swer ing answering
27. a part ment apartment
28. a pol o gize apologize
29. ap peal ing appealing

30. ap prov ing approving
31. ar gu ments arguments
32. as ser tion assertion
33. as ser tive assertive
34. as sis tant assistant
35. as stron o my astronomy
36. at tack ers attackers
37. at tack ing attacking
38. at ten tion attention
39. at ten tive attentive
40. at ti tudes attitudes
41. at trac ted attracted
42. au di o tape audiotape
43. au thor i ty authority
44. au to mat ic automatic
45. a vail a ble available
46. a void ance avoidance
47. beau ti ful beautiful
48. be ha viors behaviors
49. boss i ness bossiness
50. bril li ant brilliant
51. cal cu late calculate
52. can di date candidate
53. cap tiv i ty captivity
54. care ful ly carefully
55. ca thar sis catharsis
56. cel e brate celebrate
57. cen tu ries centuries
58. cer tain ly certainly
59. char ac ter character
60. char i ties charities
61. chem i cals chemicals
62. chem is try chemistry
63. cho co late chocolate
64. cir cui try circuitry
65. civ i lized civilized
66. cog ni tive cognitive
67. com mit ted committed
68. com pan ies companies
69. com pe tent competent
70. com pe ting competing
71. con ceit ed conceited
72. con di tion condition
73. con du cive conducive
74. con duc ted conducted
75. con fi dent confident
76. con fu sing confusing
77. con fu sion confusion
78. con nec ted connected
79. con sid ers considers
80. con so ling consoling
81. con tin ued continued
82. con tin ues continues
83. co op er ate cooperate
84. cop y right copyright
85. cor rect ly correctly
86. co work ers coworkers
87. crim i nals criminals
88. crit i cism criticism
89. crit i cize criticize
90. cul ti vate cultivate
91. cu ri os i ty curiosity
92. cur rent ly currently
93. cus tom ers customers
94. dan ger ous dangerous
95. de ci sions decisions
96. de creas es decreases
97. de feat ing defeating

98. de fend ing	defending
99. de fen sive	defensive
100. de light ed	delighted

List 131

1. de mean ing	demeaning
2. de pend ing	depending
3. de sir a ble	desirable
4. de ten tion	detention
5. de ter mine	determine
6. de vel oped	developed
7. dif fer ent	different
8. dif fer ing	differing
9. dif fi cult	difficult
10. di rec tion	direction
11. di rect ive	directive
12. di rect ors	directors
13. dis a grees	disagrees
14. dis ap pear	disappear
15. dis cov er y	discovery
16. dis o beyed	disobeyed
17. di vorc ing	divorcing
18. doc u ments	documents
19. dom i nance	dominance
20. dom i na ted	dominated
21. ear nest ly	earnestly
22. ed u ca tion	education
23. ef fect ive	effective
24. e lim i nate	eliminate
25. em bar rass	embarrass
26. e mer gen cy	emergency
27. e mo tion al	emotional
28. em ploy ees	employees
29. en count er	encounter
30. en cour age	encourage
31. end less ly	endlessly
32. en dur ance	endurance
33. en er gized	energized
34. en for cing	enforcing
35. en joy ment	enjoyment
36. en ter tain	entertain
37. en vi sions	envisions
38. e qua tions	equations
39. e quip ment	equipment
40. es ti ma ted	estimated
41. e ter nal ly	eternally
42. eth i cal ly	ethically
43. ex cel lent	excellent
44. ex cep tion	exception
45. ex chang es	exchanges
46. ex er cis es	exercises
47. ex haus ted	exhausted
48. ex is tence	existence
49. ex pect ing	expecting
50. ex pen sive	expensive
51. ex plet ive	expletive
52. ex plor ing	exploring
53. ex po sures	exposures
54. ex pressed	expressed
55. ex tor tion	extortion
56. ex treme ly	extremely
57. fan ta sies	fantasies
58. fic tion al	fictional
59. fin ish ing	finishing
60. fol low ers	followers
61. fol low ing	following
62. for giv ing	forgiving

63. fort i tude	fortitude
64. gen er al ly	generally
65. gen u ine ly	genuinely
66. grad u al ly	gradually
67. grat i tude	gratitude
68. guar an tee	guarantee
69. hap pen ing	happening
70. hap pi ness	happiness
71. harm ful ly	harmfully
72. hi er arch y	hierarchy
73. hom i cides	homicides
74. hope ful ly	hopefully
75. hos pi tals	hospitals
76. hos til i ty	hostility
77. hu man i ty	humanity
78. hu mil i ate	humiliate
79. il le gal ly	illegally
80. i mag i nar y	imaginary
81. i mag i ning	imagining
82. im bal ance	imbalance
83. im i tat ing	imitating
84. im me di ate	immediate
85. im mense ly	immensely
86. im pa tient	impatient
87. im per fect	imperfect
88. im por tant	important
89. im prov ing	improving
90. in ci dents	incidents
91. in clu ding	including
92. in cor rect	incorrect
93. in creas es	increases
94. in cur a ble	incurable
95. in di ca tor	indicator
96. in dig nant	indignant
97. in flu ence	influence
98. in stant ly	instantly
99. in sult ing	insulting
100. in tense ly	intensely

List 132

1. in tens i ty	intensity
2. in ter fere	interfere
3. in ter rupt	interrupt
4. in ter vene	intervene
5. in vent ing	inventing
6. in ven tion	invention
7. in volv ing	involving
8. ir rit a ble	irritable
9. ir rit at ed	irritated
10. ir rit ates	irritates
11. just i fied	justified
12. lan guag es	languages
13. late com er	latecomer
14. li ber at ed	liberated
15. li brar i an	librarian
16. lin ger ing	lingering
17. list en ers	listeners
18. lit er al ly	literally
19. lo ca tions	locations
20. log i cal ly	logically
21. mag i cal ly	magically
22. mar riag es	marriages
23. mas ter ing	mastering
24. mea sur ing	measuring
25. me di a tion	mediation
26. meth a done	methadone
27. mil len i a	millennia

28. mis er a ble	miserable
29. mis guid ed	misguided
30. mo ti va ted	motivated
31. mu si cians	musicians
32. na tu ral ly	naturally
33. nec es sar y	necessary
34. nec es si ty	necessity
35. neg lec ted	neglected
36. ne go ti ate	negotiate
37. news pa per	newspaper
38. ob nox ious	obnoxious
39. ob tain ing	obtaining
40. ob vi ous ly	obviously
41. oc ca sions	occasions
42. oc cur ring	occurring
43. of fi cials	officials
44. op er a tion	operation
45. op po nents	opponents
46. or gan ized	organized
47. or gan iz es	organizes
48. oth er wise	otherwise
49. o ver joyed	overjoyed
50. o ver night	overnight
51. par a graph	paragraph
52. par a lyzed	paralyzed
53. pa tient ly	patiently
54. pe di at ric	pediatric
55. pen al ties	penalties
56. per fect ly	perfectly
57. per man ent	permanent
58. per mit ted	permitted
59. per sua ded	persuaded
60. poi son ous	poisonous
61. po lice men	policemen
62. po li ti cal	political
63. pon der ing	pondering
64. pow er less	powerless
65. prac tic es	practices
66. pre ce dent	precedent
67. pred at ors	predators
68. pres ent ed	presented
69. pres i dent	president
70. pre vent ed	prevented
71. prim i tive	primitive
72. prin ci pal	principal
73. prin ci ple	principle
74. pri vate ly	privately
75. pro ce dure	procedure
76. pro duc ing	producing
77. pro fes sor	professor
78. prom i nent	prominent
79. prom is ing	promising
80. pro mo ting	promoting
81. pro pos ing	proposing
82. pro tec ted	protected
83. pro vid ing	providing
84. pro vok ing	provoking
85. pun ish ing	punishing
86. pur pose ly	purposely
87. real is tic	realistic
88. re al iz ing	realizing
89. rea son ing	reasoning
90. re call ing	recalling
91. re cep tive	receptive
92. rec og nize	recognize
93. rec om mend	recommend
94. re cord ing	recording
95. re cur rent	recurrent

96. re fer ring referring
97. re fill ing refilling
98. re flec ted reflected
99. re gain ing regaining
100. re gard ing regarding

List 133

1. reg u lar ly regularly
2. re hear sal rehearsal
3. re in force reinforce
4. re jec tion rejection
5. re la tions relations
6. rel a tives relatives
7. re leas ing releasing
8. re mind ing reminding
9. re peat ing repeating
10. re sem bles resembles
11. re sent ful resentful
12. res i dents residents
13. re sist ing resisting
14. re sourc es resources
15. re spect ed respected
16. re spond ed responded
17. re spons es responses
18. re sult ing resulting
19. re tell ing retelling
20. re turn ing returning
21. re view ing reviewing
22. re ward ing rewarding
23. sar cas tic sarcastic
24. sci en tist scientist
25. seem ing ly seemingly
26. sen si tive sensitive
27. sen ten ces sentences
28. sep ar at ed separated
29. Sep tem ber September
30. se ri ous ly seriously
31. shov el ing shoveling
32. sig ni fies signifies
33. sim i lar ly similarly
34. sin cere ly sincerely
35. sit u a tion situation
36. so cial ist socialist
37. so cial ize socialize
38. so lu tions solutions
39. stim u late stimulate
40. suc ceed ed succeeded
41. suf fer ing suffering
42. sug gest ed suggested
43. sum mar ize summarize
44. su per vise supervise
45. sup por ted supported
46. sur ren der surrender
47. tem por ar y temporary
48. ter ri tor y territory
49. ter ror ism terrorism
50. ter ror ist terrorist
51. ter ror ize terrorize
52. ther a pist therapist
53. tol er ance tolerance
54. tol er at ed tolerated
55. tri bal ism tribalism
56. un in vi ted uninvited
57. va ca tions vacations
58. var i a bles variables
59. vir tu al ly virtually
60. vis u al ize visualize

61. wa ter fall	waterfall
62. will ing ly	willingly
63. won der ful	wonderful
64. won der ing	wondering
65. ab so lute ly	absolutely
66. ac cept a ble	acceptable
67. ac ci dent al	accidental
68. ac com plish	accomplish
69. ac cu rate ly	accurately
70. ac cus tomed	accustomed
71. ac tiv i ties	activities
72. ad di tion al	additional
73. ad mir a tion	admiration
74. ad o les ccnt	adolescent
75. ad ren a line	adrenaline
76. ad van tag es	advantages
77. ad vo cat ing	advocating
78. af ter wards	afterwards
79. ag gra vat ed	aggravated
80. ag gres sion	aggression
81. ag gres sive	aggressive
82. al le giance	allegiance
83. al to geth er	altogether
84. a part ments	apartments
85. a pol o giz es	apologizes
86. ap pear ance	appearance
87. ap pen di ces	appendices
88. ap pre ci ate	appreciate
89. ap proach es	approaches
90. at trac tion	attraction
91. at trac tive	attractive
92. bar gain ing	bargaining
93. be fore hand	beforehand
94. be ha vior al	behavioral
95. ben e fi cial	beneficial
96. cal cu la ted	calculated
97. can di dates	candidates
98. care less ly	carelessly
99. care ta kers	caretakers
100. cat e gor ies	categories

List 134

1. chal leng es	challenges
2. char ac ters	characters
3. cheer ful ly	cheerfully
4. com par i son	comparison
5. com pas sion	compassion
6. com pat i ble	compatible
7. com pet ence	competence
8. com pli ment	compliment
9. com pro mise	compromise
10. con cern ing	concerning
11. con clu sion	conclusion
12. con crete ly	concretely
13. con di tions	conditions
14. con fi dence	confidence
15. con firm ing	confirming
16. con nec tion	connection
17. con quer ing	conquering
18. con stant ly	constantly
19. con sult ing	consulting
20. con tin u ing	continuing
21. con tort ing	contorting
22. con tra dict	contradict
23. con tri bute	contribute
24. con verse ly	conversely
25. con vic tion	conviction

26. cor rec tive corrective
27. cour age ous courageous
28. cre a tiv i ty creativity
29. crit i cisms criticisms
30. crit i cized criticized
31. crit i ciz es criticizes
32. cul ti vates cultivates
33. def in ite ly definitely
34. def in i tion definition
35. de part ment department
36. de pend a ble dependable
37. de press ing depressing
38. de pres sion depression
39. de scri bing describing
40. de stroy ing destroying
41. de ter mined determined
42. de ter mines determines
43. de vas ta ted devastated
44. de vel op ing developing
45. dif fer ence difference
46. di rec tions directions
47. dis a bil i ty disability
48. dis ap prove disapprove
49. dis ci pline discipline
50. dis com fort discomfort
51. dis cour age discourage
52. dis cov ered discovered
53. dis cus sion discussion
54. dis tort ing distorting
55. dis trac ted distracted
56. dom i na ting dominating
57. el e ment ar y elementary
58. em pa thi zes empathizes
59. em pha sized emphasized
60. en cour aged encouraged
61. en ter tains entertains
62. en thu si asm enthusiasm
63. es pe cial ly especially
64. e vent u al ly eventually
65. ex chang ing exchanging
66. ex cite ment excitement
67. ex pe ri ence experience
68. ex per i ment experiment
69. ex plain ing explaining
70. ex pres sion expression
71. fas cin a ted fascinated
72. fin ger tips fingertips
73. force ful ly forcefully
74. for get ting forgetting
75. fre quent ly frequently
76. frus tra ted frustrated
77. gath er ings gatherings
78. gen er al ize generalize
79. gen er os i ty generosity
80. gov ern ment government
81. gym nas tics gymnastics
82. hy po the sis hypothesis
83. i den ti fied identified
84. il lus trate illustrate
85. im pa tience impatience
86. im por tance importance
87. im pos si ble impossible
88. in creas ing increasing
89. in di vid u al individual
90. in flu enced influenced
91. in flu en ces influences
92. in hib i tion inhibition
93. in struc tor instructor

94. in su la tion	insulation
95. in ter est ed	interested
96. in ter fered	interfered
97. in ter feres	interferes
98. in ter rupts	interrupts
99. in ter venes	intervenes
100. in ter views	interviews

List 135

1. in tim i date	intimidate
2. in tro duced	introduced
3. in ven tions	inventions
4. in vit a tion	invitation
5. ir rit a ting	irritating
6. ir rit a tion	irritation
7. lab or a tor y	laboratory
8. lead er ship	leadership
9. le gal iz ing	legalizing
10. like li hood	likelihood
11. med i ta tion	meditation
12. med i ta tive	meditative
13. men tion ing	mentioning
14. mis for tune	misfortune
15. mis treat ed	mistreated
16. mo tiv a tion	motivation
17. nav i ga ting	navigating
18. neg a tive ly	negatively
19. neg a tiv i ty	negativity
20. non vi o lent	nonviolent
21. op er a tions	operations
22. or gan iz ing	organizing
23. out land ish	outlandish
24. o ver ri ding	overriding
25. o ver weight	overweight
26. par tic u lar	particular
27. pe di at rics	pediatrics
28. per mis sion	permission
29. per sua ding	persuading
30. per sua sion	persuasion
31. per sua sive	persuasive
32. phys i cal ly	physically
33. plan et hood	planethood
34. pleas ant ly	pleasantly
35. po lite ness	politeness
36. post pon ing	postponing
37. prac tic ing	practicing
38. pre dic ting	predicting
39. pre dic tion	prediction
40. pre dic tors	predictors
41. pre dis pose	predispose
42. pref er a ble	preferable
43. pre tend ing	pretending
44. pre ven tion	prevention
45. pre vi ous ly	previously
46. prin ci ples	principles
47. priv i leg es	privileges
48. pro duc tive	productive
49. proph e cies	prophecies
50. pro por tion	proportion
51. pros per i ty	prosperity
52. pro tec ting	protecting
53. pro tec tion	protection
54. pro tec tive	protective
55. psy chi a try	psychiatry
56. psy chol o gy	psychology
57. pub lish ing	publishing
58. pun ish ment	punishment

59. ran dom ized randomized
60. ra tion al ly rationally
61. rea son a ble reasonable
62. rea son a bly reasonably
63. re as signed reassigned
64. re cog nized recognized
65. rec om mends recommends
66. re cord ings recordings
67. re count ing recounting
68. re cov er ing recovering
69. re cruit ing recruiting
70. re cy cla ble recyclable
71. re flec ting reflecting
72. re flec tion reflection
73. re gard less regardless
74. re group ing regrouping
75. reg u la tion regulation
76. re hears als rehearsals
77. re hears ing rehearsing
78. re in forced reinforced
79. re in for cer reinforcer
80. re in for ces reinforces
81. re lax a tion relaxation
82. re mod el ing remodeling
83. re morse ful remorseful
84. re peat ed ly repeatedly
85. rep er toire repertoire
86. re pet i tive repetitive
87. rep ri mands reprimands
88. rep u ta tion reputation
89. re quest ing requesting
90. re sent ment resentment
91. res o lu tion resolution
92. re spond ing responding
93. rest au rant restaurant
94. re tire ment retirement
95. re ver si ble reversible
96. rev o lu tion revolution
97. rid ic u lous ridiculous
98. sac ri fi ces sacrifices
99. sat is fy ing satisfying
100. sau er kraut sauerkraut

List 136

1. sci en tif ic scientific
2. sci en tists scientists
3. sen sa tions sensations
4. sep ar ate ly separately
5. sep ar a tion separation
6. sit u a tions situations
7. skill ful ly skillfully
8. smol der ing smoldering
9. sta tis tics statistics
10. stim u la ted stimulated
11. strat e gies strategies
12. sub sti tute substitute
13. suc ceed ing succeeding
14. suc cess ful successful
15. sug ges ting suggesting
16. sug ges tion suggestion
17. sum mar ized summarized
18. su per vi sor supervisor
19. sup port ing supporting
20. su port ive supportive
21. sur pris ing surprising
22. sus pi cious suspicious
23. tech nol o gy technology

24. ten der ness tenderness
25. thor ough ly thoroughly
26. tol er a ting tolerating
27. tour na ment tournament
28. tre men dous tremendous
29. trig ger ing triggering
30. un der lined underlined
31. un der stand understand
32. un em ployed unemployed
33. un ex ci ting unexciting
34. un fam il i ar unfamiliar
35. un friend ly unfriendly
36. un grate ful ungrateful
37. un pleas ant unplcasant
38. un pun ished unpunished
39. un san i tar y unsanitary
40. use ful ness usefulness
41. veg e ta bles vegetables
42. veg e tar i an vegetarian
43. vic tim ized victimized
44. vig or ous ly vigorously
45. vo cab u lar y vocabulary
46. with draw al withdrawal
47. worth i ness worthiness
48. a chieve ment achievement
49. ac know ledge acknowledge
50. ad o les cents adolescents
51. al ter na tive alternative
52. a pol o giz ing apologizing
53. ap point ment appointment
54. ap pre ci at ed appreciated
55. ap proach ing approaching
56. ap pro pri ate appropriate
57. as sert ive ly assertively
58. as sess ments assessments
59. au thor i ties authorities
60. bi o feed back biofeedback
61. blame worth y blameworthy
62. cal cu la ting calculating
63. cal cu la tion calculation
64. cel e bra ting celebrating
65. cel e bra tion celebration
66. chal leng ing challenging
67. char is mat ic charismatic
68. com fort a ble comfortable
69. com mun i cate communicate
70. com mun i ties communities
71. com pet en ces competences
72. com pet ent ly competently
73. com pet i tion competition
74. com pet i tive competitive
75. com pli ca ted complicated
76. com pro mi ses compromises
77. con cen trate concentrate
78. con clu sions conclusions
79. con scious ly consciously
80. con se quence consequence
81. con sid er ing considering
82. con tin u al ly continually
83. con trib u ted contributed
84. con vic tions convictions
85. co op er at ing cooperating
86. co op er a tion cooperation
87. co op er a tive cooperative
88. crit i ci zing criticizing
89. dan ger ous ly dangerously
90. dec lar a tion declaration
91. de lin quen cy delinquency

92. dem on strate demonstrate
93. de part ments departments
94. de riv a tives derivatives
95. des per ate ly desperately
96. de struc tive destructive
97. dev as ta ting devastating
98. de vel op ment development
99. dif fer en ces differences
100. dif fer ent ly differently

List 137

1. dis ap prov al disapproval
2. dis ap proves disapproves
3. dis cov er ies discoveries
4. dis cov er ing discovering
5. dis par ag ing disparaging
6. dis tinc tion distinction
7. dis tor tions distortions
8. dis trac ting distracting
9. dis tur bance disturbance
10. doc u ment ar y documentary
11. dras ti cal ly drastically
12. ef fec tive ly effectively
13. ef fi cient ly efficiently
14. em bar assed embarrassed
15. em bar ass es embarrasses
16. e mo tion al ly emotionally
17. em pa thi zing empathizing
18. en count ered encountered
19. en force ment enforcement
20. en gin eer ing engineering
21. en ter tained entertained
22. en ti tle ment entitlement
23. en vi ron ment environment
24. es sen tial ly essentially
25. ex as per at ed exasperated
26. ex pec ta tion expectation
27. ex pe ri enced experienced
28. ex pe ri en ces experiences
29. ex per i ments experiments
30. ex plan a tion explanation
31. ex pres sions expressions
32. fa mil i ar i ty familiarity
33. fas cin a ting fascinating
34. fas cin a tion fascination
35. fer o cious ly ferociously
36. flex i bil i ty flexibility
37. for tu nate ly fortunately
38. frus tra ting frustrating
39. frus tra tion frustration
40. func tion ing functioning
41. fur ther more furthermore
42. gov ern ments governments
43. hand i capped handicapped
44. hand wri ting handwriting
45. il lus trates illustrates
46. i mag i na tion imagination
47. im med i ate ly immediately
48. im pa tient ly impatiently
49. im pli ca tion implication
50. im pres sions impressions
51. im pul sive ly impulsively
52. in com pe tent incompetent
53. in cor por ate incorporate
54. in di vid u als individuals
55. in flu enc ing influencing
56. in form a tion information

57. in stru ments instruments
58. in tel li gent intelligent
59. in ter ac tion interaction
60. in ter change interchange
61. in ter est ing interesting
62. in ter rupt er interrupter
63. in ter viewed interviewed
64. in tim i da ted intimidated
65. key board ing keyboarding
66. leg is la tive legislative
67. main ten ance maintenance
68. man u fac ture manufacture
69. math e mat ics mathematics
70. mer ci less ly mercilessly
71. mis spell ing misspelling
72. mis trust ing mistrusting
73. nec es sar i ly necessarily
74. ne go ti a ting negotiating
75. ne go ti a tion negotiation
76. non pu ni tive nonpunitive
77. non vi o lence nonviolence
78. ob nox ious ly obnoxiously
79. ob scen i ties obscenities
80. ob ser va tion observation
81. op por tu ni ty opportunity
82. o ri ent a tion orientation
83. par a phras es paraphrases
84. par ti ci pate participate
85. per form ance performance
86. per man ent ly permanently
87. per son al i ty personality
88. per spec tive perspective
89. phil o soph er philosopher
90. pho to graphs photographs
91. pre his tor ic prehistoric
92. pre oc cu pied preoccupied
93. pro fan i ties profanities
94. pro gres sive progressive
95. pro vo ca tion provocation
96. pun ish ments punishments
97. quar ter back quarterback
98. re ap pear ing reappearing
99. re cip ro cate reciprocate
100. re cip ro ci ty reciprocity

List 138

1. re com mend ed recommended
2. re pe ti tions repetitions
3. re search ers researchers
4. re search ing researching
5. re so lu tions resolutions
6. re spon si ble responsible
7. rest au rants restaurants
8. re strict ing restricting
9. screw driv er screwdriver
10. seg re ga tion segregation
11. self ish ness selfishness
12. sig ni fi cant significant
13. stim u la ting stimulating
14. stim u la tion stimulation
15. sub cul tures subcultures
16. sub stan tive substantive
17. sub sti tutes substitutes
18. sug ges tions suggestions
19. sum mar iz ing summarizing
20. su per fi cial superficial
21. sym pa thet ic sympathetic
22. tem per a ture temperature
23. tem por ar i ly temporarily
24. ther mom e ter thermometer

25. threat en ing threatening
26. trust worth y trustworthy
27. un a vail a ble unavailable
28. un con scious unconscious
29. un der stands understands
30. un de sir a ble undesirable
31. un dis tort ed undistorted
32. un hap pi ness unhappiness
33. un im port tant unimportant
34. in in hib it ed uninhibited
35. un nec es sar y unnecessary
36. vic tim i zing victimizing
37. vol un teered volunteered
38. will ing ness willingness
39. with draw ing withdrawing
40. ac ci dent al ly accidentally
41. ac com plished accomplished
42. ac com plish es accomplishes
43. af fec tion ate affectionate
44. ag gres sive ly aggressively
45. al ter na tives alternatives
46. ap pre ci a tion appreciation
47. as so ci a tions associations
48. a vail a bil i ty availability
49. bib li o gra phy bibliography
50. cel e bra tions celebrations
51. cham pi on ship championship
52. cheer ful ness cheerfulness
53. cir cum stance circumstance
54. com ple ment ed complemented
55. con cen tra ted concentrated
56. con di tion ing conditioning
57. con grat u late congratulate
58. con se quenc es consequences
59. con sid er a bly considerably
60. con sis tent ly consistently
61. con struct ing constructing
62. con struc tion construction
63. con struc tive constructive
64. con tin u ous ly continuously
65. con trib u ting contributing
66. con trib u tion contribution
67. con ver sa tion conversation
68. co or din a tion coordination
69. dem on strates demonstrates
70. dif fer en tial differential
71. dif fi cult ies difficulties
72. dis a bil i ties disabilities
73. dis ad van tage disadvantage
74. dis a gree ment disagreement
75. dis ap point ed disappointed
76. dis ap prov ing disapproving
77. dis as sem bled disassembled
78. dis ci plin ing disciplining
79. dra mat i cal ly dramatically
80. en light en ing enlightening
81. en ter tain ing entertaining
82. en thu si as tic enthusiastic
83. es tab lish ing establishing
84. ex pec ta tions expectations
85. ex pe ri enc ing experiencing
86. ex per i ment al experimental
87. ex plan a tions explanations
88. ex tin guish es extinguishes
89. friend li ness friendliness
90. frus tra tions frustrations
91. hi er arch i cal hierarchical
92. hy po thet i cal hypothetical
93. i mag i na tions imaginations
94. im per fec tion imperfection
95. im pli ca tions implications
96. in com pat i ble incompatible
97. in de pend ence independence
98. in struc tions instructions
99. in ter sec tion intersection
100. in ter ven tion intervention

List 39

1. coun ter at tack counterattack
2. dem on stra ting demonstrating
3. de ter min a tion determination
4. de vel op ment al developmental
5. dis ad van tag es disadvantages
6. dis a gree ments disagreements
7. dis ap point ing disappointing
8. dis re spect ful disrespectful
9. dis tin guished distinguished
10. en ter tain ment entertainment
11. ex per i ment ers experimenters
12. fa cil i ta tions facilitations
13. in ap pro pri ate inappropriate
14. in stan ta ne ous instantaneous
15. in ten tion al ly intentionally
16. in ter na tion al international
17. in ter per son al interpersonal
18. ir re spon si ble irresponsible
19. mis cel la ne ous miscellaneous
20. mis un der stand misunderstand
21. neigh bor hoods neighborhoods
22. non ag gres sive nonaggressive
23. op por tu ni ties opportunities
24. or gan i za tions organizations
25. pos si bil i ties possibilities
26. post trau mat ic posttraumatic
27. prob a bil i ties probabilities
28. pro fes sion als professionals
29. psy cho log i cal psychological
30. psy chol o gists psychologists
31. real is tic al ly realistically
32. re in force ment reinforcement
33. re la tion ships relationships
34. sar cas tic al ly sarcastically
35. un com fort a ble uncomfortable
36. un der stand ing understanding
37. un for tu nate ly unfortunately
38. ac com plish ment accomplishment
39. at trac tive ness attractiveness
40. char ac ter is tic characteristic
41. con grat u la ting congratulating
42. dis ap prov ing ly disapprovingly
43. rec om mend a tion recommendation
44. rep re sent a tive representative
45. re spons i bil i ty responsibility
46. su per in tend ent superintendent
47. sus pi cious ness suspiciousness
48. whole heart ed ly wholeheartedly
49. ac com plish ment accomplishment
50. con grat u la tion congratulation
51. con sci en tious ly conscientiously
52. con tem por ar y contemporary
53. in tox i ca tion intoxication
54. in tro duc tion introduction
55. ir rit a bil i ty irritability
56. light heart ed lighthearted
57. lon gi tu din al longitudinal
58. mea sure ments measurements
59. neigh bor hood neighborhood
60. nev er the less nevertheless
61. ob ser va tions observations
62. oc ca sion al ly occasionally
63. or gan i za tion organization
64. o ver in dulged overindulged
65. o ver step ping overstepping
66. par tic u lar ly particularly
67. per form anc es performances
68. per spec tives perspectives
69. pre scrip tion prescription
70. pres i den tial presidential
71. pro duc tive ly productively
72. pro fes sion al professional
73. pro vo ca tions provocations
74. psy cho lo gist psychologist
75. re la tion ship relationship
76. re spect ful ly respectfully

77. sat is fac tion — satisfaction
78. spe cif i cal ly — specifically
79. suc cess ful ly — successfully
80. sur pri sing ly — surprisingly
81. ther mom e ters — thermometers
82. thun der storm — thunderstorm
83. tre men dous ly — tremendously
84. un em ploy ment — unemployment
85. un rea son a ble — unreasonable
86. vol un teer ing — volunteering
87. ac com plish ing — accomplishing
88. ad ren al in ized — adrenalinized
89. ap pro pri ate ly — appropriately
90. au thor i tar i an — authoritarian
91. au to mat i cal ly — automatically
92. cir cum stanc es — circumstances
93. com mun i ca ting — communicating
94. com mun i ca tion — communication
95. com pan ion ship — companionship
96. com pas sion ate — compassionate
97. com pli ment ar y — complimentary
98. con cen tra ting — concentrating
99. con grat u lates — congratulates
100. con ver sa tions — conversations

List 140

1. con tri bu tions — contributions
2. ob ser va tions — observations
3. med i cine — medicine
4. na tur al — natural
5. math e ma ti cian — mathematician
6. ge o me try — geometry
7. den si ty — density
8. il lus tra ted — illustrated
9. ca ta pults — catapults
10. ob tain — obtain
11. i den ti fy — identify
12. dis cov er ies — discoveries
13. sci en ti fic — scientific
14. as tro no mer — astronomer
15. u ni verse — universe
16. mea sure ments — measurements
17. pla ne tar y — planetary
18. dis cus sion — discussion
19. ge ni us — genius
20. chem is try — chemistry
21. e lec tri ci ty — electricity
22. mag ne tism — magnetism
23. bi o lo gy — biology
24. he re di ty — heredity
25. ad van ces — advances
26. nu cle ar — nuclear
27. su per mar kets — supermarkets
28. fac to ries — factories
29. con tin u ing — continuing
30. com pu ters — computers
31. prin ci ples — principles
32. en gin eers — engineers
33. re search — research
34. ma te ri als — materials
35. be ne fits — benefits
36. tech no lo gy — technology
37. tech ni cal — technical
38. by pro ducts — byproducts
39. de mon strate — demonstrate
40. re la tion ship — relationship
41. ex cit ing — exciting
42. an cient — ancient
43. at ti tude — attitude
44. cen tu ries — centuries
45. ob jec tives — objectives
46. li mi ta tions — limitations
47. the o ry — theory
48. in ves ti gate — investigate
49. nut crack ers — nutcrackers
50. so lu tion — solution
51. hy po the sis — hypothesis

52. lo ca tion	location
53. ex per i ments	experiments
54. var i a ble	variable
55. en clo sure	enclosure
56. po si tion	position
57. im por tant	important
58. re la ted	related
59. re mem ber	remember
60. con clu sions	conclusions
61. land marks	landmarks
62. lo gi cal	logical
63. me chan ic	mechanic
64. na tur al	natural
65. con tra dict	contradict
66. in for ma tion	information
67. pre dic tion	prediction
68. cal cu la ted	calculated
69. or bit	orbit
70. the o rized	theorized
71. o pin ion	opinion
72. un test ed	untested
73. pre sent ly	presently
74. a vail a ble	available
75. pho to graph	photograph
76. o ri gin a ted	originated
77. in ter na tion al	international
78. a gree ment	agreement
79. de ci mals	decimals
80. con ver ting	converting
81. gro cer y	grocery
82. bus i ness	business
83. au to mo bile	automobile
84. man u fac tur ers	manufacturers
85. go vern ment	government
86. mil li onth	millionth
87. pla tin um	platinum
88. wave length	wavelength
89. e mit ted	emitted
90. kryp ton	krypton
91. re de fined	redefined
92. ac cu rate	accurate
93. spe cif i cal ly	specifically
94. kil o me ter	kilometer
95. cen ti me ter	centimeter
96. mil li me ter	millimeter
97. con ver sions	conversions
98. mul ti ply	multiply
99. il lus trates	illustrates
100. for mu las	formulas

List 141

1. re fer ence	reference
2. rec tan gu lar	rectangular
3. e qua tion	equation
4. sub sti tute	substitute
5. mul ti ply ing	multiplying
6. mar gin	margin
7. grad u a ted	graduated
8. cyl in der	cylinder
9. mer cu ry	mercury
10. li quid	liquid
11. ir reg u lar ly	irregularly
12. dis place ment	displacement
13. dif fer ence	difference
14. ki lo gram	kilogram
15. av er age	average
16. ap prox i mate ly	approximately
17. tem per a ture	temperature
18. ther mo me ter	thermometer
19. Cel si us	Celsius
20. ad van tage	advantage
21. la bor a tor y	laboratory
22. de scrip tion	description
23. di ag no sing	diagnosing
24. re quire ments	requirements
25. gra du a tion	graduation
26. de vel op ment	development

27. laun dry	laundry
28. man u al	manual
29. so ci e ty	society
30. re vo lu tion	revolution
31. e lec tron ic	electronic
32. tran sis tor	transistor
33. re fri ger a tor	refrigerator
34. in te gra ted	integrated
35. cir cuit	circuit
36. fin ger nail	fingernail
37. ap pli ca tions	applications
38. bud get	budget
39. ma ga zine	magazine
40. te le vi sion	television
41. en ter tain ment	entertainment
42. e quip ment	equipment
43. broad cast	broadcast
44. pro per ties	properties
45. re li a ble	reliable
46. de fi ni tion	definition
47. re pro duce	reproduce
48. port a ble	portable
49. in dus try	industry
50. trans port a tion	transportation
51. com pu ter ized	computerized
52. re gis ters	registers
53. re ceipt	receipt
54. add i tion	addition
55. tax a ble	taxable
56. de sign ing	designing
57. con trol lers	controllers
58. pro gram ming	programming
59. phy si cian	physician
60. di ag no sis	diagnosis
61. in ter nal	internal
62. or gans	organs
63. sub stan ces	substances
64. vi bra tions	vibrations
65. res o nance	resonance
66. im ag ing	imaging
67. cross sec tion al	cross-sectional
68. de ter min ing	determining
69. po li o	polio
70. te tan us	tetanus
71. diph ther i a	diphtheria
72. non ex is tent	nonexistent
73. vac cin a tion	vaccination
74. ac quired	acquired
75. im mune	immune
76. de fi cien cy	deficiency
77. syn drome	syndrome
78. op ti cal	optical
79. sur geon	surgeon
80. op er ate	operate
81. in stru ment	instrument
82. scal pel	scalpel
83. ves sels	vessels
84. min i mum	minimum
85. re mo val	removal
86. ma te ri al	material
87. as tro nauts	astronauts
88. cal cu la tions	calculations
89. mon i tored	monitored
90. con tin u ous ly	continuously
91. ap pli ca tions	applications
92. sa tel lite	satellite
93. com mun i ca tions	communications
94. cam er as	cameras
95. en er gy	energy
96. mu si cians	musicians
97. syn the si zer	synthesizer
98. de vice	device
99. ver sa tile	versatile
100. pro duc tion	production

List 142

1. clas si cal	classical

2. re cord ing recording
3. ed it ed edited
4. pos i tive positive
5. neg a tive negative
6. nu cle ar nuclear
7. pro vid ing providing
8. de struc tive destructive
9. e ven tu al ly eventually
10. a vail a bil i ty availability
11. pur cha ses purchases
12. read i ly readily
13. re tail ers retailers
14. en force ment enforcement
15. a gen cies agencies
16. pri va cy privacy
17. in va sion invasion
18. ad van ces advances
19. ac ci dent accident
20. al ter na tive alternative
21. pe tro le um petroleum
22. car bon carbon
23. mo le cules molecules
24. chem i cals chemicals
25. si mi lar similar
26. syn thet ic synthetic
27. de ci sions decisions
28. an a lyze analyze
29. com mu ni ty community
30. gra du a tion graduation
31. as so ci a tion association
32. man age ment management
33. de creas es decreases
34. fa mi li ar familiar
35. plas ma plasma
36. cir cum stan ces circumstances
37. fluor es cent flourescent
38. con ser va tion conservation
39. de fin ite definite
40. com pres si ble compressible
41. de ter mined determined
42. con tain er container
43. sup port ing supporting
44. struc tures structures
45. pres sure pressure
46. el e va tions elevations
47. moun tain top mountaintop
48. com par i son comparison
49. ex ert exert
50. pro per ties properties
51. phys i cal physical
52. par ti cu lar particular
53. char ac ter is tic characteristic
54. re gard less regardless
55. den si ty density
56. cu bic cubic
57. ob ject object
58. grav i ty gravity
59. af fec ted affected
60. in ter act interact
61. o rig i nal original
62. dis tort ed distorted
63. ex per i enc ing experiencing
64. e las tic elastic
65. fric tion friction
66. sub stan ces substances
67. fun da ment al fundamental
68. e lec tro mag ne tism electromagnetism
69. twen ti eth twentieth
70. a tom ic atomic
71. struc ture structure
72. pro ton proton
73. neu tron neutron
74. ra di o ac tiv i ty radioactivity
75. fu el fuel
76. en er gy energy
77. kin et ic kinetic
78. po ten tial potential

79. com pressed	compressed
80. move ment	movement
81. el e ments	elements
82. vi brate	vibrate
83. mo le cu lar	molecular
84. trans for ma tion	transformation
85. pen du lum	pendulum
86. up ward	upward
87. par ti cles	particles
88. ac cel er at ed	accelerated
89. de vice	device
90. u ni verse	universe
91. dis tinc tion	distinction
92. al um i num	aluminum
93. graph i cal ly	graphically
94. co or din ates	coordinates
95. bil li ons	billions
96. sur face	surface
97. lat i tude	latitude
98. long i tude	longitude
99. li brar y	library
100. in ter sec tion	intersection

List 143

1. sub ma rine	submarine
2. di men sion al	dimensional
3. re la tiv i ty	relativity
4. tra vel ing	traveling
5. ex act ly	exactly
6. ap proach ing	approaching
7. ar chi tects	architects
8. vi su al ize	visualize
9. re pre sent a tion	representation
10. lan guage	language
11. in te ri or	interior
12. hy po the size	hypothesize
13. ev i dence	evidence
14. phys i cist	physicist
15. ed u ca tion al	educational
16. in sti tu tions	institutions
17. aer o space	aerospace
18. ca reer	career
19. com ple tion	completion
20. doc tor al	doctoral
21. dis cus sion	discussion
22. do main	domain
23. cos mic	cosmic
24. re in forced	reinforced
25. dis trib ute	distribute
26. im pos si ble	impossible
27. spe cial iz ing	specializing
28. ad jus ta ble	adjustable
29. hy drau lic	hydraulic
30. hois ted	hoisted
31. ca pa bil i ty	capability
32. pneu ma tic	pneumatic
33. re fur bished	refurbished
34. lux ur y	luxury
35. re o pened	reopened
36. re ac tions	reactions
37. re sult ed	resulted
38. pe ri od ic	periodic
39. el e ments	elements
40. ex per i ment ing	experimenting
41. com po si tion	composition
42. jew el ry	jewelry
43. car bon di ox ide	carbon dioxide
44. ho mo ge ne ous	homogeneous
45. he ter o ge ne ous	heterogeneous
46. sym bol	symbol
47. dis tri bu ted	distributed
48. si li con	silicon
49. po tas si um	potassium
50. mag ne si um	magnesium
51. min er als	minerals
52. hy dro gen	hydrogen
53. phos phor us	phosphorus

54. ox y gen oxygen
55. chlor ine chlorine
56. so di um sodium
57. sul fur sulfur
58. ni tro gen nitrogen
59. cal ci um calcium
60. co balt cobalt
61. func tion function
62. i den ti ties identities
63. par ti cles particles
64. pro por tions proportions
65. in di vid u al individual
66. vol ca noes volcanoes
67. e rupt ed erupted
68. at mo sphere atmosphere
69. gran ite granite
70. mix ture mixture
71. pro spect or prospector
72. tech nique technique
73. fil tra tion filtration
74. com po nents components
75. con di tion ers conditioners
76. fur nac es furnaces
77. sep a rat ed separated
78. va por vapor
79. dis til la tion distillation
80. e vap or a tion evaporation
81. con tain er container
82. e vap or a ted evaporated
83. so lu tion solution
84. sol vent solvent
85. sol ute solute
86. ex am ples examples
87. al loy alloy
88. a cet ic acetic
89. an ti freeze antifreeze
90. in sol u ble insoluble
91. sol u bil i ty solubility
92. dis solv ing dissolving
93. i so pro pyl isopropyl
94. al co hol alcohol
95. sus pen sion suspension
96. col loid colloid
97. a bil i ty ability
98. e mul sion emulsion
99. de o dor ant deodorant
100. com pound compound

List 144

1. or gan ic organic
2. in or gan ic inorganic
3. car bon ate carbonate
4. pre dic tion prediction
5. hy dro chlor ic hydrochloric
6. re ar range rearrange
7. re ar range ment rearrangement
8. va cuum vacuum
9. ne ga tive ly negatively
10. e lec trons electrons
11. pos i tive ly positively
12. sub a tom ic subatomic
13. oc cu pies occupies
14. sta di um stadium
15. neu trons neutrons
16. pro tons protons
17. i ma gined imagined
18. co work ers coworkers
19. i so topes isotopes
20. hea vi er heavier
21. re la tive relative
22. he li um helium
23. u ra ni um uranium
24. af fect affect
25. sum mar y summary
26. or bi tals orbitals
27. quan tum quantum
28. ex ci ta tion excitation

29. va lence valence
30. pe ri od ic periodic
31. spe cif ic al ly specifically
32. al ka li alkali
33. hal o gens halogens
34. li thi um lithium
35. ru bi di um rubidium
36. ex plo sion explosion
37. un re ac tive unreactive
38. no ble noble
39. cir cum stanc es circumstances
40. oc tet octet
41. de cor a tive decorative
42. i o dine iodine
43. an ti sep tic antiseptic
44. bac ter i a bacteria
45. po ly vi nyl polyvinyl
46. chlor ide chloride
47. cor ro sion corrosion
48. man u fac ture manufacture
49. in ter pret ing interpreting
50. non me tals nonmetals
51. con duc tiv i ty conductivity
52. mal le a bil i ty malleability
53. duc tile ductile
54. duc til i ty ductility
55. me tal lic metallic
56. me tal loids metalloids
57. mac ro mol e cule macromolecule
58. i on i za tion ionization
59. cat i on cation
60. an i on anion
61. co va lent covalent
62. i on ic ionic
63. mo lec u lar molecular
64. for mu la formula
65. sub script subscript
66. su crose sucrose
67. em pir i cal empirical
68. su per script superscript
69. ni trates nitrates
70. fer ti li zers fertilizers
71. per spir a tion perspiration
72. e lec tro lytes electrolytes
73. hy drox ide hydroxide
74. de ter gent detergent
75. am mo ni a ammonia
76. con cen tra tion concentration
77. pur i ty purity
78. in di ca tor indicator
79. lit mus litmus
80. neu tra li za tion neutralization
81. ty pi cal typical
82. dis tin guish distinguish
83. ac cu rate accurate
84. re ac tants reactants
85. pro ducts products
86. e qua tion equation
87. co ef fi cient coefficient
88. ox ide oxide
89. ne ces sar y necessary
90. de com po si tion decomposition
91. re ac tion reaction
92. pho to chem i cal photochemical
93. pho to graph y photography
94. ig nite ignite
95. ig ni tion ignition
96. ex change exchange
97. pre cip i tate precipitate
98. sul fur ic sulfuric
99. in vi si ble invisible
100. ra di a tion radiation

List 145

1. reg u late regulate
2. ab nor mal abnormal

3. ex po sure exposure
4. tech ni cian technician
5. ther a py therapy
6. bi o log i cal biological
7. scin til la tion scintillation
8. al pha alpha
9. nu cle i nuclei
10. un sta ble unstable
11. spon ta ne ous spontaneous
12. col li sion collision
13. ac cel er a tors accelerators
14. in ves ti gate investigate
15. ex ten sive extensive
16. sen si tive sensitive
17. ra di o met ric radiometric
18. or gan ism organism
19. mea sur ing measuring
20. ef fi cient ly efficiently
21. awe some awesome
22. bom bar ded bombarded
23. fis sion fission
24. fu sion fusion
25. op er ates operates
26. gen er a tor generator
27. ac cu mu late accumulate
28. cir cu late circulate
29. cool ant coolant
30. oc cur rence occurrence
31. e vac u a ted evacuated
32. mas sive massive
33. e quip ment equipment
34. hy dro car bons hydrocarbons
35. gas o line gasoline
36. pol lu tants pollutants
37. de pos its deposits
38. re fin er ies refineries
39. pol y mer i za tion polymerization
40. fac to ries factories
41. ar ti fi cial artificial
42. i den ti cal identical
43. pol y eth y lene polyethylene
44. ther mo plas tic thermoplastic
45. pol y ur e thane polyurethane
46. em bed ded embedded
47. frag ments fragments
48. pol y es ter polyester
49. in fec tion infection
50. tem por ar y temporary
51. vul can i za tion vulcanization
52. me tal lur gy metallurgy
53. in su la tor insulator
54. pur i fi ca tion purification
55. mon ox ide monoxide
56. tem per a tures temperatures
57. ma chin er y machinery
58. sur gi cal surgical
59. a vi a tion aviation
60. fra gile fragile
61. tur bines turbines
62. crys tal lize crystallize
63. fa tigue fatigue
64. ad vanced advanced
65. im pur i ties impurities
66. ap pli ca tions applications
67. com mer cial commercial
68. si li ca silica
69. am pli fi ca tion amplification
70. im plant ed implanted
71. re place ment replacement
72. por ce lain porcelain
73. ce ram ic ceramic
74. u til ize utilize
75. cor rod ing corroding
76. in su la tors insulators
77. in tense intense
78. die sel diesel
79. dis ad van tag es disadvantages
80. com pos ite composite

81. win dow pane windowpane
82. fi ber glass fiberglass
83. ti tan i um titanium
84. dur a bil i ty durability
85. bi o med i cal biomedical
86. sub sti tute substitute
87. ro bot ics robotics
88. com pres sor compressor
89. re strict ed restricted
90. e lec trodes electrodes
91. am pu tee amputee
92. coun ter clock wise counterclockwise
93. par a ly sis paralysis
94. un par a lyzed unparalyzed
95. stim u lates stimulates
96. bi o en gin eer ing bioengineering
97. phys ics physics
98. pas sen gers passengers
99. av er age average
100. div i ding dividing

Index